Instant Pot
Cookbook for Beginners

600 Simple & Easy Recipes - Every Model of Instant Pot Recipes -

30-Day Instant Pot Meal Plan Challenge

By Meghan Kalton

Table of Content

Introduction

What is in cooking beyond ingredients? Many used to believe that once you get your ingredients in the right quantities according to the recipes, you're good to go. Little did they know that a lot more is involved in having a great meal. I'm sure this is going to be an eye-opener for a lot of people.

Beyond having the right mixture of ingredients, you also need crucial culinary skills to handle your recipes right. It is ultimately important to know when and how to add each ingredient to achieve a specific taste or flavor. Even at that, you may still not get it just right.

The best and most experienced cooks, including the chef de partie or even cordon bleu, depend greatly on their tools to serve the exciting meals that they're being praised for.

It is good to now focus on one of those tools that separate two equally-skillful chefs. That's the Instant Pot. The pots that come in various sizes and models have warmed their ways into the hearts and minds of those who could do anything to prepare a sumptuous meal that will be pleasant to their taste buds and those of their family and friends.

But you will be particularly excited about how the cookbook begins. It beings by telling you all you have to know about the Instant Pot. In the chapter introducing you to the Instant Pot, you will come across the basics of pressure cooking and its benefits. I'm sure you will have some more appreciation for the Instant Pot after reading about how it works.

The Instant Pot looks like any other regular pot or pressure cooker. But there are a few definitive differences. The Instant Pot has a modified lid which that creates a seal on the pot by locking on over a rubber gasket. With this sealing, the cooker traps the heat and raises the temperature of the boiling water. That's what speeds up the boiling, braising, or steaming of water.

You need to add a minimum of one cup of water or other liquid to the food you intend cooking in the pressure cooker in order to produce sufficient steam pressure. As the high heat is applied, the pressure trapped in the pot that cannot escape because the lid is locked in place, the atmospheric pressure inside the cooker will increase by 15 psi.

Once this pressure is increased by 15 pounds above the normal sea level, the water boiling point goes from 212°F to 250°F. And the higher the temperature, the faster the food cooks. There are electric pressure cookers that operate below 15 psi. You can use a lower setting like 10 or 11 psi, which is about 235°F for delicate foods. There are pressure cookers that you can program to advance from the low temperature that you use to soak beans and whole grains, to higher temperatures that you cook on.

There usually is a gauge or a pop-up rod on top of the lid that gives an indication when the pot has reached the full pressure. The release valve is opened and allows the steam out in a regulated flow. This helps to maintain the pot's constant pressure.

In summary, the Instant Pot works with steam pressure. As a sealed pot that traps a lot of steam, it builds up high pressure when being heated, and this is what cooks your food faster. There are two basic effects of this pressure steam. First, it raises the boiling point of the water in the pot from the maximum 212°F in a regular pot to the as high as 250°F. The second effect is that the pressure forces liquid and moisture into your food more quickly and keeps it there. This also contributes to the speed of cooking. An extra effect of the extra-high heat is that it aids browning or caramelizing excellently.

I sincerely hope that this eBook will perfect your cooking as it enhances your skills.

Chapter 1: The Instant Pot – An Instant Path to Health

Instant Pot 101

The Instant Pot is a brainchild of a team of veteran food technologists from Canada who brainstormed on solutions that will serve the interest of those leading busy lifestyles so that they could be cooking at home in spite of their busy schedule. That is why it's called the Canadian brand of electronic kitchen appliances. These veterans were among the professionals who were hard-pressed for the time to spend in cooking.

They needed what can help them to prepare quality and delicious meals to their taste in less time. They could thus stop consuming fast foods and junks outside and instead eat conveniently at home. After 18 exhausting months of intense research, design, and development, they came up with the current kitchen companion in the name of the Instant Pot.

An Instant Pot comprises several cooking elements packaged together within a piece of single straightforward equipment. Such components include the rice cooker, a slow cooker, yogurt making function, and the pressure cooker. It's a machine that performs about seven functions which consist of the slow cooker, rice cooker, browning pan, yogurt maker, steamer, and warming pot, etc. The Instant Pot comes with sensors and self-regulating features for temperature and the amount of pressure.

The Instant Pot has about 10 built-in safety mechanisms and modern technologies that make it very easy to use. The safety mechanisms will prevent the Instant Pot from any scary explosions. The Instant Pot will save you lots of time and energy. For instance, using slow cookers will take approximately 4 to 8 hours for Goat Stew to be ready, while the Instant Pot takes about 30 minutes.

This kitchen cooking machine is an excellent cooking utensil. It cooks food faster and delicious. It is an electronic cooking machine that was branded to serve the stress of cooking on a stovetop. It is well programmed to give you optimum satisfaction while cooking.

Why Instant Pot

Safe To Use:

The Instant Pot has about 10 built-in safety mechanisms and technologies that make it very easy to use. The safety mechanisms will prevent the Instant Pot from making unnecessary noise or unwanted explosions.

Healthier and Succulent Food:

It allows you to make palatable and tender meals. The Instant Pot reduces the time taken for meal preparation and uses minimal liquid which makes the food to retain most of their nutrients.

Buttons of your Instant Pot and their Functions

There are several function keys on the Instant Pot pressure cooker. Some keys might have slightly different labeling on different models. Below is a general guide to the use of each of those keys.

Manual / Pressure: This is probably the most often used key on the Instant Pot. For those who aren't sure of the cooking program to set, this button gives users the opportunity to pressure cook while manually selecting the cooking time. It allows you to set the pot to the desired pressure, temperature, and time by using the "+/-" buttons. This will depend on the recipes and notes regarding the meals to cook at high or low pressure. Anything around 10.2 to 11.6 psi and 239°F to 244°F is recognized to be "High Pressure" while "Low Pressure" something around 5.8 to 7.2 psi and 229 to 233°F.

Sauté: This is the second commonest button on the Instant Pot in order of usage frequency for most users. Almost anything can be sautéed and produce the same result as you would get if cooking in an open pan or skillet. Using the "Sauté" button, you're not bound by the rule of having a specified amount of water in the pot because you're not pressure cooking. The sauté temperature can be adjusted to the range of Normal mode (320°F to 349°F), More mode (347°F to 410°F), and Less mode (275°F to 302°F).

Slow Cook: This is the button you use if you want your Instant Pot to serve as a slow cooker. Just add your food as if you're adding it to a slow cooker, close the lid, and press the "Slow Cook" button. The default cook time when using the slow cook option is 4 hours. But you can use "+/-" buttons to set the cooking time to your desired time.

Keep Warm / Cancel: When the cooking is done, and you're not ready to serve it, the "Keep Warm" / "Cancel" function on the Instant Pot will stop the cooking and keep your food warm for up to 99 hours. It will keep counting up the number of minutes or hours that your food has been kept on the "Keep Warm" / "Cancel" mode. For example, the display panel will display something like "L3:30" if the cooking has stopped for 3 hours, 30 minutes. Your food will be kept at the temperature of between 145° F to 172°F. The function key is also used to cancel a wrong option you just selected and return your Instant Pot to the standby mode.

Bean / Chili: This is the button you need to use if

you're cooking the normally time-consuming foods like beans and legumes. It makes the cooking of such foods as black beans and kidney beans faster (10-15 minutes and 20-25 minutes respectively). The default cook is a High Pressure of 30 minutes. However, it can be adjusted for "More" to "High Pressure" for 40 minutes and "Less" to "High Pressure" for 25 minutes.

Meat / Stew: The default setting when you use this button is High Pressure for 35 minutes. It's the Instant Pot setting for cooking stew or meat dish. If you want fall-off-bone meat, you can set it to "More" to have the "High Pressure" for 45 minutes. It can also be set to "Less" for 20 minutes High Pressure.

Multigrain: If you're cooking brown rice and wild rice, which takes longer than white rice to cook, this is the best setting. The rice to water ratio for brown rice should be 1:1.25 while that for water and wild rice is 1:3. The default pressure cooking time for this setting is 40 minutes at "Normal." If you need to, you can adjust it as needed to "Less" for 20 minutes of pressure cooking time. It can also be adjusted to "More" at 45 minutes of cook time.

Porridge: This is the best setting to cook rice porridge and other grains porridges. The default cook time is 20 minutes at High Pressure. But it can be adjusted to "More" for 30 minutes of High Pressure or to "Less" for 15 minutes of High Pressure. Please note that it's better to use NR when using the "Porridge" setting. The porridge may be splattered through the steam release vent if you use QR.

Poultry: Chicken and Turkey recipes do well with the "Poultry" button, which defaults to a High Pressure at 15 minutes. It can be adjusted to "More" for 30 minutes of High Pressure or to "Less" for 5 minutes of High Pressure.

Rice: Cooking rice in the Instant Pot using the rice button reduces the cooking time by half the period it takes to cook in a conventional rice cooker. Most rice can be cooked on the "Rice" setting in about 4 to 8 minutes. This function key automatically adjusts the cooking time by the quantity of food in the unit.

Soup: If you want to prepare a broth, soup, or stock, this is the function key that will do that for you. Once you press the button, the Instant Pot microprocessor will regulate the pressure and temperature so that the liquid doesn't boil too much. This setting also allows the pressure to be adjusted to either low or high, and the cooking time is between 20-40 minutes.

Steam: This is the button that enables you to steam seafood and vegetables in your Instant Pot. If you don't want to reheat your food with microwaving, you can use the Steam function using the stream rack so that your food doesn't burn or stick to the inner pot's bottom. For a more definite timing, you can use the "+" or "-" button.

Timer Button: It's a versatile button on the Instant Pot. It's used to delay the cooking. Press the timer button and adjust the delayed hours using "+/- " buttons and wait a second before pressing the "Timer" again. You can cancel the set time by pressing the "Keep Warm / Cancel" button as usual.

The Top 5 Benefits of Instant Pot

Perfectly Cooked Dishes

With the Instant Pot, you can cook all types of foods like pot roast or meat stew in one pot. You may then use the "keep warm" function using the 24-hour programmable timer to enjoy a warm meal when you want to. It also spares you from using a skillet to brown your meat, as it can sauté and sear in the juices.

In addition, you won't need to be home to switch on the "keep warm" setting after the cooking cycle is finished, since your Instant Pot will do that on its own, thus giving you the opportunity to come home to a perfectly cooked dinner that is tender and warm.

No Mess on the Kitchen and Quick Cleaning

You will end up having almost no mess to clean and wash after the cooking process is over because you needed just one pot for everything, which is so easy to clean on your own or in a dishwasher.

The instant pot comes with a removable stainless-steel cooking pot. Just simply remove it and let it wash in the dishwasher or simply rinse it with soapy water and a soft cloth. A quick wipe-down with a cloth on the outside, and it is ready to use again. Thus, It spares you from heavy cleaning of skillets and pans.

Better than Simple Pressure Cooker

A simple pressure cooker is a thing of the past now. Although a pressure cooker is very convenient to use, it might be quite dangerous too, especially if you have kids as it releases enormous amounts of hot steam. Instant pot is designed for a fully automatic cooking process that spares you from all the guesswork and cooks perfect meals in almost no time.

Energy Efficient & Eco-friendly

Instant pot is capable of preparing your foods quickly using high-pressure steam. Generating high temperature and shorter cooking time, it may reduce electric consumption by 70%. The device has been designed to use energy only during the cooking process, preventing energy waste.

Space-Saving

If you always lack free space in your kitchen, then Instant Pot is a perfect find for you. Since you can cook under pressure, sauté, slow cook, and use various cooking programs mentioned earlier, you don't need to purchase various devices as owning one Instant Pot for all cooking tasks is just enough. Its compact design requires less space, and you can easily store it in your kitchen cabinet when it's not in use.

FAQs of Instant Pot

1. I Got My Instant Pot Few Months Ago, But It's still in the Box. How can I get started?

The Instant Pot contains built-in safety features that you need to follow and has a good explanation of the safety features. Follow the guidelines and get started.

2. My Instant Pot Takes Longer Time to Come To Pressure. Why is it so?

Because of what and or how much you have inside of it, the heating mechanism has to heat up the whole pot from the bottom up to start cooking. The more you have or, the colder the insides are, the longer that will take.

3. Can The Glass Lid Be Used To Pressure Cook?

No. The glass lid is just for slow cooking, sautéing, and anything that doesn't require pressure. If your pot doesn't make the R2-D2-like jingle, this indicates that it won't come to pressure for safety reasons. But it's safe to use.

4. Is it Normal if the Handle and the Pressure Release Steam Release Is Wobbly and Loose?

Yes!!! The pressure release handle is a safety feature that allows pressure to be released manually, and yes, it is supposed to be loose. It is normal.

5. I Choose To Set High And Low Pressure. How Can I Do That?

Not all Instant Pots have a Low setting. The Instant Pot Lux model only has the High-pressure setting and other models, use either the Pressure or Pressure Level button to switch between Low and High.

For the Instant Pot Ultra model, you'll use the knob to change the pressure setting.

6. I have heard a lot about Trivet in the Instant Pot. What is it?

A trivet is a rack, and usually, this is a reference to the rack that was shipped with the Instant Pot. The trivet is an essential part of the Instant Pot.

7. Can Frozen Food be cooked Using Instant Pot?

You can, but it takes a little longer to cook.

8. Do I Need Accessories For My Instant Pot?

Accessories can only put extra convenience and capabilities, but then, you can cook meals without accessories.

Chapter 2 Breakfasts

Espresso Oatmeal

Servings: 4 , **Prep + Cook Time:** 20 minutes

Ingredients:
- Steel cut oats -1 cup
- Sugar -2 tbsp.
- Milk -1 cup
- Vanilla extract -2 tsp.
- Espresso powder -1 tsp.
- Water -2 ½ cups
- Grated chocolate - for serving
- Whipped cream - for serving
- Salt – a pinch

Directions:

1. Mix water, sugar, oats, salt, milk and espresso powder in the insert of Instant Pot.
2. Seal the lid and cook on Manual mode for 10 minutes at High.
3. Naturally, the pressure in 10 minutes then remove the lid.
4. Add vanilla extract and mix well gently.
5. Leave it for 5 minutes then serve whipped cream and grated chocolate.
6. Enjoy.

Breakfast Bell Pepper Hash

Servings: 4 , **Prep + Cook Time:** 18 minutes

Ingredients:
- Sausage, ground -8 oz.
- Hash browns; frozen -1 package
- Water -1/3 cup
- Yellow onion; chopped -1
- Green bell pepper; chopped -1
- Eggs; whisked -4
- Cheddar cheese; grated -1 cup
- Salt and black pepper - to the taste
- Salsa - for serving

Directions:

1. Choose Sauté mode on Instant Pot and add sausages.
2. Sauté for 2 minutes then drain the excess fat.
3. Stir in onion and bell pepper, then sauté for 2 minutes.
4. Add water, eggs, cheese, salt, and hash browns.
5. Seal the lid then cook for 4 minutes on Low.
6. Once done, release the pressure then serve with salsa.
7. Enjoy.

Potato Ham Hash

Servings: 4 , **Prep + Cook Time:** 20 minutes

Ingredients:
- Potatoes; peeled and roughly chopped -6
- Eggs; whisked -6
- Ham; chopped -1 cup
- Water -1/4 cup
- Olive oil - a drizzle
- Cheddar cheese, shredded -1 cup
- Salt and black pepper – desired taste
- Toasted bread - for serving

Directions:

1. Choose Sauté mode on your Instant Pot and add oil to its insert.
2. Stir in potatoes and sauté for 3 minutes.
3. Add cheese, eggs, ham, salt, water, and pepper.
4. Mix well and seal the lid. Cook on manual mode for 5 minutes at High.
5. Once done, release the pressure naturally.
6. Serve with toasted bread.
7. Enjoy.

Pumpkin Apple Medley

Servings: 18 , Prep + Cook Time: 25 minutes

Ingredients:
- Pumpkin puree -30 oz
- Apples; peeled; cored and chopped -3
- Honey -1/2 cup
- Apple cider -12 oz
- Pumpkin spice -1 tbsp.
- Sugar -1 cup
- Salt – a pinch

Directions:

1. Add pumpkin puree, pumpkin spice, sugar, honey, cider, a pinch of salt, and apple pieces to the insert of the Instant Pot.
2. Mix well then seal the lid and cook for 10 minutes at High on Manual mode.
3. Once done, release the pressure naturally in 15 minutes.
4. Add butter then refrigerate after cooling it.
5. Enjoy.

Spinach Egg Bake

Servings: 6 , Prep + Cook Time: 30 minutes

Ingredients:
- Baby spinach; chopped -3 cups
- Eggs -12
- Milk -1/2 cup
- Green onions; sliced -3
- Tomatoes sliced -4
- Parmesan; grated -1/4 cup
- Water -1 ½ cups
- Tomato; diced -1 cup
- Salt and black pepper – desired taste

Directions:
1. Add water into the insert of the Instant Pot and place the steamer basket over it.
2. Whisk eggs with milk, salt, and pepper in a bowl.
3. Spread tomatoes, green onions, and spinach in the baking dish.
4. Pour the eggs over the vegetables and top the mixture with tomato slices and parmesan.
5. Place the baking dish in the basket and seal the lid.
6. Cook for 20 minutes at high on manual mode.
7. Once done, release the pressure quickly.
8. Transfer the baking dish to a broiler and broil for 2-3 minutes until brown from top.
9. Slice and serve.

Italian Bacon Potatoes

Servings: 2 , Prep + Cook Time: 12 minutes

Ingredients:
- Gold potatoes; washed -4
- Italian seasoning -2 tsp.
- Bacon fat -1 tbsp.
- Chives; chopped for serving -1 cup
- Water
- Salt and pepper -desired taste

Directions:
1. Add potatoes to the insert of the Instant pot and pour enough water to cover them.
2. Seal the lid then cook for 10 minutes at High on manual mode.
3. Naturally, release the pressure then transfer the potatoes to a working surface.
4. Peel the potatoes and then mash the potatoes in a bowl.
5. Empty the Instant Pot and switch it to Sauté mode.
6. Add bacon fat, mashed potatoes, salt, pepper, and seasoning.
7. Mix well and seal the lid.
8. Cook for 1 minute at High on manual mode.
9. Release the pressure and garnish with chives.
10. Serve.

Sausage Eggs

Servings: 4 , **Prep + Cook Time:** 25 minutes

Ingredients:
- Sausage; ground -1 lb.
- Vegetable oil -1 tbsp.
- Eggs -4
- Water -2 cups

Directions:
1. Add eggs and 1 cup water to the Instant Pot.
2. Seal the lid and cook for 6 minutes at High on manual mode.
3. Once done, release the pressure naturally then remove the lid.
4. Transfer the boiled eggs to an ice bath then peel the eggs.
5. Place the eggs on a working surface.
6. Divide the minced sausage into 4 balls and flatten them.
7. Place one egg at the center of each sausage patty.
8. Wrap the meat around the egg and keep the balls aside.
9. Add oil to the instant pot and switch it to the Sauté mode.
10. Add the egg balls and sauté until brown from all the sides.
11. Transfer them to a plate then empty the Instant Pot.
12. Add a cup of water to the base of the Instant Pot and set the steamer basket over it.
13. Place the egg balls in the basket and seal the lid.
14. Cook for 6 minutes on manual mode at High.
15. Release the pressure quickly.
16. Enjoy.

Cinnamon Millet Meal

Servings: 4 , **Prep + Cook Time:** 20 minutes

Ingredients:
- Organic millet -2 cups
- Bay leaf -1
- Cinnamon stick -1-inch
- White onion; chopped -1
- Ghee -1 tbsp.
- Cardamom; crushed -1 tsp.
- Water -3 cups
- Cumin seeds -3 tsp.
- Salt – desired taste

Directions:
1. Add ghee to the insert of the Instant Pot and Choose Sauté mode.
2. Stir in cinnamon, cardamom, cumin, and bay leaf.
3. Sauté for 1 minute then add onion, sauté for 4 minutes.
4. Add water, salt and millet then seal the lid.
5. Cook for 1 minute on manual mode at High.
6. Allow the pressure to release naturally.
7. Fluff the mixture with a fork.
8. Serve.

Pomegranate Oatmeal

Servings: 2 , **Prep + Cook Time:** 8 minutes

Ingredients:
- Seeds from pomegranate -1
- Porridge oats -1 cup
- Water -1 cup
- Pomegranate juice -3/4 cup
- Salt – a pinch

Directions:
1. Add oats, water, pomegranate juice and a pinch of salt to the insert of the Instant Pot.
2. Seal the lid and cook on Manual mode for 2 minutes at High.
3. Once done, release the pressure naturally.
4. Garnish with pomegranate seeds.
5. Enjoy.

Breakfast Ham Quiche

Servings: 4 , **Prep + Cook Time:** 40 minutes

Ingredients:

- Ham, diced -1/2 cup
- Sausage; already cooked and ground -1 cup
- Cheese; shredded -1 cup
- Bacon slices; cooked and crumbled -4
- Water -1 ½ cups
- Green onions; chopped -2
- Milk -1/2 cup
- Eggs whisked -6
- Salt and black pepper - to taste

Directions:

1. Add water to the insert of the Instant pot and place the steamer basket over it.
2. Whisk eggs with milk, salt, pepper, ham, sausage, onions, bacon and cheese in a bowl.
3. Pour the eggs mixture into a baking dish then cover the dish with tin foil.
4. Place the baking dish in the steamer basket in the Instant Pot.
5. Seal the lid and cook for 30 minutes at High on manual mode.
6. Let the pressure release naturally in 10 minutes.
7. Open the lid and remove the baking dish.
8. Slice the cooked quiche and serve.
9. Enjoy.

Creamy Egg & Ham Breakfast

Servings: 6 , **Prep + Cook Time:** 30 minutes

Ingredients:

- Ham; cooked and crumbled -1 cup
- Kale leaves; chopped -1 cup
- Water -1 cup
- Yellow onion; finely chopped -1
- Heavy cream -1/2 cup
- Eggs -6
- Herbs de Provence -1 tsp.
- Cheddar cheese; grated -1 cup
- Salt and black pepper - to taste

Directions:

1. Whisk eggs with heavy cream, salt, pepper, kale, onion, herbs, and cheese in a heatproof dish.
2. Add a cup of water to the base of the Instant Pot and place the steamer basket in it.
3. Place the eggs dish in the basket and seal the lid.
4. Cook for 20 minutes on manual mode at High.
5. Once done, release the pressure naturally.
6. Remove the lid and slice to serve.
7. Enjoy.

Pear Walnut Oatmeal

Servings: 4 , **Prep + Cook Time:** 12 minutes

Ingredients:

- Pear; peeled and chopped -2 cups
- Milk -2 cups
- Water -1 cup
- Raisins -1/2 cup
- Walnuts; chopped -1/2 cup
- Soft butter -1 tbsp.
- Rolled oats -1 cup
- Brown sugar -1/4 cups
- Cinnamon powder -1/2 tsp.
- Salt – a pinch

Directions:

1. Mix milk with butter, sugar, oats, salt, raisins, pears, walnuts and cinnamon in a heatproof dish.
2. Add a cup of water to the base of the Instant Pot and place the steamer basket in it.
3. Place the oats dish in the basket and seal the lid.
4. Cook for 6 minutes on manual mode at High.
5. Once done, release the pressure naturally.
6. Serve fresh.

Tofu & Brussel Sprouts Medley

Servings: 4 , **Prep + Cook Time:** 15 minutes

Ingredients:

- Purple potatoes; cubed -3
- Yellow onion; chopped -1
- Brussels sprouts -1 ½ cups
- Garlic cloves; minced -2
- Carrot; chopped -1
- Ginger root; grated -1
- Firm tofu; cubed -1/2 lbs.
- Tamari -1 tbsp.
- Mexican spice blend - to the taste
- Water -3 tbsp.

Directions:

1. Choose Sauté mode on your Instant pot and add the onion.
2. Sauté for 1 minute then add ginger, potatoes, garlic, tofu, tamari, spices, water, Brussels sprouts, and carrots.
3. Mix gently then seal the lid.
4. Cook for 2 minutes on manual mode at High.
5. Release the pressure naturally.
6. Serve fresh.

Chickpeas Tahini Spread

Servings: 8, **Prep + Cook Time:** 25 minutes

Ingredients:

- Chickpeas soaked and drained -1 cup
- Water -6 cups
- Bay leaf -1
- Garlic cloves crushed -4
- Tahini paste - 2 tbsp.
- Juice of lemon -1
- Cumin -1/4 tsp.
- Chopped parsley -1/4 cup
- Paprika - a pinch
- Olive oil-extra virgin
- Salt - to the taste

Directions:

1. Add water and chickpeas to the insert of the Instant Pot.
2. Stir in bay leaf, and 2 garlic cloves then seal the lid.
3. Cook for 18 minutes on manual mode at High.
4. Release the pressure quickly then discard the bay leaf and excess liquid.
5. Reserve some of the cooking liquid aside.
6. Add tahini paste to the reserved liquid along with cumin, lemon juice, salt, and remaining garlic.
7. Transfer this mixture to the food processor along with cooked chickpeas.
8. Blend well until smooth then garnish with olive oil and paprika.
9. Enjoy.

Apple Lentil Breakfast

Servings: 4 , **Prep + Cook Time:** 35 minutes

Ingredients:

- Apples; diced -2
- Cinnamon; ground -1 tbsp.
- Red lentils; soaked for 4 hours and drained -1 cup
- Cloves; ground -1 tsp.
- Rooibos tea -3 cups
- Turmeric; ground -1 tsp.
- Maple syrup - to the taste
- Coconut milk - for serving

Directions:

1. Add lentil to the insert of the Instant Pot along with tea and mix well.
2. Seal the lid and cook for 15 minutes on manual mode at High.
3. Once done, release pressure quickly then remove the lid.
4. Add apples, cloves, turmeric, and cinnamon.
5. Mix well then seal the lid again to cook for 15 minutes on manual mode at High.
6. Once done, release the pressure quickly.
7. Divide the mixture into the serving bowls.
8. Add coconut milk and maple syrup.

Cranberry Raisins Jam

Servings: 12 , **Prep + Cook Time:** 1 hour 30 minutes

Ingredients:
- Cranberries -16 oz.
- Raisins -4 oz.
- Water -3 oz.
- Sugar -2 ½ lb.
- Strawberries; chopped -16 oz.
- Zest from lemon -1
- Salt – a pinch

Directions:
1. Toss strawberries, lemon zest, raisins and cranberries in the insert of the Instant Pot.
2. Stir in sugar and mix gently. Leave them aside for 1 hour.
3. Pour in water along with a pinch of salt then seal the lid.
4. Cook for 15 minutes on manual mode at High.
5. Release the pressure quickly then leave this mixture for 5 minutes.
6. Allow it to cool then serve with bread slices.
7. Enjoy.

Caper Mixed Chicken Liver

Servings: 8 , **Prep + Cook Time:** 20 minutes

Ingredients:
- Chicken liver -3/4 lb.
- Extra virgin olive oil -1 tsp.
- Yellow onion, roughly chopped -1
- Bay leaf -1
- Red wine -1/4 cup
- Anchovies -2
- Capers drained and chopped -1 tbsp.
- Butter -1 tbsp.
- Salt and black pepper - to the taste

Directions:
1. Add olive oil to the insert of the Instant Pot.
2. Stir in onion, chicken liver, wine, bay leaf, salt, and pepper.
3. Seal the lid then cook for 10 minutes on manual mode at High.
4. Allow the pressure to release quickly, then remove the lid.
5. Add butter, capers, and anchovies.
6. Mix well then transfer this mixture to a kitchen blender.
7. Blend well and stir in salt and pepper.
8. Mix again and serve with bread slices.
9. Enjoy.

Cheesy Butter Grits

Servings: 4 , **Prep + Cook Time:** 20 minutes

Ingredients:
- Cheddar cheese; grated -1 ¾ cup
- Half and a half -1 ¾ cup
- Coconut oil -2 tbsp.
- Stone ground grits -1 cup
- Water -3 cups
- Salt -2 tsp.
- Butter -3 tbsp.
- Butter - for serving

Directions:
1. Choose Sauté mode on your Instant pot then add grits.
2. Stir cook for 3 minutes then add half and half, oil, water, butter, salt, and cheese.
3. Mix well then seal the lid. Cook on manual mode for 10 minutes at High.
4. Allow the pressure to release naturally then mix gently.
5. Leave the grits for 15 minutes then garnish with butter.
6. Enjoy fresh.

Mixed Mushroom Cheese

Servings: 6 , **Prep + Cook Time:** 25 minutes

Ingredients:

- Dry porcini mushrooms -1 oz.
- Extra-virgin olive oil -1 tbsp.
- Shallot finely chopped -1
- White wine -1/4 cup
- Button mushrooms sliced -1 lb.
- Boiled water -1 cup
- Bay leaf -1
- Truffle oil -1 tbsp.
- Grated parmesan cheese -3 tbsp.
- Butter -1 tbsp.
- Salt and pepper - to the taste

Directions:

1. Add dry mushrooms to a bowl and pour 1 cup boiling water over mushrooms and keep them aside.
2. Choose Sauté mode on Instant Pot and add olive oil and butter to its insert.
3. Stir in shallot and sauté for 2 minutes then add the dry mushrooms, their liquid, wine, salt, pepper, bay leaf, and fresh mushrooms.
4. Mix gently then seal the lid and cook for 16 minutes on manual mode at High.
5. Once done, release the pressure quickly, then remove the lid.
6. Discard the bay leaf and ¼ cup fo the liquid.
7. Transfer this mixture to a blender and blend until smooth.
8. Stir in parmesan cheese and truffle oil.
9. Mix gently then serve.

Berries Mixed Quinoa

Servings: 6 , **Prep + Cook Time:** 20 minutes

Ingredients:

- Quinoa; rinsed -1 ½ cups
- Fresh berries - for serving
- Milk - for serving
- Maple syrup -2 tbsp.
- Water -2 ¼ cups
- Cinnamon powder -1/4 tsp.
- Vanilla extract -1/2 tsp.
- Salt - a pinch
- Almonds; sliced - for serving

Directions:

1. Add vanilla, water, quinoa, cinnamon, maple syrup and salt to the insert of the Instant Pot.
2. Mix well then seal the lid and cook for 10 minutes at High on manual mode.
3. Once done, release the pressure naturally then fluff the mixture with a fork.
4. Serve with a splash of milk and garnish with berries and almonds.
5. Enjoy.

Pectin Blackberries Jam

Servings: 4 , **Prep + Cook Time:** 30 minutes

Ingredients:

- Sugar -5 cups
- Pints' blackberries -4
- Pectin powder -3 tbsp.
- Juice of lemon -1 small

Directions:

1. Add blackberries to the insert of the Instant Pot.
2. Drizzle sugar over berries then Choose Sauté mode and stir cook for 3 minutes.
3. Transfer the berries to clean jars and seal them.
4. Add a cup of water to the base of the Instant Pot and place the steamer basket in it.
5. Place the berries jars in the basket and seal the lid.
6. Cook for 20 minutes on Canning mode.
7. Allow the jam to cool then refrigerate.
8. Serve with toasted bread and butter.

Avocado Quinoa Salad

Servings: 8 , **Prep + Cook Time:** 25 minutes

Ingredients:

- Quinoa; rinsed -1 ½ cups
- Garlic cloves; minced -2
- Mint leaves; chopped -1/3 cup
- Avocado, pitted, peeled and diced -1
- Veggie stock -3 tbsp.
- Lime juice -1/4 cup
- Scallions; finely chopped -1/2 cup
- Chickpeas, already cooked -1 ½ cups
- Parsley leaves; finely chopped -2/3 cup
- Chipotle chili pepper -1/2 tsp.
- Water -2 ¼ cups
- Tomatoes; chopped -2
- Cucumber; chopped -1
- Jalapeno pepper; chopped -1
- Corn, already cooked -1 cup
- Black pepper - to the taste
- Salt - a pinch

Directions:

1. Mix quinoa with 1 pinch of salt, water and 1 garlic clove in the insert of the Instant Pot.
2. Seal the lid and cook for 1 minute on manual mode at High.
3. Once done, release the pressure then remove the lid.
4. Fluff the quinoa with a fork then allow it to cool.
5. Toss the quinoa with cucumber, tomatoes, corn, chickpeas, scallions, jalapeno pepper, mint, parsley and avocado in a salad bowl.
6. Mix vegetable stock with lime juice, chipotle chili pepper, 1 garlic clove in another small bowl.
7. Pour this mixture into the quinoa mixture.
8. Mix well and serve fresh.

Nutmeg Banana Cake

Servings: 5 , **Prep + Cook Time:** 1 hour ,

Ingredients:

- Bananas, peeled and mashed -3
- Baking powder -2 tsp.
- Water -1 cup
- Eggs -2
- Stick butter; soft -1
- Nutmeg -1 tsp.
- Sugar -1 ½ cups
- Cinnamon -1 tsp.
- Flour -2 cups
- Salt - a pinch

Directions:

1. Whisk eggs with sugar and butter in a bowl.
2. Stir in baking powder, salt, nutmeg, and cinnamon and mix again.
3. Add flour and bananas, mix well.
4. Layer a springform pan with butter and pour the batter into the pan.
5. Cover this pan with tin foil.
6. Add a cup of water to the base of the Instant Pot and place the steamer basket over it.
7. Place the springform pan in the basket then seal the lid.
8. Cook for 55 minutes at High on manual mode.
9. Once done, release the pressure quickly, then remove the lid.
10. Allow it to cool then slice the cake.

Millet Date Pudding

Servings: 4 , **Prep + Cook Time:** 20 minutes

Ingredients:

- Millet -2/3 cup
- Coconut milk -14 oz.
- Dates; pitted -4
- Water -7 oz.
- Salt - a pinch
- Honey - for serving

Directions:

1. Add millet, dates, a pinch of salt and milk to the insert of the Instant Pot.
2. Mix and add water. Seal the lid then cook for 10 minutes on manual mode at High.
3. Once done, allow the pressure naturally then remove the lid.
4. Garnish with honey and serve to enjoy.

Chia Almond Pudding

Servings: 4 , **Prep + Cook Time:** 15 minutes

Ingredients:
- Chia seeds -1/2 cup
- Coconut; shredded -1/4 cup
- Almonds -1/4 cup
- Sugar -4 tsp.
- Almond milk -2 cups

Directions:

1. Add chia seeds, milk, coconut flakes and almonds to the insert of Instant Pot.
2. Seal the lid and cook for 3 minutes on manual mode at High.
3. Once done, release the pressure quickly, then remove the lid.
4. Garnish with sugar.
5. Enjoy.

Tofu kale Medley

Servings: 4 , **Prep + Cook Time:** 17 minutes

Ingredients:
- Tofu; cubed and baked -3 oz.
- Kale leaves; chopped -1 bunch
- Paprika -1 tsp.
- Olive oil -1 tbsp.
- Water -1/2 cup
- Sherry vinegar -2 tsp.
- Almonds; chopped -1/4 cup
- Leek, cut into halves lengthwise and thinly sliced -1
- Sat - to the taste
- Cayenne pepper - a pinch

Directions:

1. Choose Sauté mode on your Instant Pot and add oil to its insert.
2. Add leeks and sauté for 5 minutes.
3. Stir in paprika and cook for 1 minute.
4. Then add kale, salt, water, and cayenne then seal the lid.
5. Cook for 2 minutes on manual mode at High.
6. Release the pressure quickly then add vinegar and tofu.
7. Mix well then garnish with almonds.
8. Enjoy fresh.

Turkey Filled Tacos

Servings: 4 , **Prep + Cook Time:** 15 minutes

Ingredients:
- Turkey meat; ground -1 lb.
- Beef stock -1 ¼ cups
- Corn flour -2 tsp.
- Dried onions -1/4 tsp.
- Paprika -1/2 tsp.
- Onion powder -1/4 tsp.
- Garlic powder -1/4 tsp.
- Oregano; dried -1/4 tsp.
- Extra-virgin olive oil -1 tbsp.
- Cumin; ground -1 ½ tsp.
- Chili powder -1 tbsp.
- Worcestershire sauce -1 tbsp.
- Cayenne pepper - a pinch
- Salt and black pepper - to the taste
- Tacos shells - for serving

Directions:

1. Choose Sauté mode on your Instant Pot then add oil to its insert.
2. Add meat and half cup stock to the oil.
3. Stir cook for 2 minutes and remove the excess fat.
4. Add remaining stock, cumin, flour, chili powder, garlic, dried onions, paprika, salt, pepper, cayenne pepper, oregano, Worcestershire sauce
5. Mix well then seal the lid. Cook for 5 minutes on manual mode at High.
6. Allow the pressure to release naturally and remove the lid.
7. Divide the meat mixture into taco shells.
8. Serve fresh.

Morning Tofu Scramble

Servings: 4 , Prep + Cook Time: 18 minutes

Ingredients:
- Canned tomatoes, diced -12 oz.
- Yellow onion; thinly sliced -1
- Walnut oil -1 tsp.
- Garlic cloves; minced -3
- Veggie stock -1/4 cup
- Carrot; chopped -1 cup
- Firm tofu; drained -1 block
- Cumin -1 tsp.
- Red pepper; chopped -2 tbsp.
- Italian seasoning -1 tbsp.
- Nutritional yeast -1 tsp.
- Salt and black pepper - to the taste

Directions:

1. Choose Sauté mode on your Instant Pot then add oil to its insert.
2. Add carrot, garlic, and onion, sauté for 3 minutes.
3. Stir in crumbled tofu and mix well.
4. Add red pepper, stick, cumin, tomatoes, salt, pepper, and Italian seasoning.
5. Seal the lid and cook on manual mode for 4 minutes at High.
6. Allow the pressure to release quickly, then remove the lid.
7. Garnish with nutritional yeast on top.
8. Enjoy.

Mushroom Gouda Oatmeal.

Servings: 4 , Prep + Cook Time: 25 minutes

Ingredients:
- Mushroom; sliced -8 oz.
- Small yellow onion; chopped -1
- Thyme springs; chopped -3
- Steel cut oats -1 cup
- Garlic cloves; minced -2
- Butter -2 tbsp.
- Extra virgin olive oil -2 tbsp.
- Water -1/2 cup
- Gouda; grated -1/2 cup
- Canned chicken stock -14 oz.
- Salt and black pepper - to the taste

Directions:
1. Set the Instant Pot on the sauté mode and add butter to its insert.

2. Once melted add onions and sauté for 3 minutes.
3. Stir in garlic and cook for 1 minute then add oats.
4. Cook for 1 minute then add salt, pepper, water, stock, and thyme.
5. Seal the lid and cook on manual mode for 10 minutes at High.
6. Once done, release the pressure quickly and leave the pot for a few minutes.
7. Take a suitable pan and heat olive oil in it over medium heat.
8. Stir in mushrooms and sauté for 3 minutes.
9. Add the mushrooms to the Instant pot along with gouda.
10. Mix well then serve fresh.

Bread Pudding with Mustard Sauce

Servings: 6 , Prep + Cook Time: 35 minutes

Ingredients:
- Loaf and bread; cubed -14 oz.
- Water -1 cup
- Swiss cheese; grated -1 cup
- Mushrooms; sliced -1 cup
- Butter -4 tbsp.
- Onions; thinly sliced -1 cup
- Eggs; whisked -3
- Half and half cream -2 cups
- Thyme; dried -1/2 tsp.
- Mustard; dry -1/2 tsp.
- Salt and black pepper - to taste
- Ham; diced -1 cup

16

- Sugar -1/4 cup
- Cooking spray

For the sauce:
- Rice wine vinegar -1 ½ tsp.
- Mustard -1/2 cup
- Maple syrup -2 tbsp.
- Salt and black pepper - to taste

Directions:
1. Take a suitable pan and melt butter in it over medium heat.
2. Stir in onions and sauté for 2 minutes.
3. Add ham and cook for 2 minutes then remove it from the heat.
4. Grease a baking dish with cooking oil.
5. Whisk eggs with half and half, sugar, thyme, salt, pepper, half of the swiss cheese, mushroom, bread cubes, onions and ham mixture in a bowl.
6. Pour this mixture into the greased pan.
7. Add a cup of water to the base of the Instant Pot and place the steamer basket over it.
8. Place the pan in the basket and seal the lid of the Instant Pot.
9. Cook on manual mode for 25 minutes at High.
10. Meanwhile, take a small pot and add dry mustard, salt, vinegar, pepper, and maple syrup.
11. Place it over medium heat and stir cook for 3 minutes.
12. Once the Instant Pot beeps, release the pressure quickly.
13. Remove the lid and the pan from inside.
14. Drizzle cheese on top and broil the pudding in a broiler for 2 minutes.
15. Slice and pour the maple sauce on top.
16. Enjoy.

Curried Tofu Breakfast

Servings: 6 , Prep + Cook Time: 20 minutes

Ingredients:
- Firm tofu; cubed -28 oz.
- BBQ sauce -12 oz.
- Red bell pepper; chopped -1
- Yellow onion; chopped -1
- Celery stalk; chopped -1
- Green bell pepper; chopped -1
- Extra virgin olive oil -2 tbsp.
- Garlic cloves; minced -4
- Salt - to the taste
- Curry powder - a pinch

Directions:

1. Choose Sauté mode on your Instant Pot then add oil to its insert.
2. Add garlic, onion, celery, and bell peppers, salt, and curry powder.
3. Sauté for 2 minutes then add tofu. Stir cook for 4 minutes.
4. Stir in BBQ sauce then seal the lid. Cook on manual mode for 5 minutes at High.
5. Once done, release the pressure naturally then remove the lid.
6. Serve fresh.

Shredded Beef Roast

Servings: 8 , Prep + Cook Time: 50 minutes

Ingredients:
- Beef roast; cut into small chunks -4 lb.
- Brown sugar -2 tbsp.
- Garlic powder -2 ½ tsp.
- Mustard powder -2 tsp.
- Onion flakes -2 tsp.
- Paprika -2 tsp.
- Worcestershire sauce -2 tbsp.
- Butter; soft -4 tbsp.
- Hoagie rolls -8
- Balsamic vinegar -1 tbsp.
- Provolone cheese -8 slices
- Beef stock -3 cups
- Salt and black pepper - to the taste

Directions:
1. Add meat to the insert of the Instant Pot along with salt, pepper, garlic powder, paprika, mustard powder, stock, onion flakes, vinegar and Worcestershire sauce.
2. Mix well then seal the lid. Cook for 40 minutes on manual mode at High.
3. Once done, allow the pressure to release quickly.

4. Remove the lid and transfer the meat to the cutting board.
5. Strain the cooking liquid and reserve the liquid,
6. Shred the meat using a fork.

7. Spread the butter over the rolls and divide the meat over the rolls.
8. Add cheese over the meat and place the rolls in the baking sheet.
9. Broil them for 3 minutes then serve.

Peppers and Sausages Hash

Servings: 5 , **Prep + Cook Time:** 35 minutes

Ingredients:
- Green bell peppers, cut into thin strips -4
- Canned tomatoes; diced -28 oz.
- Italian sausages -10
- Tomato sauce -15 oz.
- Garlic cloves; minced -4
- Basil; dried -1 tbsp.
- Italian seasoning -1 tbsp.
- Water -1 cup

Directions:
1. Add tomatoes, basil, water, tomato sauce, sausages, garlic, Italian seasoning and bell peppers to the insert of the Instant Pot.
2. Seal the lid and cook for 25 minutes on manual mode at High.
3. Allow the pressure to release quickly.
4. Serve fresh.

Cinnamon Cream Cheese Oats.

Servings: 4 , **Prep + Cook Time:** 25 minutes

Ingredients:
- Steel oats -1 cup
- Water -3 ½ cups
- Milk -1 tsp.
- Cream cheese; soft -2 oz.
- Butter -1 tbsp.
- Salt - a pinch
- White sugar -2 tbsp.
- Cinnamon -1 tsp.
- Brown sugar -1/4 cup
- Raisins -3/4 cup

Directions:
1. Set your Instant Pot on Sauté mode and add butter to its insert.
2. Add oats and sauté for 3 minutes.
3. Stir in water and a pinch of salt.
4. Seal the lid then cook for 10 minutes on manual mode at High.
5. Once done, release the pressure naturally in 5 minutes.
6. Remove the lid then add raisins and leave the oatmeal aside.
7. Mix cinnamon with sugar in one bowl.
8. Whisk white sugar with milk and cream cheese in another.
9. Serve the oatmeal with cream cheese mixture on top.
10. Garnish with cinnamon mixture.
11. Enjoy.

Chapter 3 Poultry Recipes

Chicken Pineapple Sandwiches

Servings: 8 , **Prep + Cook Time:** 25 minutes

Ingredients:
- Canned pineapple and its juice; chopped -20 oz.
- Chicken breasts; skinless and boneless -6
- Soy sauce -1 tsp.
- Cornstarch -1 tbsp.
- Brown sugar -1/4 cup
- Hamburger buns -8
- Canned orange juice -12 oz.
- Lemon juice -2 tbsp.
- Canned peaches and their juice -15 oz.
- Grilled pineapple slices; for serving -8

Directions:
1. Mix orange juice with lemon juice, soy sauce, peaches, sugar and pineapple pieces in a bowl.
2. Add half of this sauce to the insert of the Instant Pot.
3. Place the chicken in it and pour the remaining sauce over it.
4. Seal the lid and cook for 12 minutes on Manual mode at High.
5. Once done, release the pressure quickly then place the chicken on a cutting board.
6. Shed the chicken using a fork.
7. Mix 1 tbsp cooking liquid with cornstarch.
8. Add this mixture to the mixture in the Instant Pot and stir cook on Sauté mode for 3 minutes.
9. Add chicken and mix well.
10. Serve fresh with pineapple slices, and hamburger buns.

Duck and Vegetable Stew

Servings: 8 , **Prep + Cook Time:** 50 minutes

Ingredients:
- Duck; chopped into medium pieces -1
- Wine -1 tbsp.
- Carrots; chopped -2
- Water -2 cups
- Cucumber; chopped -1
- Ginger pieces; chopped -1-inch
- Salt and black pepper - to the taste

Directions:
1. Place the duck pieces in the insert of the Instant Pot
2. Add carrots, wine, cucumber, ginger, water, salt, and pepper.
3. Mix well and seal the lid. Cook for 40 minutes on Poultry mode.
4. Once done, release the pressure quickly, then remove the lid.
5. Serve fresh.

Mushroom Cream Goose Curry

Servings: 5 , **Prep + Cook Time:** 1 hour 10 minutes

Ingredients:
- Canned mushroom cream -12 oz.
- Goose breast; fat: trimmed off and cut into pieces -1
- Goose leg; skinless -1
- Yellow onion; chopped -1
- Water -3 ½ cups
- Garlic; minced -2 tsp.
- Goose thigh; skinless -1
- Salt and black pepper - to the taste

Directions:
1. Place the goose meat in the insert of the Instant Pot.
2. Stir in onion, water, salt, pepper, and garlic.
3. Seal the lid and cook for 1 hour on Manual mode at Low.
4. Once done, release the pressure quickly, then remove the lid.
5. Add mushroom cream and cook for 5 minutes on Sauté mode.
6. Serve fresh with toasted bread.
7. Enjoy fresh.

Chicken Eggplant Curry

Servings: 4, Prep + Cook Time: 35 minutes

Ingredients:

- Chicken pieces -8
- Eggplant; cubed -1
- Garlic cloves; crushed -3
- Vegetable oil -2 tbsp.
- Cumin; ground -1/8 tsp.
- Coriander; ground -1/4 tsp.
- Canned coconut milk -14 oz.
- Bird's eye chilies; cut into halves -3
- Piece ginger; sliced -1-inch
- Cilantro; chopped -1/2 cup
- Basil; chopped -1/2 cup
- Cooked barley - for serving
- Fish sauce -1 tbsp.
- Spinach; chopped -4 cups
- Lime wedges - for serving
- Green curry paste - 2 tbsp.
- Quash; cubed -6 cups
- Salt and black pepper - to the taste

Directions:

1. Choose Sauté mode on your Instant Pot and add oil to its insert.
2. Add ginger, garlic, cumin, chilies, and coriander and stir cook for 1 minute.
3. Stir in curry paste and cook for 3 minutes then add coconut milk.
4. Cook for 1 minute then add squash, chicken, salt, pepper, and eggplant.
5. Mix well then seal the lid. Cook for 20 minutes on Manual mode at High.
6. Once done, release the pressure quickly, then remove the lid.
7. Stir in fish sauce, spinach, basil, cilantro, salt and pepper.
8. Serve fresh with lime wedges and barley.
9. Enjoy.

Colombian Potato Chicken

Servings: 4 , Prep + Cook Time: 35 minutes

Ingredients:

- Chicken; cut into 8 pieces -1
- Gold potatoes; cut into medium chunks -4
- Bay leaves -2
- Big tomatoes; cut into medium chunks -4
- Yellow onion; thinly sliced -1
- Salt and black pepper - to the taste

Directions:

1. Add potatoes, onion, tomato, bay leaves, salt, pepper and chicken to the insert of the Instant Pot.
2. Seal the lid and cook for 25 minutes on manual mode at High.
3. Once done, release the pressure quickly, then remove the lid.
4. Discard the bay leaves and add salt and pepper for seasoning.
5. Enjoy fresh.

Chicken Curry with Chickpeas

Servings: 4 , Prep + Cook Time: 35 minutes

Ingredients:

- Chicken drumsticks and thighs -3 lb.
- Yellow onion; finely chopped -1
- Butter -2 tbsp.
- Chicken stock -1/2 cup
- Canned tomatoes; crushed -15 oz.
- Lemon juice -1/4 cup
- Canned chickpeas; drained -15 oz.
- Garlic cloves; minced -4
- Spinach; chopped -1 lb.
- Heavy cream -1/2 cup
- Ginger; grated -1 tbsp.
- Cilantro; chopped -1/2 cup
- Paprika -1 ½ tsp.
- Cumin; ground -1 tbsp.
- Coriander; ground -1 ½ tsp.
- Turmeric; ground -1 tsp.

- Salt and black pepper - to the taste
- Cayenne pepper - a pinch

Directions:

1. Choose Sauté mode on your Instant Pot then add butter to its insert.
2. Add onion, garlic, and ginger, sauté for 5 minutes.
3. Stir in cumin, coriander, paprika, turmeric, cayenne, salt and pepper.
4. Stir cook for 30 seconds then add spinach and tomatoes.
5. Cook for 2 minutes then add chicken pieces, stock and half of cilantro.
6. Seal the lid and cook for 15 minutes on manual mode at High.
7. Once done, release the pressure quickly, then remove the lid.
8. Add chickpeas, lemon juice, and heavy cream.
9. Cook for 3 minutes on sauté mode.
10. Garnish with cilantro.
11. Enjoy fresh.

Saucy Teriyaki Chicken

Servings: 6 , **Prep + Cook Time:** 25 minutes

Ingredients:

- Chicken breasts; skinless and boneless -2 lbs.
- Teriyaki sauce -2/3 cup
- Honey -1 tbsp.
- Chicken stock -1/2 cup
- Green onions; chopped - a handful
- Salt and black pepper - to the taste

Directions:

1. Choose Sauté mode on your Instant Pot.
2. Add honey, and teriyaki to the insert of the Instant Pot.
3. Cook for 1 minute then add chicken, stock, salt, and pepper.
4. Mix well and seal the lid. Cook for 12 minutes on manual mode at High.
5. Once done, release the pressure quickly, then remove the lid.
6. Transfer the chicken to the cutting surface and shred it with forks.
7.
8. Remove a half cup of cooking liquid from the Instant Pot.
9. Add chicken shreds and green onions.
10. Serve fresh.

Turkey and Chickpea Chili

Servings: 4 , **Prep + Cook Time:** 20 minutes

Ingredients:

- Turkey meat; ground -1 lb.
- Chickpeas; already cooked -15 oz.
- Cumin -1 ½ tsp.
- Water -5 oz.
- Yellow onion; chopped -1
- Yellow bell pepper; chopped -1
- Garlic cloves; chopped -3
- Chili powder -2 ½ tbsp.
- Cayenne pepper - a pinch
- Veggies stock -12 oz.
- Salt and black pepper - to the taste

Directions:

1. Place the turkey meat in the insert of your Instant Pot.
2. Add water and seal the lid.
3. Cook for 5 minutes on manual mode at High.
4. Once done, release the pressure quickly, then remove the lid.
5. Add bell pepper, chickpeas, garlic, onion, cumin, chili powder, salt, cayenne, pepper, and vegetable stock.
6. Seal the lid again then cook for another 5 minutes at High on manual mode.
7. Once done, release the pressure naturally then remove the lid.
8. Add chili and serve fresh.

Chicken Shrimp Curry

Servings: 4 , Prep + Cook Time: 25 minutes

Ingredients:

- Shrimp; peeled and deveined -8 oz.
- Sausages; sliced -8 oz.
- Chicken breasts; skinless; boneless and chopped -8 oz.
- Extra virgin olive oil -2 tbsp.
- Creole seasoning -1 tsp.
- Garlic cloves; minced -3
- Yellow onion; chopped -1
- Green bell pepper; chopped -1
- Celery stalks; chopped -3
- White rice -1 cup
- Chicken stock -1 cup
- Canned tomatoes; chopped -2 cups
- Parsley; chopped -3 tbsp.
- Thyme; dried -2 tsp.
- Cayenne pepper - a pinch
- Worcestershire sauce -2 tsp.
- Tabasco sauce -1 dash

Directions:

1. Mix Creole seasoning with cayenne and thyme to a bowl.
2. Choose Sauté mode on your Instant Pot then add oil to its insert.
3. Add chicken and cook until brown from all the sides.
4. Stir in sausage slices and cook for 3 minutes.
5. Add half of the seasoning mixture and shrimp.
6. Cook for 2 minutes then transfer this mixture to a bowl.
7. Add celery, bell pepper, onions, and garlic to the Instant Pot.
8. Stir in remaining seasoning mix and stir cook for 10 minutes.
9. Add stock, tomatoes, rice, Worcestershire sauce, and Tabasco sauce.
10. Mix well and seal the lid. Cook for 8 minutes on manual mode at High.
11. Once done, release the pressure quickly, then remove the lid.
12. Add the chicken-shrimp mixture to the Instant Pot.
13. Leave the mixture for 5 minutes.
14. Serve fresh.

Ground Duck Chili

Servings: 4 , Prep + Cook Time: 1 hour, 10 minutes

Ingredients:

- Northern beans, soaked and rinsed -1 lb.
- Yellow onion; cut into half -1
- Garlic heat; top trimmed off -1
- Cloves -2
- Bay leaf -1
- Water -6 cups
- Salt - to the taste

For the duck:

- Duck; ground -1 lb.
- Canned tomatoes and their juices; chopped -15 oz.
- Canned green chilies and their juice -4 oz.
- Brown sugar -1 tsp.
- Vegetable oil -1 tbsp.
- Yellow onion; minced -1
- Carrots; chopped -2
- Salt and black pepper - to the taste
- Cilantro; chopped - a handful

Directions:

1. Add beans to the insert of the Instant Pot.
2. Add garlic head, cloves, whole onion, water, salt, and bay leaf.
3. Seal the lid and cook for 25 minutes on Manual mode at High.
4. Once done, release the pressure quickly, then remove the lid.
5. Discard all the solids and transfer the beans to a bowl.
6. Take a suitable pan and heat oil in it over medium-high heat.
7. Add onion, salt, pepper, and carrots. Stir cook for 5 minutes.
8. Stir in duck and cook for 5 minutes then add tomatoes and chilies.
9. Cook this mixture to a simmer then remove it from the heat.
10. Add this mixture to the Instant Pot then seal the lid.
11. Cook for 5 minutes on manual mode at High.

12. Once done, release the pressure naturally then remove the lid.
13. Add beans, brown sugar, and more salt and pepper if needed.
14. Mix gently then garnish with cilantro.
15. Serve fresh.

Chicken Lentil Stew

Servings: 4 , Prep + Cook Time: 35 minutes

Ingredients:
- Chicken pieces -2 ½ lb.
- Bacon; chopped -8 oz.
- Yellow onion; chopped -1 cup
- Lentils; dried -8 oz.
- Carrots; chopped -2
- Parsley springs; chopped -12
- Extra virgin olive oil -2 tbsp.
- A drizzle of olive oil - for serving
- Bay leaves -2
- Chicken stock -1-quart
- Sherry vinegar -2 tsp.
- Salt and black pepper - to the taste

Directions:
1. Choose Sauté mode on your Instant Pot.
2. Add oil to the insert of the Instant pot and add bacon.
3. Stir cook for 1 minute then add onions, sauté for 2 minutes.
4. Stir in carrots, lentils, parsley, chicken pieces, bay leaves, parsley, salt, pepper, and stock.
5. Seal the lid then cook for 20 minutes on Manual mode at High.
6. Once done, release the pressure quickly, then remove the lid.
7. Transfer the chicken to a cutting board and remove the skin and bones.
8. Shred the chicken and return it to the Instant Pot.
9. Switch the Instant Pot to the sauté mode and cook for 7 minutes.
10. Add salt, pepper, and vinegar.
11. Mix well and garnish with olive oil.
12. Enjoy.

Saucy Goose Satay

Servings: 4 , Prep + Cook Time: 25 minutes

Ingredients:
- Goose breast half, skinless; boneless and cut into thin slices -1
- Sweet chili sauce -1/4 cup
- Sweet onion; chopped -1
- Garlic; chopped -2 tsp.
- Extra virgin olive oil -1/4 cup
- Salt and black pepper - to the taste

Directions:
1. Choose Sauté mode on your Instant Pot then add oil to its insert.
2. Add garlic and onion, sauté for 3 minutes.
3. Stir in goose breast slices, pepper, and salt.
4. Cook for 2 minutes per side then add chili sauce.
5. Seal the lid and cook for 5 minutes on manual mode at High.
6. Once done, release the pressure quickly, then remove the lid.
7. Serve fresh.

Lemongrass Chicken Curry

Servings: 5 , Prep + Cook Time: 30 minutes

Ingredients:

- Lemongrass; rough bottom removed and trimmed -1 bunch
- Piece ginger root; chopped -1-inch
- Garlic cloves; crushed -4
- Coconut aminos -3 tbsp.
- Chinese five spice -1 tsp.
- Chicken drumsticks -10
- Coconut milk -1 cup
- Cilantro; finely chopped -1/4 cup
- Yellow onion; chopped -1
- Lime juice -1 tbsp.
- Fish sauce -2 tbsp.
- Ghee -1 tsp.
- Salt and black pepper - to the taste

Directions:

1. Add lemongrass, garlic, ginger, five spice, fish sauce, and aminos to a food processor.
2. Add coconut milk and blend until smooth.
3. Choose Sauté mode on your Instant Pot then add ghee to its insert.
4. Stir in onion and sauté for 5 minutes.
5. Add salt, pepper and chicken pieces. Stir cook for 1 minute.
6. Pour in the lemongrass mixture.
7. Adjust seasoning with salt, black pepper, and lime juice.
8. Garnish with cilantro.
9. Enjoy fresh.

Sesame Chicken Satay

Servings: 4 , Prep + Cook Time: 18 minutes

Ingredients:

- Chicken breasts; skinless; boneless and chopped -2 lbs.
- Yellow onion; chopped -1/2 cup
- Vegetable oil -1 tbsp.
- Water -3 tbsp.
- Sesame oil -2 tsp.
- Honey -1/2 cup
- Cornstarch -2 tbsp.
- Red pepper flakes -1/4 tsp.
- Green onions; chopped -2
- Sesame seeds; toasted -1 tbsp.
- Garlic cloves; minced -2
- Soy sauce -1/2 cup
- Ketchup -1/4 cup
- Salt and black pepper - to the taste

Directions:

1. Choose Sauté mode on your instant Pot then add oil to its insert.
2. Stir in onion, garlic, salt pepper, and chicken.
3. Sauté for 3 minutes then add soy sauce, pepper flakes, and ketchup.
4. Seal the lid and cook for 3 minutes on manual mode at High.
5. Once done, release the pressure quickly, then remove the lid.
6. Add honey and sesame oil.
7. Mix cornstarch water and pour the mixture into the Instant Pot.
8. Garnish with sesame seeds and green onions.
9. Serve fresh.

Moroccan Cranberry Chicken

Servings: 4 , Prep + Cook Time: 35 minutes

Ingredients:

- Chicken thighs -6
- Cloves -1 tsp.
- Extra virgin olive oil -2 tbsp.
- Cardamom pods -10
- Cumin -1/2 tsp.
- Ginger -1/2 tsp.
- Parsley; finely chopped -1/2 cup
- Turmeric -1/2 tsp.
- Cinnamon; ground -1/2 tsp.
- Bay leaves -2
- Coriander -1/2 tsp.
- Yellow onions; chopped -2
- Tomato paste -2 tbsp.
- Garlic cloves; chopped -5
- Cranberries; dried -1/4 cup
- Juice of lemon -1
- Green olives -1 cup
- Chicken stock -1 cup
- Paprika -1 tsp.
- White wine -1/4 cup

Directions:

1. Mix cardamom, bay leaf, coriander, cloves, cumin, ginger, cinnamon, paprika, and turmeric in a bowl.
2. Choose Sauté mode on your Instant Pot and add oil to its insert.
3. Add chicken thighs and sauté for 3 minutes per side until golden brown.
4. Add onion to the pot, stir and cook for 4 minutes
5. Add garlic, stir and cook for 1 minute.
6. Stir in wine, stock, chicken, spice mixture and tomato paste.
7. Seal the lid and cook for 15 minutes on manual mode at High.
8. Once done, release the pressure quickly, then remove the lid.
9. Discard the cardamom, bay leaf, and cloves.
10. Add lemon juice, parsley, cranberries, and olives.
11. Mix well and serve fresh.

Chicken with Romano Cheese

Servings: 4 , Prep + Cook Time: 25 minutes

Ingredients:

- Chicken things; boneless and skinless and cut into medium chunks -6
- Chicken bouillon granules -1 tsp.
- Romano cheese; grated -1 cup
- Yellow onion; chopped -1
- Mushrooms; sliced -4 oz.
- Garlic; minced -1 tsp.
- White flour -1/2 cup
- Vegetable oil -2 tbsp.
- Tomato sauce -10 oz.
- Basil; dried -1 tsp.
- White wine vinegar -1 tsp.
- Sugar -1 tbsp.
- Oregano; dried -1 tbsp.
- Salt and black pepper - to the taste

Directions:

1. Choose Sauté mode on your Instant Pot then add oil to its insert.
2. Stir in chicken pieces and sauté for 2 minutes until golden brown.
3. Stir in garlic and onion, cook for 3 minutes.
4. Add flour, salt, and pepper while stirring the mixture well.
5. Now add vinegar, tomato sauce, sugar, mushrooms, oregano, basil and bouillon granules.
6. Seal the lid then cook for 10 minutes on manual mode at High.
7. Once done, release the pressure naturally in 10 minutes.
8. Add cheese and serve fresh.

Chicken Dumplings with Celery Stick

Servings: 6 , **Prep + Cook Time:** 35 minutes

Ingredients:
- Chicken breasts, skinless and bone-in -2 lbs.
- Carrots; chopped -4
- Yellow onion; chopped -1
- Thyme; dried -1/2 tsp.
- Eggs -2
- Milk -2/3 cup
- Chives -1 tbsp.
- Baking powder -1 tbsp.
- Flour -2 cups
- Celery stalks; chopped -3
- Chicken stock -3/4 cup
- Salt and black pepper - to the taste

Directions:
1. Add chicken, carrots, onion, celery, thyme, salt, pepper and stock to the insert of the Instant Pot.
2. Seal the lid and cook for 15 minutes at Low on manual mode.
3. Once done, release the pressure quickly, then remove the lid.
4. Transfer the chicken to a bowl then keep it aside.
5. Whisk eggs with milk, salt, and baking powder.
6. Stir in flour gradually and mix well.
7. Switch the Instant Pot to sauté mode and cook the mixture to a boil.
8. Make 6 dumplings from the flour mixture then place them in the boiling stock.
9. Seal the lid and cook for 7 minutes on manual mode at High.
10. Once done, release the pressure quickly, then remove the lid.
11. Shred the cooked chicken and add to the dumpling mixture.
12. Garnish with chives.
13. Enjoy fresh.

Chicken Drumsticks with Corn

Servings: 4 , **Prep + Cook Time:** 35 minutes

Ingredients:
- Chicken drumsticks -8
- Tomato sauce -8 oz.
- Chicken bouillon -1 tbsp.
- Yellow onion; chopped -1/2
- Tomato; chopped -1
- Cilantro; chopped -1/4 cup
- Garlic clove; minced -1
- Corn on the cob; husked and cut into halves -2
- Extra virgin olive oil -1 tsp.
- Garlic powder -1/2 tsp.
- Scallions; chopped -3
- Water -2 cups
- Cumin; ground -1/2 tsp.
- Salt and black pepper - to the taste

Directions:
1. Select the Sauté mode on your Instant Pot and add oil to its insert.
2. Add scallions, tomato, onions, and garlic, sauté for 3 minutes.
3. Stir in cilantro and cook a minute.
4. Add cumin, tomato sauce, water, bouillon, garlic powder, salt, pepper, chicken, and corn.
5. Seal the lid then cook for 20 minutes on manual mode at High.
6. Once done, release the pressure quickly, then remove the lid.
7. Adjust seasoning with salt and pepper.
8. Serve fresh.

Coconut Chicken Curry

Servings: 4 , **Prep + Cook Time:** 30 minutes

Ingredients:
- Chicken breast; chopped -15 oz.
- Canned coconut cream -5 oz.
- Extra-virgin olive oil -1 tbsp.
- Yellow onion; thinly sliced -1
- Potatoes; cut into halves -6
- Chicken curry base -1 bag
- Coriander; chopped -1/2 bunch

Directions:
1. Choose Sauté mode on your Instant Pot then add oil to its insert.
2. Add chicken and sauté for 2 minutes until brown.
3. Stir in onion, and cook for 1 minute.
4. Mix coconut cream and curry base in a bowl.
5. Add this mixture to the chicken along with potatoes.
6. Mix well and seal the lid and cook for 15 minutes on manual mode at High.
7. Once done, release the pressure quickly, then remove the lid.
8. Garnish with coriander.

Chicken Liver with Anchovies

Servings: 8 , **Prep + Cook Time:** 20 minutes

Ingredients:
- Extra virgin olive oil -1 tsp.
- Chicken liver -3/4 lb.
- Yellow onion; roughly chopped -1
- Bay leaf -1
- Red wine -1/4 cup
- Anchovies -2
- Capers; drained and chopped -1 tbsp.
- Butter -1 tbsp.
- Salt and black pepper - to the taste

Directions:
1. Add olive oil to the insert of the Instant Pot.
2. Choose Sauté mode and add onion, chicken liver, bay leaf, wine, salt, and pepper.
3. Seal the lid then cook for 10 minutes on manual mode at High.
4. Once done, release the pressure quickly, then remove the lid.
5. Add butter, capers, and anchovies.
6. Transfer the mixture to a food blender and blend well.
7. Adjust seasoning with salt and pepper.
8. Serve with bread slices.
9. Enjoy fresh.

Italian Mushroom Chicken

Servings: 6 , **Prep + Cook Time:** 30 minutes

Ingredients:
- Chicken breasts; skinless and boneless -2 lbs.
- Extra-virgin olive oil -1 tbsp.
- Marinara sauce -3/4 cup
- Pesto -2 tbsp.
- Mushrooms; sliced -3/4 cup
- Green bell pepper; chopped -1/2 cup
- Red bell pepper; chopped -1/2 cup
- Salt and black pepper - to the taste
- Yellow onion; diced -3/4 cup
- Cheddar cheese, shredded - for serving

Directions:
1. Choose Sauté mode on your Instant Pot then add oil to its insert.
2. Add bell pepper, onion, salt, and pepper, sauté for 4 minutes.
3. Stir in pesto, chicken and marinara sauce.
4. Seal the lid and cook for 12 minutes on manual mode at High.
5. Once done, release the pressure quickly, then remove the lid.
6. Transfer the chicken to a cutting board and shred the chicken using a fork.
7. Remove 2/3 of the cooking liquid from the Instant pot and add mushrooms.
8. Switch the Instant Pot to Sauté mode and cook for 3 minutes.
9. Return the chicken to the pot then mix well.
10. Serve fresh with cheese on top.

Balsamic Chicken Salad

Servings: 2 , Prep + Cook Time: 60 minutes

Ingredients:
- Chicken breast, skinless and boneless -1
- Extra virgin olive oil -3 tbsp.
- Mustard -1 tbsp.
- Garlic cloves; minced -3
- Balsamic vinegar -1 tbsp.
- Honey -1 tbsp.
- Mixed salad greens
- Cherry tomatoes; cut into halves - a handful
- Water -3 cups
- Salt and black pepper - to the taste

Directions:
1. Take a large bowl and mix 2 cups water with salt in it.
2. Add chicken to the bowl and mix well. Refrigerate for 45 minutes.
3. Add a cup of water to the base of the instant place the steamer basket over it.
4. Place the chicken in the basket and seal the lid.
5. Cook for 5 minutes on manual mode at High.
6. Once done, release the pressure quickly, then remove the lid.
7. Seal the lid and cook for 5 minutes at High on manual mode.
8. Once done, release the pressure quickly, then remove the lid.
9. Transfer the chicken to a plate then slice it into strips.
10. Mix garlic, salt, pepper, vinegar, honey, olive oil and mustard in a bowl.
11. Toss the chicken strips with tomatoes and salad greens.
12. Pour the vinaigrette over the salad.
13. Mix well and serve fresh.

Chicken Broccoli Stew

Servings: 6 , Prep + Cook Time: 25 minutes

Ingredients:
- Chicken breasts; skinless and boneless -2
- Butter -1 tbsp.
- Extra-virgin olive oil -1 tbsp.
- Broccoli; steamed and chopped -3 cups
- Parsley; dried -1 tbsp.
- Water -2 tbsp.
- Cornstarch -2 tbsp.
- Cheddar cheese; shredded -1 cup
- Cream cheese; cubed -4 oz.
- Yellow onion; chopped -1/2 cup
- Canned chicken stock -14 oz.
- Salt and black pepper - to the taste
- Red pepper flakes - a pinch

Directions:
1. Choose Sauté mode on Instant Pot and add butter and oil to its insert.
2. Place chicken in the insert and drizzle salt and pepper on top.
3. Cook for 2-3 minutes per side until golden brown then transfer to a plate.
4. Add onion and sauté for 5 minutes.
5. Stir in parsley, pepper, salt, pepper flakes, stock, and chicken.
6. Seal the lid and cook for 5 minutes on manual mode at High.
7. Once done, release the pressure quickly, then remove the lid.
8. Transfer the chicken to a cutting board and dice it.
9. Mix cornstarch with water, cream cheese and cheese in a bowl.
10. Add this mixture to the Instant Pot then add broccoli.
11. Switch the Instant Pot to the Sauté mode and cook for 5 minutes.
12. Serve fresh.

Sausage Wrapped Chicken

Servings: 2 , Prep + Cook Time: 40 minutes

Ingredients:

- Chicken breasts, skinless and boneless and butterflied -2
- Bacon strips -16
- Asparagus spears -6
- Ham; halved and cooked -1-piece
- Water -2 cup
- Mozzarella cheese slices -4
- Salt and black pepper - to taste

Directions:

1. Add 1 cup water to a large bowl and add salt.
2. Mix well and place the chicken breasts in it.
3. Cover the chicken and refrigerate for 30 minutes.
4. Remove the chicken from the brine and pat it dry.
5. Spread the chicken breasts on a working surface.
6. Place 2 slices mozzarella, 1 ham piece and 3 asparagus pieces over each chicken breast.
7. Drizzle salt and pepper then roll up the chicken.
8. Wrap each roll in 8 bacon strips.
9. Add a cup of water to the base of the Instant Pot and place steamer basket over it.
10. Place the chicken rolls in the basket and seal the lid.
11. Cook for 10 minutes on manual mode at High.
12. Once done, release the pressure quickly, then remove the lid.
13. Empty the pot and switch it to Sauté mode.
14. Place the rolls in the insert and cook until golden brown.
15. Serve warm.

Chicken with Apricot Sauce

Servings: 4 , Prep + Cook Time: 30 minutes

Ingredients:

- Chicken; cut into medium pieces -1
- White wine -1/4 cup
- Extra-virgin olive oil -1 tbsp.
- Paprika -1/2 tsp.
- Marjoram; dried -1/2 tsp.
- Chicken stock -1/4 cup
- Salt and black pepper - to the taste

For the sauce:

- Ginger root; grated -1 ½ tsp.
- Apricot preserves -1/4 cup
- Honey -2 tbsp.
- White vinegar -2 tbsp.

Directions:

1. Choose Sauté mode on the Instant pot and add oil to its insert.
2. Add chicken pieces and sear them until golden brown from both the sides.
3. Transfer the chicken to a suitable bowl.
4. Add salt, pepper, paprika, and marjoram. Mix well to coat.
5. Remove the fat from the insert of the Instant Pot and add wine and stock to it.
6. Cook for 2 minutes on Sauté mode.
7. Add the chicken and seal the lid.
8. Cook for 9 minutes on manual mode at High.
9. Once done, release the pressure quickly, then remove the lid.
10. Transfer the chicken to the serving plates
11. Add apricot preserves, vinegar, ginger, and honey to the remaining mixture in the pot.
12. Cook for 10 minutes on Sauté mode.
13. Pour this sauce over the chicken and enjoy.

Honey Braised Chicken Wings

Servings: 6 , Prep + Cook Time: 35 minutes

Ingredients:
- Chicken wings; cut into 24 pieces -12
- Yogurt -1 cup
- Parsley; finely chopped -1 tbsp.
- Hot sauce -4 tbsp.
- Water -1 cup
- Tomato puree -1/4 cup
- Celery; cut into thin matchsticks -1 lb.
- Honey -1/4 cup
- Salt - to the taste

Directions:
1. Add a cup of water to the base of the Instant Pot.
2. Place a steamer basket over the water.
3. Arrange chicken wings in the basket and seal the lid.
4. Cook for 19 minutes on manual mode at High.
5. Meanwhile, mix tomato purees with salt, honey and hot sauce in a bowl.
6. Once the Instant Pot is done, release the pressure quickly, then remove the lid.
7. Transfer the chicken to a baking sheet and pour the sauce over it.
8. Broil the wings for 5 minutes in the broiler.
9. Mix yogurt with parsley.
10. Serve the wings with yogurt and celery sticks.
11. Enjoy warm.

Chicken & Cabbage Mix

Servings: 3 , Prep + Cook Time: 40 minutes

Ingredients:
- Chicken thighs, boneless -1 ½ lb.
- Coconut milk -10 oz.
- Green cabbage; roughly chopped -1
- White wine -1/2 cup
- Yellow onion; chopped -1
- Garlic cloves; chopped -4
- Curry paste -3 tbsp.
- Fish sauce -1 tbsp.
- Vegetable oil -1 tbsp.
- Salt and black pepper - to the taste
- Chili peppers; chopped -2
- Cayenne pepper - a pinch

Directions:
1. Choose Sauté mode on your Instant Pot then add oil to its insert.
2. Add chicken, salt and pepper to the oil.
3. Cook well until brown then transfer to a suitable bowl.
4. Add chili peppers, garlic, and onions to the Instant Pot.
5. Sauté for 4 minutes then add the curry paste.
6. Cook for 2 minutes then add cabbage, wine, coconut milk, fish sauce, cayenne, salt, pepper and chicken pieces.
7. Seal the lid then cook for 20 minutes on manual mode at High.
8. Once done, release the pressure naturally then remove the lid.
9. Serve warm.

Bleu Cheese Buffalo Chicken

Servings: 6 , Prep + Cook Time: 35 minutes

Ingredients:
- Chicken stock -1/2 cup
- Celery; chopped -1/2 cup
- Small yellow onion; chopped -1
- Buffalo sauce -1/2 cup
- Bleu cheese; crumbled -1/4 cup
- Chicken breasts; skinless, boneless and cut into thin strips -2 lbs.

Directions:
1. Add everything to the insert of your Instant Pot.
2. Seal its lid and cook on manual mode for 12 minutes at High.
3. Once done, release the pressure quickly, then remove the lid.
4. Remove 2/3 cup of the cooking liquid from the Instant Pot.
5. Add crumbled cheese and mix well.
6. Serve fresh.

Citrus Glazed Turkey Wings

Servings: 4, Prep + Cook Time: 30 minutes

Ingredients:

- Turkey wings -4
- Walnuts -1 cup
- Orange juice -1 cup
- Yellow onions; sliced -1
- Thyme; roughly chopped -1 bunch
- Butter -2 tbsp.
- Vegetable oil -2 tbsp.
- Cranberries -1 ½ cups
- Salt and black pepper - to the taste

Directions:

1. Choose Sauté mode on your Instant Pot then add butter and oil to its insert.
2. Add turkey wings, salt, and pepper to the oil.
3. Cook for few minutes until golden brown.
4. Remove the chicken wings to a plate.
5. Add walnuts, onion, thyme, and cranberries.
6. Stir cook for 2 minutes then add orange juice.
7. Return the turkey wings to the Instant Pot and mix well.
8. Seal the lid then cook for 20 minutes on Manual mode at High.
9. Once done, release the pressure naturally then remove the lid.
10. Switch the Instant Pot to Sauté mode.
11. Cook for 5 minutes then serve warm.

Turkey Meatball Gravy

Servings: 8, Prep + Cook Time: 50 minutes

Ingredients:

- Turkey meat; ground -1 lb.
- Egg; whisked -1
- Milk -1/4 cup
- Parmesan cheese; grated -1/4 cup
- Panko bread crumbs -1/2 cup
- Yellow onion; minced -1
- Chicken stock -1 cup
- Extra virgin olive oil -2 tbsp.
- Soy sauce -2 tsp.
- Fish sauce -1 tsp.
- Butter -2 tbsp.
- Oregano; dried -1 tsp.
- Cremini mushrooms; chopped -12
- Dried shiitake mushrooms; soaked in water, drained and chopped -3
- Cornstarch mixed -2 tbsp.
- Water -2 tbsp.
- Garlic cloves; minced -4
- Parsley; chopped -1/4 cup
- Salt and black pepper - to the taste
- Sherry wine - a splash

Directions:

1. Mix turkey meat with salt, pepper, parmesan cheese, garlic, onion, parsley, bread crumbs, egg, milk, oregano, 1 tsp fish sauce and 1 tsp soy sauce in a bowl.
2. Make 16 small balls out of this mixture.
3. Take a suitable pan and heat 1 tbsp oil in it over medium heat.
4. Add meatballs and cook for 1 minute per side until brown.
5. Transfer the meatballs to a plate.
6. Pour the stock into the pan and deglaze the pan then turn off the heat.
7. Choose Sauté mode on your Instant Pot then add 1 tbsp oil and 2 tbsp butter to its.
8. Add salt, pepper, and cremini mushrooms.
9. Stir cook for 10 minutes.
10. Add sherry wine, soy sauce, and dried mushroom
11. Toss in the seared meatballs and seal the lid again.
12. Cook for 6 minutes on manual mode at High.
13. Once done, release the pressure quickly, then remove the lid.
14. Mix cornstarch with water and pour the mixture into Instant Pot.
15. Mix well and serve warm.

Zesty Chicken Luncheon

Servings: 8 , **Prep + Cook Time:** 45 minutes

Ingredients:

- Whole chicken, cut into pieces -1
- Cumin powder -1 tbsp.
- Lemon zest -1 ½ tbsp.
- Chicken stock -1 cup
- Thyme leaves -1 tbsp.
- Cinnamon powder -1/2 tsp.
- Garlic powder -2 tsp.
- Coriander powder -1 tbsp.
- Extra-virgin olive oil -1 tbsp.
- Salt and black pepper - to the taste

Directions:

1. Mix cumin, cinnamon, garlic, salt, pepper, lemon zest and coriander in a bowl.
2. Rub the chicken with half of the oil and half of the spice mixture.
3. Choose Sauté mode on your Instant pot then add rest of the oil to its insert.
4. Add chicken and sear it for 5 minutes.
5. Stir in thyme and stock. Seal the lid.
6. Cook for 25 minutes on manual mode at High.
7. Once done, release the pressure naturally then remove the lid.
8. Serve warm.

Chicken with Pomegranate Molasses

Servings: 6 , **Prep + Cook Time:** 25 minutes

Ingredients:

- Chicken pieces -10
- Walnuts -2 cups
- Sugar -2 tbsp.
- Juice of lemon -1/2
- Yellow onion; chopped -1
- Extra virgin olive oil -3 tbsp.
- Cinnamon; ground -1/2 tsp.
- Pomegranate molasses -2/3 cup
- Water -3/4 cup
- Cardamom; ground -1/4 tsp.
- Salt and black pepper - to the taste
- Pomegranate seeds - for serving

Directions:

1. Take a suitable pan and place it over medium heat.
2. Add walnuts and toast them for 5 minutes.
3. Transfer them to the food processor and grind them well.
4. Add them to a bowl and leave it aside.
5. Select the Sauté mode on Instant Pot and add 2 tbsp oil to its insert.
6. Season the chicken with black pepper and salt.
7. Sear the chicken until brown from all the sides and keep them aside in a plate.
8. Add the remaining oil to the pot and add the onion. Sauté for 3 minutes.
9. Stir in cinnamon and cardamom, sauté for 1 minute.
10. Add pomegranate molasses, lemon juice, sugar, chicken, and ground walnuts.
11. Seal the lid and cook for 7 minutes on manual mode at High.
12. Allow the pressure to release quickly, then remove the lid.
13. Adjust seasoning with salt and pepper.
14. Garnish with pomegranate seeds.
15. Enjoy.

Ginger Thai Chicken

Ingredients:

- Chicken thighs; boneless and skinless -2 lbs.
- Fish sauce -1/2 cup
- Lime juice -1 cup
- Coconut nectar -2 tbsp.
- Ginger; grated -1 tsp.
- Cilantro; finely chopped -2 tsp.
- Mint; chopped -1 tsp.
- Extra virgin olive oil -1/4 cup

Directions:

1. Place the chicken thighs in the insert of the Instant Pot.
2. Mix lime juice, olive oil, fish sauce, mint, ginger, cilantro and coconut nectar in a bowl.
3. Pour this mixture over the chicken and seal the lid.
4. Cook for 10 minutes on manual mode at High.
5. Allow the pressure to release quickly.
6. Serve fresh.

Asian Jalapeno Chicken

Ingredients:

- Chicken thighs, skinless and boneless -10
- Canned tomatoes and their juice; chopped -28 oz.
- Jalapeno peppers; chopped -2
- Cumin seeds; toasted and ground -2 tsp.
- Heavy cream -3/4 cup
- Garam masala -2 tsp.
- Greek yogurt -3/4 cup
- Cornstarch -2 tbsp.
- Water -2 tbsp.
- Cilantro; chopped -1/4 cup
- Cumin; ground -2 tsp.
- Ginger; chopped -2 tbsp.
- Butter -1/2 cup
- Salt and black pepper - to the taste

Directions:

1. Blend tomatoes with jalapenos and ginger in a food processor.
2. Switch the Instant Pot to Sauté mode then add butter to its insert.
3. Add chicken and sear it for 3 minutes per side.
4. Stir in ground cumin and paprika, sauté for 10 seconds.
5. Add salt, pepper yogurt, tomato mix, and heavy cream.
6. Seal the lid and cook for 5 minutes on manual mode at High.
7. Allow the pressure to release naturally in 15 minutes.
8. Mix cornstarch with water, cumin seeds and garam masala in a bowl.
9. Pour this mixture into the Instant Pot.
10. Mix well and garnish with cilantro.
11. Enjoy with naan bread.

Turkey Vegetable Medley

Servings: 3 , **Prep + Cook Time:** 60 minutes

Ingredients:

- Turkey quarters -2
- Gold potatoes; cut into halves -5
- Yellow onion; chopped -1
- Parmesan cheese; grated -2 tbsp.
- Extra virgin olive oil -2 tbsp.
- Cream -3.5 oz.
- Bay leaves -2
- Sage; dried - a pinch
- Thyme; dried - a pinch of
- Rosemary; dried - a pinch
- Cornstarch -3 tbsp.
- Water -2 tbsp.
- Butter -2 tbsp.
- Carrot; chopped -1
- Garlic cloves; minced -3
- Celery stalk; chopped -1
- Chicken stock -1 cup
- Salt and black pepper - to the taste
- White wine - a splash

Directions:

1. Rub the turkey with salt and pepper.
2. Choose Sauté mode on your Instant pot then add a tbsp of oil to its insert.
3. Add turkey and sear the pieces for 4 minutes per side.
4. Transfer the seared turkey to a plate and keep them aside.
5. Add half cup stock to the pot and mix well.
6. Add a tbsp oil and onion. Cook for 1 minute.
7. Stir in garlic and cook for 20 seconds.
8. Add carrot, salt, pepper, and celery and cook for 7 minutes.
9. Stir in thyme, 2 bay leaves, rosemary, and sage.
10. Stir cook for 1 minute. Add turkey, wine, and remaining stock.
11. Place the steamer basket over the mixture and set the potatoes in it.
12. Seal the lid then cook for 20 minutes on Manual mode at High.
13. Once done, release the pressure naturally in 10 minutes.
14. Transfer the potatoes to a bowl and mash them.
15. Stir in salt, pepper, cream, parmesan, and butter.
16. Divide the turkey into serving plates.
17. Switch the Instant Pot to sauté mode.
18. Add cornstarch and stir cook for 3 minutes.
19. Pour this sauce over the cooked turkey and serve with mashed potatoes.
20. Enjoy.

Creamy Ranch Chicken

Servings: 6 , **Prep + Cook Time:** 30 minutes

Ingredients:

- Chicken breasts; skinless and boneless -2 lbs.
- Cream cheese -4 oz.
- Ranch seasoning -1 oz.
- Slices bacon; chopped -2
- Chicken stock -1 cup
- Green onions; chopped - for serving

Directions:

1. Choose Sauté mode on your Instant Pot then add bacon.
2. Cook for 4 minutes then add chicken, seasoning, and stock.
3. Seal the lid and cook for 12 minutes on manual mode at High.
4. Once done, release the pressure quickly, then remove the lid.
5. Transfer the chicken to a cutting board and shred it using a fork.
6. Remove 2/3 cup liquid and add cream cheese.
7. Switch the Instant pot to sauté mode then cook for 3 minutes.
8. Return the chicken to the insert of Instant Pot and mix well.
9. Garnish with green onions.
10. Serve fresh.

Chapter 4 Meat Recipes

Simple Lamb and Veggies mix

Servings: 8 , **Prep + Cook Time: 1 hour and 15 minutes**

Ingredients:
- Tomato paste, 2 tbsps.
- Salt
- Chopped yellow onion, 1.
- Black pepper
- Minced garlic cloves, 6.
- Vegetable oil, 1 tsp.
- Sliced carrots, 2
- Bone-in lamb meat, 1 ½ lbs.
- Chopped tomatoes, 4.
- Dried oregano, 1 tsp.
- Mushrooms, ½ lbs.
- A handful of chopped parsley

Directions:

1. Switch the instant pot to sauté mode to heat the oil for browning the meat evenly.
2. Mix in onion, tomatoes, oregano, garlic, mushrooms, tomato paste, carrots and water to cover everything.
3. Stir in the seasonings then cook for 1 hour at high pressure with the lid sealed
4. Once cooked, perform a quick release of pressure then remove the bones from meat and shred it.
5. Put the shredded meat back to the pot, stir in parsley, adjust the seasoning and serve immediately.

Cheesy Beef & Pasta Casserole

Servings: 4 , **Prep + Cook Time: 30 minutes**

Ingredients:
- Chopped celery stalk, 1.
- Chopped carrot, 1.
- Black pepper
- Ground beef, 1 lb.
- Tomato puree, 16 oz.
- Chopped yellow onion, 1.
- Butter, 2 tbsps.
- Pasta, 17 oz.
- Shredded mozzarella cheese, 13 oz.
- Red wine, 1 tbsp.
- Salt

Directions:

1. Adjust the instant pot to sauté mode to melt the butter.
2. Stir in the celery, carrot, and onion to cook for 5 minutes.
3. Mix in the beef and some seasonings to cook for 10 minutes.
4. Add in the wine to cook for 1 more minute.
5. Stir in the water, pasta, and tomato puree to cook for 6 minutes at high pressure with the lid sealed.
6. Perform a quick pressure release once the timer clicks and open the lid.
7. Give the meal a gentle stir then serve.

Coconut Beef Curry

Servings: 4 , **Prep + Cook Time: 30 minutes**

Ingredients:
- Canned coconut milk, 10 oz.
- Diced potatoes, 3
- Curry powder, 2½ tbsps.
- Chopped yellow onions, 2.
- Extra virgin olive oil, 2 tbsps.
- Tomato sauce, 2 tbsps.
- Salt
- Cubed beef steak, 2 lbs.
- Black pepper
- Wine mustard, 1 tbsp.
- Minced garlic cloves, 2.

Directions:

1. Switch the instant pot to sauté mode to heat the oil.
2. Stir in the garlic and onion to cook for 4 minutes
3. Mix in the potatoes and mustard to cook for 1 more minute.
4. Put in the beef to brown evenly.
5. Add the seasonings and curry powder to cook for 2 minutes.
6. Gently stir in the coconut milk and tomato sauce then cook for 10 minutes at high pressure with the lid sealed.
7. Once the timer is over, perform a quick release of pressure then serve the meal immediately.

Instant pot Hominy

Servings: 6 , Prep + Cook Time: 40 minutes

Ingredients:
- Chili powder, 2 tbsps.
- Drained hominy, 30 oz.
- Vegetable oil, 2 tbsps.
- Chicken stock, 4 cups
- Water, ¼ cup.
- Boneless pork shoulder, 1¼ lbs.
- Black pepper
- Cornstarch, 2 tbsps.
- Minced garlic cloves, 4.
- Avocado slices for serving
- Lime wedges for serving
- Chopped white onion, 1
- Salt

Directions:
1. Turn the instant pot to sauté mode then heat 1 tablespoon of oil.
2. Put in the pork with some seasonings to brown evenly then set in a bowl.
3. Put the remaining oil to the pot to heat up then fry in the onion, garlic, and chili powder for 4 minutes.
4. Stir in ½ of the stock to cook for 1 more minute
5. Add the remaining stock then put the pork back to the pot to cook for 30 minutes at high pressure with the lid covered.
6. Perform a quick release of pressure naturally for 10 minutes once the timer clicks then put the pork in a chopping board to shred it using 2 forks.
7. Mix cornstarch and water then pour the mixture to the pot.
8. Switch the instant pot to sauté mode, add the hominy, shredded pork and some seasonings to cook for 2 minutes as you stir gently.
9. Serve the meal on bowls topped with avocado slices and lemon wedges.

Instant pot Bacon and Collard.

Servings: 6 , Prep + Cook Time: 40 minutes

Ingredients:
- Black pepper
- Kosher salt, ½ tsp.
- Sliced bacon, ¼ lb.
- Water, ½ cup.
- Trimmed collard greens, 1 lb.

Directions:
1. Arrange the bacon in the bottom of the Instant Pot inner pot.
2. Adjust the instant pot to sauté mode to cook the bacon for 5 minutes until browned and crispy.
3. Mix in a big handful of collard greens to coat with bacon grease until slightly wilted.
4. Top up the remaining collards.
5. Sprinkle some seasonings on top the pour the water.
6. Switch the steam release valve sealing to cook for 20 minutes at high pressure with the lid sealed.
7. Turn the steam valve to venting once the time clicks to perform a quick release of pressure then open the lid.
8. Serve the meal sprinkled with freshly ground black pepper.

Simple Kalua Pork

Servings: 5, Prep + Cook Time: 1 hour 30 minutes

Ingredients:

- Liquid smoke, 1 tbsp.
- Water, ½ cup
- Steamed green beans for serving
- Salt
- Halved pork shoulder, 4 lbs.
- Black pepper
- Vegetable oil, 2 tbsps.

Directions:

1. Adjust the instant pot to Sauté mode to heat the oil.
2. Add the meat with some seasoning to brown evenly on both sides then reserve on a plate.
3. Pour the water and liquid smoke to the pot and stir gently.
4. Put the meat back to the pot to cook for 90 minutes at high pressure with the lid sealed.
5. Once the timer clicks, release the pressure naturally for 15 minutes then turn the valve to venting to release the remaining pressure then open the lid.
6. Put the meat on a chopping board to shred using 2 forks.
7. Serve the meal topped with the sauce and steamed green beans as a side.

Garlic Pork Carnitas

Servings: 8 , Prep + Cook Time: 1 hour and 10 minutes

Ingredients:

- Chicken stock, 2 cups.
- Oregano, 1 tsp.
- Minced garlic cloves, 3.
- Black pepper
- Chopped yellow onion, 1.
- Extra virgin olive oil, 2 tbsps.
- Chopped poblano pepper, 1.
- Quartered tomatillos, 1 lb.
- Cumin, 1 tsp.
- Chopped pork shoulder, 3 lbs.
- Bay leaves, 2.
- Shredded cheddar cheese
- Salt
- Chopped jalapeno pepper, 1.
- Chopped green bell pepper, 1.
- Flour tortillas for serving
- Chopped red onion for serving, 1

Directions:

1. Turn the instant pot to sauté mode to heat the oil.
2. Fry the pork pieces with some seasonings to brown evenly, about 3 minutes
3. Stir in onion, bay leaves, jalapeno, poblano pepper, stock, green bell pepper, garlic, oregano, cumin, and tomatillos.
4. Set the cook time to 55 minutes at high pressure to cook with the lid closed.
5. Perform a natural release of the pressure for 10 minutes then unlid the instant pot then put the meat on a chopping board to shred.
6. Pulse the remaining mixture in the pot with a hand blender.
7. Distribute the mixture on flour tortillas topped with cheese and red onion.

Korean Style Beef

Servings: 6 , Prep + Cook Time: 35 minutes

Ingredients:

- Cubed zucchini, 1
- Korean soybean paste, ¼ cup
- Red pepper flakes, ¼ tsp.
- Cubed extra firm tofu, 12 oz.
- Black pepper
- Quartered shiitake mushroom caps, 1 oz.
- Chicken stock, 1 cup
- Sliced yellow onion, 1
- Stripped beefsteak, 2 lbs.
- Chopped scallion, 1.

- Salt
- Sliced chili pepper, 1

Directions:
1. Switch the instant pot to sauté mode then add soybean paste and stock to simmer for 2 minutes.
2. Mix in the beef, pepper, pepper flakes, and salt to cook for 15 minutes at high pressure with the lid closed.
3. Immediately the timer beeps, quickly release the pressure.
4. Stir in the mushrooms, tofu, zucchini and onion to boil for 4 minutes at high pressure with the lid sealed.
5. Again, release the pressure then remove the lid.
6. Stir in chili, some seasonings, and scallions then serve right away.

Instant pot Beef Chili

Servings: 6, Prep + Cook Time: 50 minutes

Ingredients:
- Chipotle powder, 1 tsp.
- Beef stock, 17 oz.
- Pale ale, 12 oz.
- Chopped carrots, 4.
- Ground beef, 1½ lbs.
- Black pepper
- Chopped sweet onion, 1.
- Chili powder, 3 tbsps.
- Soaked and drained mixed beans, 16 oz.
- Bay leaf, 1
- Vegetable oil, 2 tbsps.
- Chopped garlic cloves, 6.
- Diced jalapeno peppers, 7
- Chopped canned tomatoes, 28 oz.
- Salt

Directions:

1. Turn the instant pot to sauté mode to heat the oil.
2. Stir in the beef to cook for 8 minutes until browned evenly then reserve on a bowl.
3. Heat the remaining oil in the pot to sauté the garlic, carrots, onion, and jalapeno for 4 minutes.
4. Mix in tomatoes, ale, stock, chipotle powder, beef, bay leaf, beans, pepper, salt, and chili powder.
5. Give the mix a gentle stir then set to cook for 25 minutes at high pressure with the lid sealed.
6. Carefully release the pressure naturally and remove the lid.
7. Stir the chili gently then serve immediately.

Asian Style Short Ribs

Servings: 4 , Prep + Cook Time: 60 minutes

Ingredients:
- Rice wine, ¼ cup.
- Pear juice, ¼ cup
- Soy sauce, ½ cup
- Sliced ginger, 3
- Short ribs, 4 lbs.
- Vegetable oil, 1 tbsp.
- Chopped green onions, 2.
- Sesame oil, 2 tsps.
- Water, ½ cup
- Minced garlic cloves, 3.

Directions:

1. Turn the instant pot to sauté mode to heat the oil
2. Stir in ginger, green onions, and garlic to cook for 1 minute
3. Mix in the wine, ribs, water, sesame oil, soy sauce, ribs, and pear juice to cook for 3 minutes as you stir gently.
4. With the pot sealed, cook for 45 minutes at high pressure.
5. When the timer beeps, release the pressure naturally for 15 minutes then unlid.
6. Serve the ribs on plates topped with the sauce from the pot.

Delicious Meatloaf

Servings: 6, Prep + Cook Time: 50 minutes

Ingredients:
- Panko breadcrumbs, ½ cup
- Ketchup, ¼ cup
- Grated yellow onion, 1
- Whisked eggs, 2
- Water, 2 cups
- Salt
- Ground meat, 2 lbs.
- Black pepper
- Milk, 1/3 cup

Directions:
1. Stir together milk and breadcrumbs then reserve for 5 minutes
2. Mix in the eggs, pepper, salt, and ground meat
3. Transfer the combination on a well-greased tin foil and shape of a loaf hen top with ketchup.
4. Pour the water in the instant pot then set the meatloaf in the steamer basket to cook at high pressure for 35 minutes with the lid sealed.
5. Perform a natural release of pressure for 10 minutes then turn the valve to venting to release the remaining pressure then remove the lid.
6. Let the loaf cool down for 5 minutes before slicing to serve.

Chipotle Pork Tamales

Servings: 24 , Prep + Cook Time: 1 hour and 45 minutes

Ingredients:
- Chipotle chili powder, 1 tbsp.
- Crushed garlic cloves, 2.
- Chili powder, 2 tbsps.
- Water, 4 cups
- Cumin, 1 tsp.
- Dried corn husks, 8 oz.
- Black pepper
- Baking powder, 1 tbsp.
- Masa, 4 cups
- Corn oil, ¼ cup
- Chopped pork shoulder, 3 lbs.
- Shortening, ¼ cup
- Salt
- Chopped yellow onion, 1

Directions:
1. Put cumin, 2 cups water, salt, onion, chili powder, chipotle powder, pepper, and garlic in the instant pot.
2. Stir in the pork o cook for 75 minutes at high pressure with the lid closed
3. When the timer beeps, release the pressure naturally for 10 minutes then unlid the pot.
4. Put the meat on a chopping board to shred using 2 forks.
5. Transfer the shredded meat to a bowl then add some seasonings and 1 tablespoon of oil then reserve for some time.
6. Stir together masa, baking powder, salt, oil, shortening and pepper in a medium bowl using a mixer.
7. Mix in the cooking liquid from the pot and process again.
8. Pour 2 cups of water to the instant pot and place the steamer basket inside
9. Unfold 2 corn husks then set them on a clean surface.
10. Mix ¼ cup of masa mix near the top of the husk then press into a square and leaves 2 inches at the bottom
11. Put 1 tablespoon of pork in the center of the masa then bind the husk around the dough and place standing up in the steamer basket.
12. Perform the same process with other husks.
13. With the lid sealed, cook for 20 minutes at high pressure.
14. When the timer click, release the pressure naturally for 15 minutes then switch the valve to venting to release the remaining pressure and open the lid.

Cinnamon Potatoes and Cubed Goat

Servings: 5 , Prep + Cook Time: 60 minutes

Ingredients:

- Halved potatoes, 3
- Cardamom pods, 3
- Chopped onions, 3.
- Cinnamon stick, 2
- Chopped tomatoes, 2.
- Chopped coriander, 1 tsp.
- Cubed goat meat, 2 ½ lbs.
- Minced garlic cloves, 4.
- Chopped green chilies, 2.
- Chili powder, ¾ tsp.
- Vegetable oil, 5 tbsps.
- Sugar, 1 tsp.
- Cloves, 4
- Black pepper
- Turmeric powder, 3 tsps.
- Grated ginger, 1
- Salt
- Water, 2 ½ cups.

Directions:

1. In a sizable bowl, combine goat cubes, turmeric, pepper and salt, to coat evenly and reserve for 10 minutes.
2. Adjust the instant pot to sauté mode to heat the oil and ½ of the sugar as you stir.
3. Mix in the potatoes to fry for a few minutes then put on a bowl.
4. Put the cardamom, cloves, and cinnamon stick to cook for 3 minutes
5. Mix in the chili powder and tomatoes to cook for 5 minutes.
6. Now, add the meat and cook for 10 minutes
7. Stir in 2 cups of water then cook for 15 minutes at high pressure with the lid sealed.
8. When the timer is over, quick release the pressure then open the lid carefully.
9. Adjust the seasoning then add the remaining sugar, ½ cup of water, and potatoes.
10. With the lid in position, cook for 5 minutes at high pressure.
11. Immediately the timer is over, release the pressure then remove the lid.
12. Serve the meal right away topped with chopped parsley.

Cinnamon Beef Brisket

Servings: 6 , Prep + Cook Time: 60 minutes

Ingredients:

- Halved cinnamon sticks, 4
- Water, 17 oz.
- Sliced oranges, 2
- Dried dill, 1 tbsp.
- Black pepper
- Bay leaves, 3
- Beef brisket, 4 lbs.
- Minced garlic cloves, 2.
- Sliced yellow onions, 2
- Salt
- Sliced celery, 11 0z.

Directions:

1. In a medium bowl, combine soak the beef in water, leave for some hours then drain and put to the instant pot
2. Mix in onions, bay leaves, orange slices, celery, garlic, pepper, dill, cinnamon, salt and dill and 17 oz. water then stir gently.
3. Cook for 50 minutes at high pressure with the lid sealed.
4. When the timer is over, quick release the pressure then let the meat to cool down for 5 minutes.
5. When cooled, put on the chopping board to slice.
6. Serve the meal sprinkled with juice and the vegetables from the pot.

Creamy Lamb Curry

Servings: 6 , **Prep + Cook Time:** 35 minutes

Ingredients:
- Dry white wine, 3 oz.
- Curry powder, 3 tbsps.
- Pure cream, 3 tbsps.
- Water, 3 tbsps.
- Cubed lamb shoulder, 1½ lbs.
- Chopped yellow onion, 1.
- Parsley, 1 tbsp.
- Salt
- Coconut milk, 2 oz.
- Black pepper
- Vegetable oil, 2 tbsps.

Directions:
1. Stir together half of the curry powder with coconut milk, pepper, and salt in a bowl.
2. Adjust the instant pot to sauté mode to heat the oil for frying the onions for 4 minutes.
3. Stir in the remaining curry powder to cook for 1 minute.
4. Add the meat to brown well for 3 minutes the mix in wine, water and the seasonings.
5. With the lid sealed, cook for 20 minutes at high pressure.
6. Perform a quick release of pressure when the timer goes off.
7. Stir in the coconut milk then simmer to boil for 5 minutes
8. Serve the meal on plates topped with chopped parsley.

One pot Pork & Brown Rice

Servings: 6 , **Prep + Cook Time:** 35 minutes

Ingredients:
- Butter, 3 tbsps.
- Brown sugar, 1/3 cup
- Chopped onion, 1 cup.
- Peppercorns, 1 tbsp.
- Water, 2 cups
- Brown rice, 2 cups
- Pork chops, 2 lbs.
- Bay leaves, 2
- Crushed hot peppers, 2.
- Salt, 1/3 cup.
- Beef stock, 2½ cups
- Ice, 2 cups
- Salt
- Crushed garlic cloves, 4.
- Black pepper

Directions:
1. Put water in a pan to heat over medium heat.
2. Stir in brown sugar and salt until it dissolves.
3. Remove from fire then add the ice, garlic, hot peppers, bay leaves and peppercorns.
4. Put in the pork meat to coat evenly then refrigerate for 4 hours.
5. Wash the pork the dry with paper towels
6. Switch the instant pot to sauté mode to melt the butter.
7. Add the pork chops to cook until browned evenly then reserve.
8. Fry the onions in the instant pot for 2 minutes then stir in rice to cook for 1 minute
9. Mix in pork chops, and stock
10. Cook for 22 minutes at high pressure with the lid sealed.
11. When the timer goes off, release the pressure naturally for 10minutes then unlid.
12. Adjust the seasoning then serve the meal right away.

Beef with Mixed Veggies & Rice Soup

Servings: 6 , **Prep + Cook Time:** 25 minutes

Ingredients:
- Frozen peas, ½ cup
- Minced garlic cloves, 3.
- Chopped yellow onion, 1.
- Canned garbanzo beans, 15 oz.
- Black pepper
- Crushed canned tomatoes, 14 oz.
- Spicy V8 juice, 12 oz.
- Ground beef meat, 1 lb.
- Sliced carrots, 2
- White rice, ½ cup.
- Vegetable oil, 1 tbsp.
- Chopped celery rib, 1.
- Cubed potato, 1
- Salt
- Canned beef stock, 28 oz.

Directions:
1. Switch the instant pot to sauté mode to cook the beef until it browns evenly then reserve on a plate.
2. Heat the oil in the pot to fry the onion and celery for 5 minutes
3. Stir in garlic to cook for another minute.
4. Mix in rice, V8 juice, pepper, tomatoes, potatoes, beans, beef, stock, salt and carrots.
5. Set to cook for 5 minutes at high pressure with the lid closed
6. When the timer clicks, release the pressure then remove the lid.
7. Add the seasoning and the peas to cook on simmer mode.
8. Serve the meal while still hot.

Instant Pot Spiced Beef

Servings: 4 , **Prep + Cook Time:** 40 minutes

Ingredients:
- Chopped carrots, 2.
- Chopped yellow onion, 1.
- Cubed beef stew meat, 1 ½ lbs.
- Minced garlic cloves, 2.
- Water, 2 cups
- Chopped potatoes, 4.
- White flour, 4tbsps.
- Black pepper
- Chopped celery stalks, 2.
- Bay leaf, 1
- Extra virgin olive oil, 2 tbsps.
- Dried thyme, ½ tsp.
- Chopped parsley; ½ bunch.
- Beef stock, 2 cups.
- Red wine, 2 tbsps.
- Salt

Directions:
1. Rub the beep with the seasonings the mix with ½ of the flour.
2. Adjust the instant pot to sauté mode to melt the oil

3. Add the beef to brown evenly for about 2minutes then reserve on a bowl.
4. Put the onions to the pot to cook for 3 minutes then add garlic to cook for another minute.
5. Mix in the wine to cook for 15 seconds then add the remaining flour to cook for 2 minutes
6. Put the meat back to the pot the add water, thyme, bay leaf and stock.
7. Cook at high pressure for 12 minutes with the lid sealed.
8. Quick release the pressure when the timer stops then remove the lid.
9. Stir in the potatoes, celery, and carrots to cook for 5 minutes at high pressure.
10. For 10 minutes release the pressure naturally when the timer stops.
11. Shift the valve to venting to release the remaining pressure then open the lid
12. Serve the meal topped with chopped parsley.

Herbed Lamb and Beans

Servings: 4 , **Prep + Cook Time:** 50 minutes

Ingredients:

- Chopped onion, 1 cup.
- Black pepper
- Chopped leek, 1 cup.
- Minced garlic, 2 tbsps.
- Soaked and drained white beans, 1½ cups
- Herbs de Provence, 1 tsp.
- Lamb chops, 4
- Water, 3 cups
- Worcestershire sauce, 2 tsps.
- Salt
- Chopped canned tomatoes, 2 cups.

Directions:

1. In the instant pot, put the lamb chops
2. Stir in tomatoes, water, onion, pepper, leek, garlic, salt, beans, herbs de Provence, and Worcestershire sauce.
3. Cook for 40 minutes at high pressure with the lid sealed.
4. Perform a quick release of the pressure then open the lid
5. Serve the meal right away

Cheesy Instant Pot Meatballs

Servings: 6 , **Prep + Cook Time:** 20 minutes

Ingredients:

- Whisked egg, 1
- Bread crumbs, ½ cup
- Extra-virgin olive oil, 1 tbsp.
- Tomato puree, 2¾ cups
- Milk, ½ cup
- Chopped onion, 1.
- Chopped celery stalk, ½
- Ground meat, 1 lb.
- Chopped carrot, 1.
- Dried oregano, ½ tsp.
- Water, 2 cups
- Salt
- Grated parmesan, 1/3 cup
- Black pepper

Directions:

1. Combine cheese with bread crumbs, meat, salt, half of the onion, egg, oregano, ½ of the onion milk, and pepper in a bowl.
2. Switch the instant pot to sauté mode to heat the oil for frying the onions for 3 minutes.
3. Stir in tomato puree, salt, carrot, celery, and water
4. Mould meatballs out of the mixture then arrange them in the pot.
5. Cook at high pressure for 5 minutes with the lid closed.
6. For 10 minutes naturally release the pressure when the timer goes off.
7. Shift the valve to venting to release the remaining pressure then open the lid.
8. Enjoy the meal with your favorite spaghetti

Orange Pork & Honey

Servings: 4 , **Prep + Cook Time:** 1 hour 10 minutes

Ingredients:

- Dried rosemary, 1 tsp.
- Minced garlic cloves, 3.
- Cloves, 2
- Water, ½ cup
- Soy sauce, 2 tbsps.
- Sliced ginger, 1 tbsp.
- Grape seed oil, 1 tbsp.
- Honey, 1 tbsp.
- Chopped pork shoulder, 1½ lbs.
- Maple syrup, 1 tbsp.
- Orange juice, 1 tbsp.
- Cinnamon stick, 1
- Salt
- Sliced yellow onion, 1
- Cornstarch, 1 ½ tbsps.
- Black pepper

Directions:

1. Switch the instant pot to sauté mode to heat the grape seed oil.
2. Put in the pork and some seasonings to brown evenly for about 5 minutes then reserve on a plate.
3. Put the ginger, onions, and seasonings to cook for 1 minute then stir in garlic to cook for 1 more minute.
4. Mix in soy sauce, pork pieces, water, cloves, honey, maple syrup, cinnamon, orange juice, and rosemary.
5. Cook for 50 minutes at high pressure with the lid sealed.
6. Release the pressure naturally once the timer clicks.
7. Remove the lid and get rid of the cloves and cinnamon.
8. In a small bowl, combine water and cornstarch then pour the mixture back to the pot.
9. Cook on sauté mode until the sauce thickens.
10. Serve the pork with the sauce and enjoy.

Pork Meatball

Servings: 8 , Prep + Cook Time: 20 minutes

Ingredients:

- Worcestershire sauce, 1tsp.
- Chopped parsley, 2 tbsps.
- Large egg, 1
- Bay leaf, 1
- Ground pork meat, 1½ lbs.
- Minced garlic cloves, 2.
- Soaked bread slices, 2
- Cubed potatoes, 2
- Fresh peas, ¾ cup
- Paprika, ½ tsp.
- White wine, ¼ cup
- Black pepper
- Beef stock, ¾ cup.
- Nutmeg, ½ tsp.
- Extra virgin olive oil, 2 tbsps.
- Chopped carrots, 2.
- Salt
- Flour, ¼ cup

Directions:

1. Stir together ground meat with egg, soaked bread, paprika, salt, nutmeg, parsley, pepper, and garlic in a bowl.
2. Pour in Worcestershire sauce and 1 tablespoon of stock.
3. Mould the mixture into meatballs then dust with flour.
4. Switch the instant pot to sauté mode to eat the oil.
5. Add the meatballs to brown evenly
6. Mix in the potatoes, peas, wine, bay leaf, stock and carrots.
7. Cook at high pressure for 6 minutes with the lid sealed.
8. Release the pressure once the timer clicks then remove the lid.
9. Remove the bay leaf and serve the meatballs immediately.

Balsamic Brussels Sprouts.

Servings: 6, Prep + Cook Time: 35 minutes

Ingredients:

- Balsamic reduction, 2 tbsps.
- Chopped slices bacon, 5
- Water, 2 tbsps.
- Pepper
- Soft goat cheese, ¼ cup
- Chopped Brussels sprouts; 6 cups
- Salt, ¼ tsp.

Directions:

1. Turn the instant pot to sauté mode then cook the bacon until crispy
2. Stir in the Brussels sprouts and to coat with the bacon fat.
3. Mix in the water and sprinkle with the seasonings.
4. Cook for 6 minutes as you stir occasionally until the Brussels sprouts are crisp.
5. Once cooked well, put into a serving dish sprinkled with balsamic reduction and crumbled goat cheese.

Delight Pork Sausages with Potato mash

Servings: 6, Prep + Cook Time: 30 minutes

Ingredients:

For the potatoes:
- Grated cheddar cheese, 1 tbsp.
- Mustard powder, 1tsp.
- Black pepper
- Warm milk, 4 oz.
- Water, 6 oz.
- Cubed potatoes, 4
- Sat
- Butter, 1 tbsp.

For the sausages:
- Red wine, 3 oz.
- Extra virgin olive oil, 2tbsps.
- 1 tbsp. cornstarch mixed with 1 tbsp. water
- Pork sausages, 6
- Onion jam, ½ cup
- Black pepper
- Water, 3 oz.
- Salt

Directions:

1. Add potatoes in your instant pot with pepper, 6 oz. water, and salt
2. Stir gently then cook for 5 minutes at high pressure with the lid covered.
3. Release the pressure quickly once the timer beeps then drain potatoes and reserve in a bowl.
4. Mix in the butter, warm milk, pepper, salt, and mustard, then mash well
5. Stir in the cheese and reserve.
6. Turn the instant pot to sauté mode to heat the oil for browning the sausages evenly.
7. Mix in wine, onion jam, and 3 oz. water.
8. Adjust the seasoning then cook for 8 minutes at high pressure with the lid covered.
9. Quickly release the pressure once the timer s over and serve the sausages on plates
10. Pour the cornstarch mix to the pot and give it a gentle stir
11. Sprinkle the sauce over the sausages and enjoy with mashed potatoes.

Thyme Veal and Veggies

Servings: 4 , Prep + Cook Time: 45 minutes

Ingredients:
- Extra virgin olive oil, 3 ½ tbsps.
- Veal shoulder, 2 lbs.
- Chopped shallots, 16 oz.
- Beef stock, 9 oz.
- Black pepper
- Sliced button mushrooms, 3½ oz.
- White wine, 2 oz.
- Sliced shiitake mushrooms, 3½ oz.
- White flour, 1 tbsp.
- Thyme, 1/8 tsp.
- Minced garlic cloves, 2.
- Chopped potatoes, 17 oz.
- Dried sage, 1 tsp.
- Salt
- Chopped chives, 2 tbsps.

Directions:

1. Turn the instant pot to sauté mode to heat 1½ tablespoon of oil.
2. Mix in the veal with some seasonings to brown evenly for 5 minutes then reserve in a bowl.
3. Put the remaining oil to the pot and heat then fry the mushrooms for 3 minutes
4. Stir in the garlic to cook for 1 minute and transfer everything to a bowl.
5. Mix the flour and wine to the pot to cook for 1 minute.
6. Add sage, stock, and thyme then return the meat to pot.
7. With the lid sealed, cook at high pressure for 20 minutes.
8. Release the pressure quickly then open the lid
9. Return the mushrooms and garlic.
10. Mix in the shallots and potatoes.
11. Cook for 4 minutes at high pressure with the lid covered.
12. Again, release the pressure then remove the lid
13. Stir in the seasonings and the chives and serve right away.

Mexican Stewed Lamb

Servings: 4 , **Prep + Cook Time:** 60 minutes

Ingredients:

- Extra virgin olive oil, 2 tbsps.
- Chopped yellow onion, 1
- Chopped cilantro, ½ bunch
- Corn tortillas
- Cubed lamb shoulder, 3 lbs.
- Lime wedges
- Refried beans
- Minced garlic cloves, 3.
- Salt
- Enchilada sauce, 19 oz.

Directions:

1. Combine the lamb and enchilada sauce in a bowl to marinade for 24 hours
2. Switch the instant pot to sauté mode to heat the oil
3. Stir in the garlic and onions to cook for 5 minutes
4. Mix in the lamb, salt and its marinade.
5. Boil for 45 minutes at high pressure with the lid sealed.
6. Release the pressure quickly once the timer goes off.
7. Put the meat on a chopping board to cook before shredding and put in a bowl.
8. Add cooking sauce to it and stir.
9. Put meat on tortillas then sprinkle cilantro on each.
10. Top with beans, squeeze lime juice, roll and serve.

Spicy Pork & Mashed Potatoes

Servings: 6, **Prep + Cook Time:** 35 minutes

Ingredients:

- Cubed yellow onion, 1
- Chopped garlic cloves, 3.
- Mixed rosemary, sage, oregano and thyme, 1 bunch
- White flour, 2 tbsps.
- Black pepper
- Chicken stock, 2 cups
- Butter, 2 tbsps.
- Smoked paprika, 1 tsp.
- Boneless pork chops, 6
- Salt
- Cubed potatoes, 2 lbs.

Directions:

1. In the instant pot, add potatoes, ½ of the onion, stock, garlic, and the herbs
2. Arrange the pork chops on top then sprinkle pepper, paprika, and salt.
3. Cook for 15 minutes at high pressure with the lid closed.
4. In the meantime, melt the butter on a pan over medium heat to cook the flour for 2 minutes then remove from heat.
5. Quickly release the pressure then transfer the pork to a platter and remove herbs.
6. Combine the potatoes to a bowl then mix with salt, some of the cooking liquid, pepper using your hand mixer.
7. Cook for 2 minutes on simmer mode
8. Stir in the butter until it thickens.
9. Serve the pork chops on plates with mashed potatoes as a side topped with the gravy from the pot all over.

Sherry BBQ Pork

Servings: 6 , **Prep + Cook Time:** 60 minutes

Ingredients:

- Peanut oil, 1 tsp.
- Dry sherry, 2 tbsps.
- Sesame oil, 2 tsps.
- Honey, 2 tbsps.
- Char siu sauce, 8 tbsps.
- Pork belly, 2 lbs.
- Soy sauce, 4 tbsps.
- Chicken stock, 1 quart

Directions:

1. Switch the instant pot to simmer mode then add soy sauce, sherry, stock, and half of char siu sauce to cook for 8 minutes
2. Stir in the pork then cook for 30 minutes at high pressure with the lid sealed.
3. Naturally release the pressure then put pork to a chopping board to cool before slicing.
4. Set the pan on fire to heat the peanut oil over medium heat to cook for a few minutes.
5. In the meantime, combine sesame oil with the remaining char siu sauce and honey.
6. Rub the pork from the pan with this mix then cook for 10 minutes.
7. Set another pan on fire over medium heat to simmer the cooking liquid from the pot for 3 minutes then remove from heat.
8. Serve the pork topped with the sauce.

Cajun Sausage and Red beans

Servings: 8 , **Prep + Cook Time:** 45 minutes

Ingredients:

- Soaked and drained red beans, 1 lb.
- Chopped garlic clove, 1.
- Ground cumin, ¼ tsp.
- Chopped green bell pepper; ½
- Dried parsley, 1 tsp.
- Chopped yellow onion, 1.
- Black pepper
- Sliced smoked sausage, 1 lb.
- Chopped celery stalk, 1.
- Bay leaf, 1
- Water, 5 cups
- Cajun seasoning, 2 tbsps.
- Salt

Directions:

1. Combine beans with bay leaf, bell pepper, water, Cajun seasoning, celery, salt, pepper, sausage, parsley, cumin, garlic, and onion in an instant pot
2. Cook for 30 minutes at high pressure with the lid closed
3. Release the pressure quickly then remove the lid.
4. Serve the meal into bowls while still hot.

Parmesan Meatloaf

Servings: 8 , **Prep + Cook Time:** 35 minutes

Ingredients:

- Dried parsley, 2 tbsps.
- Water, 2 cups
- Whisked eggs, 3
- Bread slices, 3
- Black pepper
- BBQ sauce, ½ cup
- Ground beef, 2 lbs.
- Milk, ½ cup
- Parmesan, ¾ cup
- Salt
- Bacon slices, 8

Directions:

1. Combine milk with bread slices then reserve for 5 minutes
2. Stir in pepper, parsley, cheese, salt, meat, and eggs.
3. Mould the mixture into a loaf then put on a tin foil.
4. Top with bacon slices, tuck them underneath and spread half of the BBQ sauce all over.
5. In the pot, add 2 cups of water and set the meatloaf in the steamer basket.
6. With the lid sealed, cook at high pressure for 20 minutes.
7. Release the pressure quickly then remove the lid
8. Put the meat loaf to a pan and spread the remaining BBQ sauce over it
9. Put in the preheated broiler for 5 minutes then put on platter to slice for serving.

Chapter 5 Fish and Seafood

Lentils And Spinach Stew

Servings: 4, **Prep +Cook time:** 50 minutes

Ingredients:

- Baby spinach- 6 cups
- Salt
- Black pepper
- Chopped yellow onion- 1
- Minced garlic- 4 cloves
- Chopped carrots- 2
- Olive oil- 2 tsp.
- Chopped celery stalk- 1
- Turmeric- 1 tsp.
- Rinsed brown lentils- 1 cup
- Thyme- 1 tsp.
- Cumin- 2 tsp.
- Veggie stock- 4 cups

Directions:

1. Press the 'Sauté' button on the Instant Pot to preheat the pot then pour in the oil.
2. Mix in the carrots, celery, and onions to fry for 5 minutes then add the thyme, salt, pepper, garlic, and turmeric to cook for 1 minute.
3. Pour in the lentils and the veggie stock and seal the pot to cook for 12 minutes at high pressure.
4. Natural release the pressure for 15 minutes then move the valve to venting to release the remaining steam.
5. Mix in the spinach and season with salt and pepper.
6. Serve into bowls.

Spicy Spinach With Potato And Sausage Soup

Servings: 4, **Prep +Cook time:** 35 minutes

Ingredients:

- Cubed big-sized potato- 1
- Salt
- Black pepper
- Chopped carrots- 2
- Bay leaves- 2
- Chopped spinach- 5 oz.
- Chopped Italian sausage- 1 Ib.
- Chopped yellow onion- 1
- Turkey stock- 5 cups
- Dried thyme- 1 tsp.
- Chopped celery stalks- 2
- Minced garlic- 2 cloves
- Dried oregano- 1 tsp.
- Dried basil- 1 tsp.
- Red pepper flakes- 1 tsp.

Directions:

1. Press the 'Sauté' button on the Instant Pot to heat it then add the sausage to brown then remove and set aside.
2. Mix in the carrots, onion, and celery and let cook for 2 minutes.
3. Mix in the potatoes and let it cook for 2 minutes then add in the pepper flakes, basil, oregano, garlic, stock, spinach, bay leaves, and thyme.
4. Seal the pot and let it cook for 4 minutes at high pressure.
5. Natural release the pressure for 15 minutes then set the valve to venting to let out the rest of the steam.
6. Remove the bay leaves and serve into bowls.

Cheesy Potato Soup With Bacon

Servings: 6, **Prep +Cook time:** 30 minutes

Ingredients:
- Cubed potatoes- 6 cups
- Water- 2 tbsp.
- Cornstarch- 2 tbsp.
- Red pepper flakes- 1/8 tsp.
- Shredded cheddar cheese- 1 cup
- Corn- 1 cup
- Dried parsley- 2 tbsp.
- Cooked and crumbled bacon- 6 bacon slices
- Butter- 2 tbsp.
- Salt and black pepper
- Chicken stock- 28 oz.
- Cubed cream cheese- 3 oz.
- Half and half- 2 cups
- Chopped yellow onion- ½ cup

Directions:
1. Press 'Sauté' on the Instant Pot and add the butter to it then add the onions to fry for 5 minutes.
2. Pour half of the chicken stock into the pot then add the parsley, pepper flakes, salt, and pepper and mix.
3. Place the potatoes on a steamer basket and put it in the pot. Seal the lid to cook for 4 minutes on high pressure.
4. Natural release the pressure for 15 minutes then move the valve to venting to release the rest of the steam.
5. Remove the potatoes and set aside.
6. Mix the water and cornstarch in a bowl.
7. Let the pot simmer then add the cheddar cheese, cream cheese, and the cornstarch mix then mix it well.
8. Pour the half and half, remaining stock, bacon, and corn and mix it well.
9. Serve into bowls.

Spicy Bourbon Stew With Beef And Veggies

Servings: 4, **Prep +Cook time:** 55 minutes

Ingredients:
- Cubed meat- 1 Ib.
- Salt
- Black pepper
- Olive oil- 2 tbsp.
- Minced garlic- 4 cloves
- Beef stock- 2 cups
- White flour- ½ cup
- Cooked and crumbled bacon- 2 slices
- Bay leaves- 2
- Peeled Cipollini onions- 1 cup
- Chopped rosemary- 1 bunch
- Tomato paste- 1 tbsp.
- Chopped carrots- 4
- Chopped thyme- 1 bunch
- Bourbon- ½ cup
- Diced rutabaga – 1

Directions:
1. Combine the salt and pepper with the flour in a bowl.
2. Dip the meat in the flour mix to coat and set aside.
3. Press the 'Sauté' button on the Instant Pot then pour the oil into the pot and add the meat to brown all around.
4. Pour in the bourbon, stock, carrots, rutabaga, garlic, thyme, onions, and rosemary then mix it and let it cook for 2 minutes.
5. Put the beef in the pot then seal the lid to cook for 10 minutes at high pressure.
6. Natural release the pressure for 15 minutes then move the valve to venting and open the pot.
7. Mix in the bacon, peas, salt, pepper, and bay leaves and seal the lid to cook for 12 minutes on low pressure.
8. Release the pressure and remove the bay leaves.
9. Serve into bowls.

Chili Endive And Rice Soup

Servings: 4, **Prep +Cook time**: 45 minutes

Ingredients:
- Salt and black pepper
- Veggie stock- 6 cups
- Chopped garlic- 3 cloves
- Trimmed and roughly chopped endives- 3
- Soy sauce- 1 ½ tbsp.
- Canola oil- 1 tbsp.
- Sesame oil- 2 tsp.
- Grated ginger- 1 tbsp.
- Chopped scallions- 2
- Chili sauce- 1 tsp.
- Uncooked rice- ½ cup

Directions:
1. Press the 'Sauté' button on the Instant Pot and add the sesame and canola oil to the pot.
2. Mix in the garlic and scallions to fry for 4 minutes.
3. Mix in the ginger and the chili sauce and let it cook for 1 minute, then pour in the soy sauce and the stock to cook for 2 minutes.
4. Mix in the rice then seal the lid to cook at high pressure for 15 minutes.
5. Natural release the pressure for 15 minutes then set the valve to venting.
6. Season with salt and pepper and add in the endives. Seal and set to cook for 5 minutes at high pressure.
7. Release the pressure and serve into bowls.

Garlic Chicken Meatball With Vegetable Soup

Servings: 6, **Prep +Cook time**: 40 minutes

Ingredients:
- Nutritional yeast-2 tbsp.
- Salt
- Black pepper
- Arrowroot powder- 2 tbsp.
- Onion powder- 1 tsp.
- Dried basil- ½ tbsp.
- Crushed red pepper- ½ tsp.
- Garlic powder- 1 tsp.
- Ground chicken breast- 1 ½ Ib.

Soup:
- Chicken stock- 6 cups
- Chopped kale- 1 bunch
- Chopped celery stalks- 4
- Whisked eggs- 2
- Chopped carrots- 3
- Chopped yellow onions- 2
- Crushed red pepper- ½ tsp.
- Dried thyme- 2 tsp.
- Minced garlic- 2 cloves

Ingredients:
1. Press the 'Sauté' button on the Instant Pot to heat it then pour in some oil.
2. Put the carrots, celery, and onions and let it cook for 3 minutes then mix in the kale, stock, garlic, thyme, salt, pepper, and red pepper flakes to cook for some minutes.
3. Combine the chicken with the chicken spices and mix well then shape into meatballs and put it into the soup in the pot.
4. Seal the pot and let it cook for 15 minutes at high pressure.
5. Natural release the pressure for 15 minutes then quick release the remaining pressure by moving the valve to venting.
6. Let it cook on 'Sauté' and add the eggs slowly and let it cook for 2 minutes.
7. Serve into soup bowls.

Cheesy Chickpeas And Tomatoes Stew

Servings: 4, **Prep +Cook time:** 45 minutes

Ingredients:

- Drained chickpeas- 1 Ib.
- Salt
- Black pepper
- A drizzle of olive oil for serving
- Water- 22 oz.
- Chopped yellow onion- 1
- Red pepper flakes- ½ tsp.
- Dried oregano- 1 tsp.
- Grated parmesan cheese- 2 tbsp.
- Chopped canned tomatoes- 22 oz.
- Bay leaves- 3
- 1 garlic head; halved
- Olive oil- 2 tbsp.
- Chopped carrots- 2

Directions:

1. Mix the chickpeas, tomatoes, onions, t tablespoons of olive oil, salt, pepper, bay leaves, onions, and carrots in the Instant Pot and seal the pot.
2. Set to cook for 25 minutes at high pressure then quick release the pressure.
3. Serve into bowls and top with pepper flakes and parmesan then drizzle the olive oil over it.

Creamy Artichoke And Potatoes Soup

Servings: 4, **Prep +Cook time:** 40 minutes

Ingredients:

- Washed and trimmed artichoke hearts- 4
- Chopped gold potatoes- 8 oz.
- Salt
- Crushed black peppercorns- ¼ tsp.
- Cream- ¼ cup
- Chicken stock- 12 cups
- Bay leaf- 1
- Sliced leek- 1
- Butter- 5 tbsp.
- Thyme sprigs- 2
- Parsley sprigs- 4
- Minced garlic- 6 cloves
- Chopped shallots- ½ cup

Directions:

1. Press the 'Sauté' button on the Instant Pot then put the butter in It to melt.
2. Mix in the leek, garlic, artichoke hearts, and the shallots and let it brown for 3-4 minutes.
3. Mix in the stock, parsley, peppercorns, salt, potatoes, thyme, and salt and let it cook for 15 minutes at high pressure.
4. Natural release the pressure for 15 minutes then quick release the remaining pressure by setting the valve to venting position.
5. Open and blend with a dipping blender then mix in the cream and season with pepper and salt.
6. Serve into bowls.

Cheesy Beans And Vegetable Pasta Soup Bowls

Servings: 8, **Prep +Cook time:** 35 minutes

Ingredients:

- Uncooked pasta- 1 cup
- Salt and black pepper
- Canned chicken stock- 29 oz.
- Minced garlic- 4 cloves
- Canned kidney beans- 15 oz.
- Peeled and chopped tomatoes- 3 Ib.
- Chopped zucchini- 1
- Chopped basil- 2 tbsp.
- Grated asiago cheese -1 cup
- Corn kernels- 1 cup
- Extra-virgin olive oil- 1 tbsp.
- Chopped celery stalk- 1
- Chopped carrots- 2
- Chopped onions- 1
- Baby kernels- 1 cup
- Italian seasoning- 1 tsp.

Directions:

1. Press 'Sauté' on the Instant Pot and add the oil to heat then mix in the onion and let it fry for 5 minutes.
2. Mix in the zucchini, corn, celery, carrots, and garlic and cook for 5 minutes.
3. Add the pasta, tomatoes, stock, Italian seasoning, salt, and pepper and mix well.

Seal the lid and set to cook for 4 minutes at high pressure.
4. Natural release the pressure for 15 minutes then quick release the remaining pressure by moving the valve to venting position.
5. Mix in the spinach, beans, and basil then season with salt and pepper.
6. Serve topped with cheese.

Cranberry Turkey and Veggies Stew

Servings: 4, **Prep +Cook time**: 50 minutes

Ingredients:

- Chopped yellow onion- 1
- Turkey meat; cooked and shredded- 3cups
- Avocado oil- 1 tbsp.
- Cranberry sauce- 1 tbsp.
- Chopped carrots- 2
- Turkey stock- 5 cups
- Dried garlic; minced- 1 tsp.
- Chopped canned tomatoes- 15 oz.
- Chopped potatoes- 2 cups
- Chopped celery stalks- 3
- Salt
- Black pepper

Directions:
1. Pour the oil into the Instant Pot and heat on 'Sauté' mode.
2. Mix in the onions, carrots, and celery and let it fry for 3 minutes.
3. Pour in the stock then add the tomatoes, potatoes, cranberry sauce, meat, and garlic then seal the lid.
4. Set to cook at Low pressure for 30 minutes.
5. Natural release the pressure for 15 minutes then turn the valve to venting position to release the remaining pressure.
6. Season with black pepper and salt and serve.

Spicy Vinegar Lamb Stew

Servings: 4, **Prep +Cook time**: 50 minutes

Ingredients:

- Cubed lamb shoulder- 2 Ib.
- Black pepper and salt
- Dried basil- 1 tsp.
- Dried oregano- 1 tsp.
- Chopped green bell pepper- 1
- Chopped red bell pepper- 1
- Chopped canned tomatoes- 14 oz.
- Red wine vinegar- ¼ cup
- Minced garlic- 1 tbsp.
- Tomato paste- 2 tbsp.
- Chopped parsley- 1/3 cup
- Chopped yellow onions- 2
- Olive oil- 1 tbsp.
- Bay leaves- 2

Directions:

1. Pour the oil in the pot on 'Sauté' mode to heat it then add the garlic and onions to fry for 2 minutes.
2. Mix in the vinegar and let it cook for 2 minutes then add the lamb, tomato paste, basil, salt, pepper, tomatoes, and the bay leaves and seal the lid.
3. Let it cook at high pressure for 12 minutes.
4. Natural release the pressure for 15 minutes then move the valve to venting to release the remaining pressure.
5. Remove the bay leaves then add the red and green bell peppers and season with pepper and salt as needed then mix and seal the lid.
6. Set to cook at high pressure for 8 minutes then quick release the pressure.
7. Mix in the parsley and serve into bowls.

Curry Potatoes And Celery Soup

Servings: 2, **Prep +Cook time:** 35 minutes

Ingredients:
- Chopped potatoes- 3
- Salt
- Black pepper
- A handful of parsley
- Veggie stock- 4 cups
- Chopped yellow onion- 1
- Curry powder- 1 tbsp.
- Chopped celery stalks- 7
- Extra virgin olive oil- 1 tsp.
- Celery seeds- 1 tsp.

Directions:
1. Pour the oil into the Instant Pot and set to 'Sauté' mode to heat.
2. Mix in the celery seeds, curry powder, and onions and let it cook for 1 minute.
3. Add the potatoes and the celery and cook for 5 minutes then pour in the stock and season with pepper and salt and seal the lid.
4. Set to cook for 10 minutes at high pressure.
5. Natural release the pressure for 15 minutes and move the valve to venting to release the remaining pressure.
6. Use a dipping blender to puree the mix then mix in the parsley.
7. Serve into soup bowls.

Leeks and Corn Soup

Servings: 4, **Prep +Cook time:** 35 minutes

Ingredients:
- Ears of corn with kernels removed and cobs set aside- 6
- Chopped leeks- 2
- Salt
- Black pepper
- Minced garlic- 2 cloves
- A drizzle of extra virgin olive oil
- Chopped chives- 1 tbsp.
- Chicken stock- 4 cups
- Chopped tarragon- 4 sprigs
- Butter- 2 tbsp.
- Bay leaves- 2

Directions:
1. Press the 'Sauté' button on the Instant Pot and put the butter in it to melt.
2. Mix in the leeks and garlic and let fry for 4 minutes then add the cobs, bay leaves, tarragon, corn, and chicken stock then seal the lid.
3. Cook for 15 minutes at high pressure then, natural release the pressure for 15 minutes then move the valve to venting position to release the remaining steam.
4. Remove the corn cobs and the bay leaves then put everything in a blender.
5. Blend till smooth then pour the stock and blend again to mix.
6. Sprinkle with salt and pepper and serve into soup bowls topped with olive oil and chives.

Creamy Bacon And Fish Porridge

Servings: 4, **Prep +Cook time:** 30 minutes

Ingredients:
- Haddock fillets- 1 Ib.
- Chopped yellow onion- 1
- Chopped bacon- ¾ cup
- Chopped celery ribs- 2
- Chopped garlic- 2 cloves
- Chopped carrot- 1
- Salt and white pepper
- Frozen corn- 1 cup
- Cubed potatoes- 3 cups
- Heavy cream- 2 cups
- Potato starch- 1 tbsp.
- Chicken stock – 4 cups
- Butter- 2 tbsp.

Directions:

1. Press the 'Sauté' button on the Instant Pot and add the butter to it to melt then put in the chopped bacon to brown until crispy.
2. Mix in the onion, celery, and garlic to cook for 3 minutes.
3. Pour in the stock then add the potatoes, corn, fish fillets, pepper, and salt and mix it well then seal the lid.
4. Set to cook for 5 minutes at high pressure.
5. Mix the potato starch and the heavy cream in a bowl and then natural release the pressure and add the heavy cream mix to the pot and simmer on low heat for 3 minutes.
6. Serve into bowls.

Cheesy Rice With Bacon And Veggies Soup

Servings: 6, **Prep +Cook time**: 30 minutes

Ingredients:
- Chopped bacon- 4 slices
- Salt and black pepper
- Basmati rice- 4 tbsp.
- Chopped spinach- 2 cups
- Small broccoli heads; chopped- 2
- Grated parmesan- 1 tbsp.
- Olive oil- 1 tsp.
- Veggie stock- 4 cups
- Chopped leek- 1
- Celery rib; chopped- 1

Directions:

1. Press the 'Sauté' button on the Instant Pot then add the olive oil and bacon to brown till crispy then set aside.
2. Pour in the veggie stock and add the celery, spinach, broccoli, leek, and rice. Season with pepper and salt then seal the lid to cook for 6 minutes at high pressure.
3. Natural release the pressure for 15 minutes then move the valve to venting to release the remaining pressure.
4. Sprinkle some more salt and pepper into the soup, if desired then add the crispy bacon.
5. Serve into soup bowls.

Chicken With Beans And Vegetable Soup

Servings: 8, **Prep +Cook time**: 30 minutes

Ingredients:
- Salt
- Black pepper
- Chorizo with casings removed- 9 oz.
- Chicken stock- 4 cups
- Baby kale- 5 oz.
- Bay leaves- 2
- Chopped potatoes- 3
- Chopped chicken thighs- 4
- Drained Garbanzo beans- 14 oz.
- Chopped canned tomatoes- 15 oz.
- Olive oil- 2 tbsp.
- Chopped yellow onions- 2
- Minced garlic- 4 cloves

Directions:

1. Press the 'Sauté' button on the Instant Pot and add the olive oil to heat then put the chicken thighs, onion, and chorizo to cook for 5 minutes.
2. Mix in the garlic to cook for 1 minute then add the tomatoes, bay leaves, and chicken stock, potatoes, kale, salt, and pepper and seal the lid.
3. Set to cook for 4 minutes at high pressure.
4. Natural release the pressure for 15 minutes then quick release the rest of the pressure by moving the valve to venting position.
5. Add the beans then season with more salt and pepper if desired.
6. Serve into bowls.

Dark Beet Soup With Lentils

Servings: 4, **Prep +Cook time:** 30 minutes

Ingredients:

- Chopped beets- 3
- Salt and black pepper
- Chopped parsley- 1 ½ tbsp.
- Dark miso- 3 tbsp.
- Sesame oil- 1 tbsp.
- Red lentils- 1 cup
- Chopped carrots- 2
- Chopped red onion- 1
- Chopped thyme leaves- ½ tsp.
- Veggie stock- 6 cups
- Bay leaves- 3

Directions:

1. Press the 'Sauté' button on the Instant Pot and add the oil. When hot, put in the chopped onion to fry for 5 minutes.
2. Mix in the remaining ingredients and seal the lid.
3. Cook for 5 minutes at high pressure then natural release the pressure for 15 minutes and move the valve to venting to release the remaining steam then remove the bay leaves.
4. Blend with a dipping blender then mix the miso with some water and pour it in the pot then season with salt and pepper and the parsley.
5. Serve into soup bowls.

Creamy Asparagus Soup

Servings: 4, **Prep +Cook time:** 45 minutes

Ingredients:

- Green asparagus; trimmed with tips cut off into medium pieces- 2 Ib.
- Salt and white pepper
- Chicken stock- 6 cups
- Chopped yellow onion- 1
- Butter- 3 tbsp.
- Crème fraiche- ½ cup
- Lemon juice- ¼ tsp.

Directions:

1. Press 'Sauté' on the Instant Pot and put the butter in it to melt then mix in the asparagus and season with pepper and salt and cook for 5 minutes.
2. Pour in 5 cups of stock and seal the lid to cook for 15 minutes on low pressure.
3. Natural release the pressure for 15 minutes then move the valve to venting to release the rest of the pressure.
4. Pour the pot contents in a blender and blend till smooth.
5. Let it simmer and mix in the crème Fraiche and the remaining stock and the lemon juice then season with salt and pepper.
6. Serve into soup bowls.

Beer Lamb And Potatoes Soup

Servings: 6, **Prep +Cook time:** 45 minutes

Ingredients:

- Lamb shoulder; cut into medium chunks- 3 Ib.
- Salt
- Black pepper
- Chopped carrots- 2
- Water- 2 cups
- Dark beer- 6 oz.
- Roughly chopped big potatoes- 2
- Chopped onions- 2
- Minced parsley- ¼ cup
- Chopped thyme sprigs- 2

Directions:

1. In the Instant Pot, put the lamb and the onions then add the pepper, salt, thyme, beer, carrots, water, and potatoes then seal the lid.
2. Let it cook for 15 minutes for high pressure.
3. Natural release the pressure for 15 minutes then move the valve to venting to release the rest of the pressure.
4. Season with salt and pepper and mix in the parsley then serve into bowls.

Tomato Soup With Parmesan And Basil

Servings: 6, **Prep +Cook time:** 60 minutes

Ingredients:

Roasted tomatoes:
- Cherry tomatoes; halved- 3 Ib.
- Salt and black pepper
- Red pepper flakes- ½ tsp.
- Extra virgin olive oil- 2 tbsp.
- Crushed garlic- 14 cloves

Soup:
- Heavy cream- 1 cup
- Chopped yellow onion- 1
- Olive oil- 2 tbsp.
- Red pepper flakes- ½ tsp.
- Dried basil- ½ tsp.
- Chopped red bell pepper- ½ tbsp.
- Tomato paste- 3 tbsp.
- Chopped celery ribs- 2
- Chicken stock- 2 cups
- Garlic powder- 1 tsp.
- Onion powder- 1 tsp.
- Salt and black pepper

For serving:
- Chopped basil leaves
- Grated parmesan- ½ cup

Directions:
1. Put the garlic and tomatoes on a baking tray and season with all the tomatoes ingredients and mix well.
2. Place the tray in the oven to roast for 25 minutes at 425°F then remove and set aside.
3. Press the 'Sauté' button on the Instant Pot and pour the oil for the soup into it. Mix in the celery, bell pepper, and onion then season with salt and pepper, garlic powder, dried basil, onion powder, and pepper flakes to cook for 3 minutes.
4. Mix in the roasted tomatoes, garlic, stock, and tomato paste and let it cook for 10 minutes at high pressure.
5. Natural release the pressure and cook on 'Sauté' mode then pour in the heavy cream.
6. Blend with a dipping blender then serve into bowls topped with cheese and basil leaves.

Garlicky Sausage And Bacon Soup With Potatoes And Spinach

Servings: 8, **Prep +Cook time:** 40 minutes

Ingredients:
- Ground chicken sausage- 1 Ib.
- A pinch of red pepper flakes
- Chopped bacon slices- 6
- Salt and black pepper
- Chicken stock- 40 oz.
- Butter- 1 tbsp.
- Evaporated milk- 12 oz.
- Shredded parmesan- 1 cup
- Chopped spinach- 2 cups
- Chopped yellow onion- 1 cup
- Minced garlic- 3 cloves
- Cubed potatoes- 3

Directions:
1. Press 'Sauté' on the Instant Pot and add in the bacon to cook till crispy and set aside.
2. Add in the sausage and brown on all sides then set aside.
3. Put the butter in the pot to melt then add the onion to fry for 5 minutes then add the garlic to cook for 1 minute.
4. Pour in 1/3 of the stock and sprinkle some pepper and salt into it and mix.
5. Put the potatoes on a steaming rack then place it above the soup then seal the lid to cook for 4 minutes at high pressure.
6. Natural release the pressure for 15 minutes then move the valve to venting position and remove the potatoes.
7. Mix in cornstarch with the evaporated milk then pour it into the pot with the remaining stock to simmer.
8. Mix in the sausage, bacon, spinach, potatoes, parmesan, pepper, and salt.
9. Serve into bowls.

Cheesy Cauliflower Soup

Ingredients:

- Cauliflower head; separated and chopped- 1
- Salt and black pepper
- Grated cheddar cheese- 1 cup
- Cubed cream cheese- 4 oz.
- Half and half- ½ cup
- Butter- 2 tbsp.
- Chicken stock- 3 cups
- Garlic powder- 1 tsp.
- Chopped small onion- 1

Directions:

1. Press 'Sauté' on the Instant Pot and put the butter in it to melt then add the onion to fry for 3 minutes.
2. Mix in the garlic powder, cauliflower, stock, salt, and pepper then seal the lid to cook for 5 minutes at high pressure.
3. Natural release the pressure for 15 minutes then move the valve to venting position to let out the remaining steam.
4. Use a dipping blender to blend the contents then season with some salt and pepper if needed, half and half, grated cheese, and cream cheese.
5. Mix and let simmer for 2 minutes and serve into soup bowls.

Chicken Noodle Soup With Celery Rib And Carrots

Ingredients:

- Cooked and shredded chicken- 2 cups
- Egg noodles; already cooked
- Sliced carrots- 4
- Salt and black pepper
- Chopped yellow onion- 1
- Chopped celery rib- 1
- Butter- 1 tbsp.
- Chicken stock- 6 cups

Directions:

1. Press 'Sauté' on the Instant Pot and add the butter to melt then put in the onions to fry for 2 minutes.
2. Mix in the carrots and celery to cook for 5 minutes then mix in the chicken stock and the chicken.
3. Seal the lid and set to cook for 5 minutes at high pressure.
4. Natural release the pressure for 15 minutes then move the valve to venting position.
5. Open the pot and season with pepper and salt.
6. Serve the noodles into soup bowls and add the soup over them.

Spicy Sweet Potato With Lentils And Carrots Soup

Ingredients:

- Cubed sweet potato- 1
- Salt and black pepper
- Chopped canned tomatoes- 14 oz.
- Green lentils- 1 cup
- Chopped big onion- 1
- Red lentils- ½ cup
- Chopped carrots- 2
- Raisins- ¼ cup
- Chopped garlic- 3 cloves
- Veggie stock- 2 cups
- Chopped celery stalk- 1

Spice blend:

- A pinch of chili flakes
- Cinnamon- ½ tsp.
- A pinch of cloves
- Grated ginger- ¼ tsp.
- Cumin- 1 tsp.
- Turmeric- 1 tsp.
- Coriander- 2 tsp.
- Paprika- 1 tsp.

Directions:

1. Press the 'Sauté' button on the Instant Pot then add the onions to brown for 2 minutes pouring in some stock occasionally.
2. Mix in the garlic and let cook for 1 minute then add the raisins, celery, carrot, and sweet potatoes to cook for 1 minute.
3. Add the stock, tomatoes, green and red lentils, turmeric, cinnamon, salt and pepper, coriander, cumin, ginger, paprika, chili flakes, and cloves then mix and seal the lid to cook for 15 minutes at high pressure.
4. Natural release the pressure for 15 minutes then move the valve to venting and open the lid.
5. Mix the stew and season with pepper and salt.
6. Serve into bowls.

Chicken With Butternut Squash Soup

Servings: 6, **Prep +Cook time**: 35 minutes

Ingredients:

- Butternut squash; baked, peeled and cubed- 1 ½ Ib.
- Chopped green onion to serve
- Salt
- Black pepper
- Canned chicken stock- 29 oz.
- Dried red pepper flakes- 1/8 tsp.
- Cooked orzo- 1 cup
- Chopped celery- ½ cup
- Chopped carrots- ½ cup
- Half and half- 1 ½ cup
- Cooked and shredded chicken meat- 1 cup
- Butter- 3 tbsp.
- Grated nutmeg- 1/8 tsp.
- Chopped canned tomatoes with its juice- 15 oz.
- Minced garlic- 1 clove
- Italian seasoning- ½ tsp.

Directions:

1. Press 'Sauté' on the Instant Pot and add the butter to melt then mix in the onions, celery, and carrots to cook for 3 minutes.
2. Add in the garlic to fry for 1 minute then mix in the stock, tomatoes, squash, pepper flakes, nutmeg, Italian seasoning, salt, and pepper.
3. Seal the lid to cook for 10 minutes at high pressure then natural release the pressure for 15 minutes.
4. Move the valve to venting then blend the mix with a dipping blender.
5. Let it simmer and pour in the half and half, chicken, and orzo for 3 minutes.
6. Serve sprinkled with green onions.

Cheesy Fennel And Leek Soup

Servings: 3, **Prep +Cook time**: 35 minutes

Ingredients:

- Chopped fennel bulb- 1
- Salt and black pepper
- Chopped leek- 1
- Vegetable bouillon- ½ cube
- Water- 2 cups
- Bay leaf- 1
- Grated parmesan cheese- 2 tsp.
- Extra virgin olive oil- 1 tbsp.

Directions:

1. Combine leek, fennel, vegetable bouillon, water, and bay leaf in the Instant Pot then seal the lid.
2. Set to cook at high pressure for 15 minutes.
3. Natural release the pressure for 15 minutes then move the valve to venting and open the lid.
4. Mix in the oil, cheese, pepper, and salt.
5. Serve into bowls.

Chili Chicken Soup With Beans And Tomatoes

Servings: 4, **Prep +Cook time:** 40 minutes

Ingredients:
- Skinless and boneless chicken breasts- 4
- Salt and black pepper
- Minced garlic- 3 cloves
- Chili powder-1 tbsp.
- Dried parsley- 2 tbsp.
- Onion powder- 1 tbsp.
- Jarred chunky salsa- 16 oz.
- Peeled and chopped canned tomatoes- 29 oz.
- Canned chicken stock- 29 oz.
- Chopped onion- 1
- Canned black beans; drained- 32 oz.
- Frozen corn- 15 oz.
- Garlic powder- 1tsp.
- Extra virgin olive oil- 2 tbsp.

Directions:

1. Press 'Sauté' on the Instant Pot then pour in the oil and the onions to fry for 5 minutes.
2. Mix in the garlic to cook for 1 minute then add the salsa, tomatoes, chicken breasts, garlic powder, stock, parsley, chili powder, onion powder, salt, and pepper and mix again.
3. Seal the lid and set to cook at high pressure for 8 minutes.
4. Natural release the pressure for 15 minutes then move the valve to venting to release the remaining steam.
5. Put the chicken on a cutting board and shred it and put it back into the pot.
6. Mix in the corn and the beans then simmer for 2-3 minutes.
7. Serve into bowls.

Spicy Chicken And Beans Soup With Tortilla Chips

Servings: 4, **Prep +Cook time:** 50 minutes

Ingredients:
- Skinless and boneless chicken breasts- 1 Ib.
- Salt and black pepper
- Chopped jalapeno pepper- 1
- Chicken stock- 3 cups
- Crushed red pepper flakes- ½ tsp.
- Olive oil- 2 tbsp.
- Chopped white onion- 1
- Drained canned cannellini beans- 30 oz.
- Minced garlic- 4 cloves
- Cumin- 1 tsp.
- Dried oregano- 2 tsp.
- Chopped cilantro for serving
- Lime wedges for serving
- Tortilla chips for serving

Directions:
1. Press the 'Sauté' button on the Instant Pot then pour in the olive oil and add the onion and jalapeno to cook for 3 minutes.
2. Mix in the garlic to cook for 1 minute then add the beans, salt and pepper, cumin, chicken, oregano, and pepper flakes to cook for 30 minutes on low pressure.
3. Natural release the pressure for 15 minutes then move the valve to venting. Remove the chicken and shred the meat then mix it into the pot and season with pepper and salt.
4. Serve into bowls topped with cilantro and lime wedges with tortilla chips on the side.

Sweet and Creamy Carrot Soup

Servings: 4, **Prep +Cook time:** 35 minutes

Ingredients:
- Chopped carrots- 1 Ib.
- Canned coconut milk- 14 oz.
- Salt and black pepper
- Sriracha- 1 tbsp.
- Chicken stock- 2 cups
- Vegetable oil- 1 tbsp.
- Butter- 1 tbsp.
- Minced garlic- 1 clove

- Grated ginger piece; small size- 1
- Chopped onion- 1
- Brown sugar- ¼ tsp.
- Chopped cilantro for serving

Directions:
1. Press 'Sauté' on the Instant Pot and add the oil and butter to melt then add the onions to fry for 3 minutes.
2. Mix in the garlic and ginger to fry for 1 minute then add the carrots, sugar, salt and pepper to cook for 2 minutes.
3. Pour in the stock, coconut milk, and the Sriracha sauce then mix and let it cook for 6 minutes at high pressure.
4. Natural release the pressure for 15 minutes then quick release the rest of the pressure by moving the valve to venting.
5. Blend the soup with a dipping blender and season with salt and pepper as desired.
6. Serve topped with cilantro.

Rum and Cream Chestnut Soup With Potatoes

Servings: 4, **Prep +Cook time:** 45 minutes

Ingredients:
- Drained and rinsed canned chestnuts- 1 Ib.
- Chopped celery stalk- 1
- A pinch of nutmeg
- Salt and white pepper
- Chopped sage sprig- 1
- Chopped yellow onion- 1
- Butter- 4 tbsp.
- Chopped potato- 1
- Bay leaf- 1
- Rum- 2 tbsp.
- Chicken stock- 4 cups
- Chopped sage leaves for serving
- Whole cream for serving

Directions:
1. Press 'Sauté' on the Instant Pot and add the butter to melt then mix in the sage, celery, onion, salt, and pepper to cook for 5 minutes.
2. Mix in the potato, bay leaf, stock, and chestnuts to cook on low pressure for 20 minutes.
3. Natural release the pressure for 15 minutes then move the valve to venting.
4. Remove the bay leaf and add the rum and the nutmeg then blend the soup with a dipping blender.
5. Serve the soup topped with sage and whole cream.

Beef with Carrot And Potatoes Soup

Servings: 8, **Prep +Cook time:** 50 minutes

Ingredients:
- Cubed beef- 2 Ib.
- Water- 2 cups
- Salt and black pepper
- Beef bouillon cubes- 2
- Cornstarch- 2 tsp.
- Vegetable oil- 1 tbsp.
- Chopped carrots- 5
- Chopped yellow onion- 1
- Cubed potatoes- 8
- Cornstarch- 2 tsp.

Directions:
1. Press the 'Sauté' button on the Instant Pot then add the oil.
2. Put the onion and the beef to brown on all sides.
3. Add the water, bouillon, and the carrots to the pot then seal the lid and set to cook at medium pressure for 20 minutes.
4. Boil some salt and water in a pot on medium high then add the potatoes to cook for 10 minutes.
5. Natural release the pressure for 15 minutes then move the valve to venting position.
6. Mix the cornstarch with some water, pepper and salt and pour it into the pot and mix in the potatoes.
7. Boil for some minutes then serve.

Okra and Tomatoes Beef Stew

Servings: 4, **Prep +Cook time**: 40 minutes

Ingredients:
- Cubed beef meat- 1 Ib.
- Frozen okra- 14 oz.
- Juice of half lemon
- Salt and black pepper
- Cardamom pod- 1
- Chicken stock- 2 cups
- A drizzle of olive oil
- Chopped yellow onion- 1
- Chopped parsley- ½ cup
- Minced garlic- 1 clove

Marinade:
- A pinch of salt
- Onion powder- ½ tsp.
- 7-spice mix- 1 tbsp.
- Garlic powder- ½ tsp.

Directions:

1. Coat the meat with a mixture of the marinade ingredients and set aside.
2. Pour some oil in the Instant Pot on 'Sauté' mode and add the onions to fry for 2 minutes.
3. Mix in the cardamom and the garlic to cook for 1 minute.
4. Put the meat in the pot to brown for 2 minutes then add the okra, tomato sauce, stock, salt and pepper and mix.
5. Seal to cook on low pressure for 20 minutes.
6. Natural release the pressure for 15 minutes then move the valve to venting to release the remaining pressure.
7. Season with more pepper and salt as needed and add the parsley and lemon juice.
8. Serve into bowls.

Sausage With Potatoes And Greens Stew

Servings: 6, **Prep +Cook time**: 40 minutes

Ingredients:
- Andouille sausage; crumbled- 1 Ib.
- Chopped sweet onion- 1
- Salt and black pepper
- Juice of half lemon
- Cherry tomatoes; halved- ½ Ib.
- Chicken stock- 1 cup
- Collard greens; thinly sliced- ¾ Ib.
- Cubed gold potatoes- 1 ½ Ib.

Directions:
1. Press the 'Sauté' button on the Instant Pot then add the sausage to cook for 8 minutes then mix in the tomatoes and onions to cook for another 4 minutes.
2. Mix in the greens, potatoes, stock, salt and pepper and seal the lid to cook for 10 minutes on high pressure.
3. Natural release the pressure for 15 minutes then move the valve to venting to release the steam.
4. Season with more pepper and salt, if desired then mix in the lemon juice.
5. Serve into bowls.

Braised Oxtail With Vegetables Soup

Servings: 4, **Prep +Cook time**: 60 minutes

Ingredients:
- Oxtails- 5 Ib.
- Chopped yellow onions- 2
- Sugar to taste
- Salt and black pepper
- Water- 1 cup
- Chopped celery stalks- 3
- Chopped tomatoes- 1 cup
- Chopped parsley- 1 bunch
- Chopped garlic- 1 clove
- Red wine- 2 cups

Directions:
1. Combine all the ingredients in the Instant Pot then seal the lid to cook on medium pressure for 40 minutes.
2. Natural release the pressure for 15 minutes then move the valve to venting position.
3. Serve the soup into bowls.

Creamy Vegetable Soup

Servings: 4, **Prep +Cook time**: 30 minutes

Ingredients:

- Chopped carrots- 3
- Broccoli head with florets separated and chopped- 1
- Cream- 2 tbsp.
- Chopped chives- 1 tbsp.
- Minced garlic- 5 cloves
- Chicken stock- 2 cups
- Olive oil- 1 tbsp.
- Chopped yellow onion- 1
- Chopped potato- 1
- Grated cheddar cheese for serving
- Salt and black pepper to taste

Directions:

1. Press the 'Sauté' button on the Instant Pot and pour in the oil, garlic and onion to fry for 2 minutes.
2. Mix in the carrots, broccoli, stock, potato, salt and pepper and seal the lid to cook at high pressure for 5 minutes.
3. Natural release the pressure for 15 minutes then move the valve to venting position.
4. While simmering, add the cream, chives, and cheddar cheese to cook for 2 minutes then serve.

Mushroom and Vegetable Soup

Servings: 4, **Prep +Cook time**: 25 minutes

Ingredients:

- Chopped tomatoes- 1 cup
- Chopped parsley
- Salt and black pepper
- A handful of dried porcini mushrooms
- Roughly chopped kale leaves- 3.5 oz.
- Chopped celery sticks- 2
- Chopped carrots- 2
- Chopped zucchini- 1
- Veggie stock- 4 cups
- Big mushrooms; sliced- 4
- Minced garlic- 4 cloves
- Chopped brown onion- 1
- Half red chili; chopped
- Lemon zest- ½ tsp.
- Coconut oil- 1 tbsp.
- Bay leaf- 1

Directions:

1. Press 'Sauté' on the Instant Pot and pour in the oil then add the carrots, onion, celery, salt and pepper to cook for 1 minute.
2. Mix in the mushrooms, chili, and garlic to cook for 2 minutes then add the bay leaf, tomatoes, stock, zucchini, and kale leaves.
3. Seal the lid to cook at high pressure for 10 minutes.
4. Natural release the pressure for 15 minutes then move the valve to venting position.
5. Serve into soup bowls topped with parsley and lemon zest.

Barley Beef Stew With Mushrooms And Veggies

Servings: 4, **Prep +Cook time**: 45 minutes

Ingredients:

- Chopped beef stew meat- 1 ½ Ib.
- Chopped potato- 1
- Salt and black pepper
- Dried thyme- ½ tsp.
- Water- 1 cup
- Vegetable oil- 2 tbsp.
- Beef stock- 6 cups
- Baby bell mushrooms; quartered- 10
- Mixed onion, celery, and carrots- 3 cups
- Bay leaves- 2
- Barley- 2/3 cup
- Minced garlic- 8 cloves

Directions:

1. Press 'Sauté' n the Instant Pot and add oil, meat, salt and pepper to cook for 3 minutes then set aside.

2. Brown the mushrooms for 2 minutes then set aside too.
3. Pour in the mixed veggies to cook for 4 minutes then add the meat and the mushrooms with the bay leaf, stock, water, thyme, salt and pepper to cook for 16 minutes on high pressure.

4. Natural release the pressure for 15 minutes then move the valve to venting position.
5. Add the barley and potatoes then seal to cook on low heat for 1 hour.
6. Release the pressure then serve into bowls.

Beef With Celery And Mushrooms Stew

Servings: 6, **Prep +Cook time**: 45 minutes

Ingredients:
- Cubed beef- 2 Ib.
- Chopped celery stalk- 1
- Chopped rosemary- 1 tsp.
- Chopped red onion- 1
- Olive oil- 1 tbsp.
- Flour- 2 tbsp.
- Beef stock- 1 cup
- Red wine- ½ cup
- Dried porcini mushrooms; chopped- 1 oz.
- Chopped carrots- 2
- Butter- 2 tbsp.
- Red wine- ½ cup
- Salt and black pepper

Directions:

1. Press 'Sauté' on the Instant Pot and add the oil and beef to brown for 5 minutes then mix in the stock, rosemary, salt, wine, onion, carrots, mushrooms, and celery.
2. Seal the lid to cook at high pressure for 15 minutes.
3. Natural release the pressure for 15 minutes then move the valve to venting position.
4. Set on simmer then put a pan over medium heat and melt the butter.
5. Mix in 6 tablespoons of cooking liquid and the flour then pour it in the stew.
6. Mix well and cook for 5 minutes then serve into bowls.

Cheesy Tomato Soup

Servings: 8, **Prep +Cook time**: 26 minutes

Ingredients:
- Tomatoes; peeled, cored and quartered- 3 Ib.
- Salt and black pepper
- Tomato paste- 1 tbsp.
- Chopped basil- ¼ cup
- Minced garlic- 2 cloves
- Shredded parmesan cheese- ½ cup
- Half and half- 1 cup
- Chopped celery stalks- 2
- Chicken stock- 29 oz.
- Chopped yellow onion- 1
- Butter- 3 tbsp.
- Chopped carrot- 1

Directions:

1. Press the 'Sauté' button on the Instant Pot and add the butter to melt then add the celery, carrots, and onion to cook for 3 minutes.
2. Mix in the garlic to cook for 1 minute then add the basil, tomato paste, stock, tomatoes, salt and pepper and seal the lid to cook for 5 minutes at high pressure.
3. Natural release the pressure for 15 minutes then move the valve to venting position.
4. Blend the soup with a dipping blender and pour in the cheese and half and half. Mix well then simmer for some minutes.
5. Serve into bowls.

Spinach Chicken Sausage And Lentils Soup

Servings: 4, **Prep +Cook time:** 50 minutes

Ingredients:
- Lentils- 1 cup
- Spinach- 2 cups
- Chopped canned tomatoes- 15 oz.
- Ground chicken sausage- ½ Ib.
- Chopped carrots- 2
- Chopped celery stalks- 2
- Chopped small onion- 1
- Minced garlic- 2 tsp.
- Beef stock- 3 ½ cups
- Olive oil- 1 tbsp.
- Salt and black pepper

Directions:
1. Press 'Sauté' on the Instant Pot and add the oil to heat then add the carrots, onion, and celery to cook for 4 minutes.
2. Mix in the chicken sausage to cook for 5 minutes then add the garlic, tomatoes, lentils, stock, spinach, salt and pepper to cook for 25 minutes at high pressure.
3. Natural release the pressure for 15 minutes then move the valve to venting position.
4. Serve the soup into bowls.

Soy Burger Veggie Soup

Servings: 4, **Prep +Cook time:** 30 minutes

Ingredients:
- Chopped cabbage head- 1
- Salt and black pepper
- Soy burger- 12 oz.
- Olive oil- 2 tbsp.
- Baby carrots- 12 oz.
- Chopped celery stalks- 3
- Veggie soup mix- 1 packet
- Chopped onion- ½
- Chicken stock- 4 cups
- Chopped cilantro- ¼ cup
- Minced garlic- 3 tsp.

Directions:
1. Combine all the ingredients except the cilantro in the Instant Pot and seal the lid to cook on high pressure for 5 minutes.
2. Natural release the pressure for 15 minutes then move the valve to venting position.
3. Mix in the cilantro and salt and pepper and serve into soup bowls.

Minty Ham With White Beans And Tomatoes Soup

Servings: 8, **Prep +Cook time:** 25 minutes

Ingredients:
- White beans; soaked for 1 hour and drained- 1 Ib.
- Water- 4 cups
- Salt and black pepper
- Chopped carrot- 1
- Minced garlic- 3 cloves
- Peeled and chopped tomato- 1
- Chopped onion- 1
- Dried thyme- 1 tsp.
- Paprika- 1 tsp.
- Dried mint- 1 tsp.
- Chopped ham- 1 Ib.
- Extra virgin olive oil- 1 tbsp.
- Veggie stock- 4 cups

Directions:
1. Press 'Sauté' on the Instant Pot and heat it then add the tomato, carrot, garlic, and onion to cook for 5 minutes.
2. Mix in the paprika, ham, beans, mint, thyme, stock, water, salt and pepper to cook for 15 minutes at high pressure.
3. Natural release the pressure for 15 minutes then move the valve to venting position.
4. Serve into bowls.

Chapter 6 Side dishes

Baked Bread And Celery Dish

Servings: 4, **Prep +Cook time:** 30 minutes

Ingredients:
- Cubed and toasted bread loaf- 1
- Salt and black pepper
- Water- 1 ½ cups
- Sage- 1 tsp.
- Chopped yellow onion- 1
- Poultry seasoning- 1 tsp.
- Chopped celery- 1 cup
- Butter- ½ cup
- Turkey stock- 1 ¼ cup

Directions:
1. Press the 'Sauté' button on the Instant Pot then add the butter to melt.
2. Pour in the stock and mix in the seasoning, celery, onion, salt and pepper then add the bread cubes and cook for 1 minute.
3. Pour the mix in a Bundt pan and cover with a tin foil.
4. Clean the Instant Pot and pour some water in the pot. Place the Bundt pan on a steaming rack then place the rack above the water in the Instant Pot.
5. Seal the lid and cook at high pressure for 15 minutes.
6. Quick release the pressure and remove the pan. Put it in the oven to bake for 5 minutes at 350°F.
7. Serve hot.

Quinoa Topped With Parsley

Servings: 4, **Prep +Cook time:** 12 minutes

Ingredients:
- Quinoa- 2 cups
- Salt to taste
- Extra virgin olive oil- 2 tbsp.
- Ground cumin- 2 tsp.
- Chopped parsley- 1 handful
- Minced garlic- 2 cloves
- Turmeric- 2 tsp.
- Water- 3 cups

Directions:
1. Press 'Sauté' on the Instant Pot then add the oil and the garlic to cook for 30 seconds.
2. Pour in the water and add the cumin, turmeric, quinoa, and salt then mix and seal the lid to cook for 1 minute at high pressure.
3. Natural release the pressure for 10 minutes then move the valve to venting to remove remaining steam.
4. Flip the quinoa with a fork then sprinkle with some salt, if needed.
5. Serve topped with parsley.

Garlic Black Beans

Servings: 8, **Prep +Cook time:** 15 minutes

Ingredients:
- Black beans; soaked overnight, rinsed and drained- 1 cup
- Minced garlic- 2 cloves
- Salt
- Water- 2/3 cup
- Kombu seaweed- 1 piece
- Cumin seeds- ½ tsp.
- Epazote- 1

Directions:
1. Combine all the ingredients in an Instant Pot then seal the lid to cook at high pressure for 5 minutes.
2. Quick release the pressure and remove the Epazote and the seaweed.
3. Serve seasoned with salt.

Garlic Potatoes

Servings: 4, **Prep +Cook time:** 16 minutes

Ingredients:

- Peeled and thinly sliced potatoes- 1 Ib.
- Salt and black pepper
- Extra virgin olive oil- 1 tbsp.
- Dried rosemary- ¼ tsp.
- Minced garlic- 2 cloves
- Water- 1 cup

Directions:

1. Pour the water into the Instant Pot and put the potatoes on a steaming rack then place it above the water in the pot and close the lid.
2. Set to cook at high pressure for 4 minutes.
3. Mix the garlic, oil, and rosemary in a heat-resistant dish and put it in a microwave for 1 minute.
4. Quick release the pressure from the potatoes and remove the water from the potatoes then spread it on a lined baking sheet.
5. Add some salt and pepper to the garlic mix and coat with the potatoes.
6. Serve.

Creamy and Cheesy Rice With Mushrooms

Servings: 4, **Prep +Cook time:** 25 minutes

Ingredients:

- Risotto rice- 2 cups
- Chicken stock- 4 cups
- Crushed garlic- 2 cloves
- Finely chopped basil- 1 oz.
- Grated parmesan cheese- 2 tbsp.
- Heavy cream- 4 oz.
- Sliced mushrooms- 8 oz.
- Sherry vinegar- 4 oz.
- Chopped yellow onions- 1
- Extra virgin olive oil- 2 oz.

Directions:

1. Press 'Sauté' on the Instant Pot and pour in the olive oil then mix in the garlic, mushrooms, and onions to cook for 3 minutes.
2. Pour in the vinegar and then stock and mix in the rice then seal the lid.
3. Set to cook at high pressure for 10 minutes then quick release the pressure and open the lid.
4. Pour in the heavy cream and the grated parmesan cheese then mix.
5. Serve sprinkled with basil.

Herby Polenta With Tomatoes

Servings: 6, **Prep +Cook time:** 20 minutes

Ingredients:

- Polenta- 1 cup
- Veggie stock- 4 cups
- Finely chopped parsley- 2 tbsp.
- Bay leaf- 1
- Minced garlic- 2 tsp.
- Extra virgin olive oil- 2 tbsp.
- Finely chopped rosemary- 1 tsp.
- Finely chopped basil- 3 tbsp.
- Chopped sun-dried tomatoes- 1/3 cup
- Finely chopped oregano- 2 tsp.
- Chopped yellow onion- ½ cup

Directions:

1. Press 'Sauté' on the Instant Pot and add the oil and onions to fry for 1 minute then mix in the garlic and fry for another minute.
2. Pour in the stock and add the oregano, half of the basil, half of the parsley, polenta, rosemary, bay leaf, salt, and the tomatoes without mixing.
3. Seal the lid and cook at high pressure for 5 minutes the natural release the pressure for 10 minutes.
4. Remove the bay leaf and mix the polenta carefully then add the basil and the remaining parsley and season with more salt.
5. Serve.

Hot and Spicy Anchovies With Eggplant

Servings: 4, **Prep +Cook time:** 25 minutes

Ingredients:
- Cubed eggplants- 2
- Chopped oregano- 1 bunch
- A pinch of hot pepper flakes
- Chopped anchovies- 2
- Water- ½ cup
- Crush garlic- 1 clove
- Extra virgin olive oil- 2 tbsp.

Directions:
1. Sprinkle some salt on the eggplant then press them on a strainer to drain them.
2. Press 'Sauté' on the Instant Pot then add the oil and garlic to fry for 1 minute then add the pepper flakes, anchovies, and oregano to cook for 5 minutes.
3. Remove the garlic and add the eggplants and the salt and pepper to cook for 5 minutes.
4. Pour in some water then seal the lid and set to cook for 3 minutes at high pressure.
5. Quick release the pressure and serve the anchovies and eggplant.

Buttery Quinoa With Almonds And Celery

Servings: 4, **Prep +Cook time:** 20 minutes

Ingredients:
- Rinsed quinoa- 1 ½ cups
- Almonds; toasted and sliced- ½ cup
- Salt and black pepper
- Water- ¼ cup
- Butter- 1 tbsp.
- Finely chopped yellow onion- ½ cup
- Chicken stock- 14 oz.
- Chopped celery stock- 1
- Chopped parsley- 2 tbsp.

Directions:
1. Press 'Sauté' on the Instant Pot and add the butter, then mix in the celery and onion to cook for 5 minutes.
2. Add in the stock, water, quinoa, salt and pepper and mix. Seal the lid to cook for 3 minutes at high pressure.
3. Natural release the pressure for 5 minutes then move the valve to venting to release the remaining pressure.
4. Loosen the quinoa with a fork and mix in the almonds and the parsley.
5. Serve.

Mashed Apple And Butternut Squash Dish

Servings: 4, **Prep +Cook time:** 25 minutes

Ingredients:
- Butternut squash; peeled and cut into medium chunks- 1
- Salt
- Thinly sliced yellow onion- 1
- Water- 1 cup
- Sliced apples- 2
- Apple pie spice- ½ tsp.
- Brown butter- 2 tbsp.

Directions:
1. Place the apple, squash, and onions on a steaming rack and pour the water in the Instant Pot.
2. Place the rack above the water in the pot then seal the lid to cook for 8 minutes at high pressure.
3. Quick release the pressure and remove the basket contents into a bowl then mash with a potato masher.
4. Sprinkle with apple pie spice, brown butter, and salt and mix well.
5. Serve.

Creamy and Cheesy Herb Sweet Potatoes

Servings: 8, **Prep +Cook time:** 20 minutes

Ingredients:

- Sweet potatoes; peeled and chopped- 3 Ib.
- Water- 1 ½ cups
- Dried parsley- ½ tsp.
- Salt and black pepper
- Butter- 2 tbsp.
- Grated parmesan- ½ cup
- Dried thyme- ½ tsp.
- Dried rosemary- ½ tsp.
- Dried sage- ½ tsp.
- Garlic- 2 cloves
- Milk- ¼ cup

Directions:

1. Put the potatoes on a steaming basket then pour the water into the Instant Pot and place the rack above the water.
2. Seal the lid to cook for 10 minutes at high pressure.
3. Quick release the pressure and remove the water. Put the potatoes in a bowl and add the garlic then mash with a mixer.
4. Mix in the parmesan, butter, parsley, sage, rosemary, milk, thyme, salt and pepper and mix well.
5. Serve.

Mashed Turmeric Cauliflower With Chives

Servings: 4, **Prep +Cook time:** 15 minutes

Ingredients:

- Cauliflower with florets separated- 1
- Salt and black pepper
- Finely chopped chives- 3
- Turmeric- ½ tsp.
- Butter- 1 tbsp.
- Water- 1 ½ cups

Directions:

1. Pour the water into the Instant Pot and place the cauliflower on a steaming rack and place above the water in the pot to cook for 6 minutes at high pressure.
2. Natural release the pressure for 2 minutes then quick release the remaining steam.
3. Put the cauliflower in a bowl and mash it then add the butter, turmeric, salt and pepper and mix.
4. Serve topped with chives.

Minty Farro With Cherries

Servings: 6, **Prep +Cook time:** 50 minutes

Ingredients:

- Whole grain farro- 1 cup
- Salt
- Cherries; pitted and halved- 2 cups
- Apple cider vinegar- 1 tbsp.
- Chopped dried cherries- ½ cup
- Chopped green onions- ¼ cup
- Chopped mint leaves- 10
- Extra virgin olive oil- 1 tbsp.
- Water- 3 cups
- Lemon juice- 1 tsp.

Directions:

1. Mix the water with the farro in the Instant Pot then seal the lid to cook at high pressure for 40 minutes.
2. Quick release the pressure and mix in all the other ingredients.
3. Serve.

Breadcrumbs Topped Cheesy Potatoes

Servings: 6, **Prep +Cook time:** 27 minutes

Ingredients:

- Peeled and sliced potatoes- 6
- Sour cream- ½ cup
- Salt and black pepper
- Monterey Jack cheese-; shredded- 1 cup
- Chopped yellow onion- ½ cup
- Chicken stock- 1 cup
- Butter- 2 tbsp.

Topping:

- Bread crumbs- 1 cup
- Melted butter- 3 tbsp.

Directions:

1. Press 'Sauté' on the Instant Pot and add the butter to melt then mix in the onion to cook for 5 minutes.
2. Pour in the stock then sprinkle with salt and pepper. Place the potatoes on a steaming rack and set it above the liquid in the pot.
3. Seal the lid and set to cook at high pressure for 5 minutes.
4. Combine the breadcrumbs with butter in a bowl and set aside.
5. Quick release the steam and put the potatoes on a bowl then mix the cheese and sour cream into the Instant Pot then add the potatoes to the pot and mix.
6. Sprinkle the bread crumbs over the dish and broil in a preheated broiler for 7 minutes.
7. Serve hot.

Ginger Bok Choy

Servings: 4, **Prep +Cook time:** 20 minutes

Ingredients:

- Bok Choy with the ends cut- 5
- Salt
- Coconut oil- 1 tbsp.
- Grated ginger- 1 tsp.
- Minced garlic- 2 cloves
- Water- 5 cups

Directions:

1. Place the Bok Choy in the Instant Pot and add the water then seal the lid to cook for 7 minutes at high pressure.
2. Quick release the pressure and remove the water then chop the Bok Choy.
3. Put the oil in a pan over medium heat then mix in the Bok Choy to cook for 3 minutes.
4. Season with some salt, ginger, and garlic and let it cook for 2 minutes.
5. Serve with meat.

Pureed Hot Beans

Servings: 4, **Prep +Cook time:** 30 minutes

Ingredients:

- Pinto beans; soaked for 4 hours and drained- 3 cups
- Salt and black pepper
- Yellow onion; halved- 1
- Ground cumin- 1/8 tsp.
- Chopped jalapeno- 1
- Vegetable stock- 9 cups
- Minced garlic- 2 tbsp.

Directions:

1. Combine all the ingredients in the Instant Pot and seal the lid to cook for 20 minutes at high pressure.
2. Natural release the pressure and remove the onion halves then drain the beans but reserve some of the liquid.
3. Put the beans in a blender to puree while adding some of the liquid.
4. Serve as side.

Green Beans And Mushrooms With Bacon

Servings: 4, **Prep +Cook time:** 18 minutes

Ingredients:

- Trimmed green beans- 1 Ib.
- Sliced mushrooms- 8 oz.
- Salt and black pepper
- A splash of balsamic vinegar- minced garlic- 1 clove
- Chopped small yellow onion- 1
- Minced garlic- 1 clove
- Chopped bacon- 6 oz.

Directions:

1. Pour the beans in the Instant Pot and add enough water to cover the beans then seal the lid to cook at high pressure for 3 minutes.
2. Natural release the pressure and drain the beans and set aside.
3. Press 'Sauté' on the Instant Pot and add the bacon to brown for 1-2 minutes.
4. Mix in the onion and garlic to cook for 2 minutes then add the mushrooms and cook until soft.
5. Mix in the beans, vinegar, and salt and pepper.
6. Serve.

Cheesy Barley Cauliflower

Servings: 4, **Prep +Cook time:** 1 hour 10 minutes

Ingredients:

- Cauliflower head with florets separated- 1
- Salt and black pepper
- Chopped yellow onion- 1
- Pearl barley- 1 cup
- Extra virgin olive oil- 4 tbsp.
- Minced garlic- 2 cloves
- Grated parmesan- ½ cup
- Chicken stock- 3 cups
- Butter- 1 tbsp.
- Chopped parsley- 2 tbsp.
- Thyme sprigs- 2

Directions:

1. Place the florets on a lined baking dish and 3c tablespoons of oil then sprinkle with salt and pepper. Mix to coat and set in the oven to bake for 20 minutes at 425°F flipping after 10 minutes.
2. Sprinkle the cauliflower with ¼ of the parmesan cheese then bake for 5 minutes.
3. Press 'Sauté' on the Instant Pot and pour in 1 tablespoon of oil then add the onion to cook for 5 minutes.
4. Mix in the garlic to cook for 1 minute then add the barley, stock, and thyme. Seal the lid to cook for 25 minutes at high pressure.
5. Quick release the pressure and mix the contents then remove the thyme and add the rest of the parmesan, roasted cauliflower, parsley, butter, salt, and pepper.
6. Mix well and serve.

Cheesy Rice And Peas Dish

Servings: 6, **Prep +Cook time:** 27 minutes

Ingredients:

- Salt and black pepper
- Grated lemon zest- 1 tsp.
- Chicken stock- 3 ½ cups
- Peas- 1 ½ cups
- Lemon juice- 2 tbsp.
- Extra virgin olive oil- 1 tbsp.
- Chopped yellow onion- 1
- Finely grated parmesan- 2 tbsp.
- Butter- 2 tbsp.
- Rice- 1 ½ cup

Directions:

1. Press 'Sauté' on the Instant Pot and add 1 tablespoon of the butter then mix in the onions to cook for 5 minutes.

2. Mix in the rice to cook for 3 minutes and add the lemon juice and 3 cups of stock. Seal the lid and set to high pressure for 5 minutes.
3. Quick release the pressure and let it simmer on low pressure, then add the remaining

stock and the peas then mix it to cook for 2 minutes .
4. Mix in the remaining butter, zest, salt and pepper, parsley, and parmesan .
5. Serve.

Beans with Celery And Parsley

Servings: 4, **Prep +Cook time:** 25 minutes

Ingredients:
- Garbanzo beans soaked overnight and drained- 1 cup
- Cranberry beans soaked overnight and drained- 1 cup
- Chopped celery- 2 stalks
- Chopped parsley- 1 bunch
- Salt and black pepper
- Water- 4 cups
- Bay leaf- 1
- Crushed garlic- 1 clove
- Chopped small red onion- 1
- Green beans- 1 ½ cups
- Sugar- 1 tbsp.
- Apple cider vinegar- 5 tbsp.
- Extra virgin olive oil- 4 tbsp.

Directions:

1. Pour the water into the Instant Pot and add the garbanzo beans, garlic, and bay leaf.
2. On a steaming basket, wrap the green beans in a tin foil and put in the basket. Put the cranberry beans on the basket too then seal the lid.
3. Set to cook at high pressure for 15 minutes.
4. Natural release the pressure for 10 minutes then quick release the rest of the pressure by moving the valve to venting.
5. Drain the beans in the liquid and put all the beans in a bowl and set aside.
6. Combine the sugar, onion, and vinegar in a bowl and set aside for some minutes then add it to the beans and mix well.
7. Mix in the olive oil, parsley, celery, salt and pepper and serve.

Creamy Cinnamon Potato Dish Topped With Nutty Mix

Servings: 4, **Prep +Cook time:** 25 minutes

Ingredients:
- Scrubbed sweet potatoes- 3 Ib.
- Salt to taste
- Coconut milk- ¼ cup
- Water- 1 cup
- Coconut flour- 2 tbsp.
- Cinnamon- 1 tsp.
- Ground nutmeg- ½ tsp.
- Palm sugar- 1/3 cup
- Allspice- ¼ tsp.

Topping:
- A pinch of salt
- Almond flour- ½ cup
- Pecans; soaked, drained, and ground- ¼ cup
- Shredded coconut- ¼ cup
- Salted butter- 5 tbsp.
- Ground cinnamon- 1 tsp.
- Chia seeds- 1 tbsp.

- Walnuts; soaked, drained, and ground- ½ cup

Directions:
1. Pour the water into the Instant Pot then prick the potatoes with a fork and put it on a steaming rack and place the rack above the water to cook for 20 minutes at high pressure.
2. Combine the topping ingredients in a bowl and set aside.
3. Natural release the pressure and peel the potatoes then pour a ½ cup of water into the pot.
4. Chop the potatoes and put it on a baking dish then add the topping mix and put it on the steaming rack in the pot and seal the lid.
5. Set to cook at high pressure for 10 minutes then quick release the pressure and remove the dish.
6. Let it cool then slice and serve.

Sautéed Garlic Beets

Servings: 4, **Prep +Cook time:** 25 minutes

Ingredients:
- Beets with greens cut and washed- 3
- Salt
- Water
- Lemon juice- 1 tsp.
- Extra virgin olive oil- 1 tbsp.
- Minced garlic- 2 cloves

Directions:
1. Put the beets in the Instant Pot and pour enough water to cover the beets and season with some salt. Seal the lid and cook at high pressure for 15 minutes.
2. Natural release the pressure for 10 minutes then release the rest of the steam by moving the valve to venting.
3. Drain the water from the beets, then peel and chop them roughly.
4. Pour oil in a pan over medium –high heat and mix in the beets to cook for 3 minutes.
5. Season with some salt and add the garlic and the lemon juice.
6. Remove and serve.

Maple Syrup Brussels Sprouts

Servings: 8, **Prep +Cook time:** 15 minutes

Ingredients:
- Brussels sprouts- 2 Ib.
- Salt and black pepper
- Buttery spread- 1 tbsp.
- Orange juice- ¼ cup
- Grated orange zest- 1 tsp.
- Maple syrup- 2 tbsp.

Directions:
1. Combine all the ingredients in the Instant Pot and seal the lid. Set to cook for 4 minutes at high pressure.
2. Natural release the pressure, then serve the Brussels sprouts on a plate.

Green Beans With Tomatoes

Servings: 4, **Prep +Cook time:** 15 minutes

Ingredients:
- Trimmed green beans- 1 Ib.
- Salt
- Crushed garlic- 1 clove
- Extra virgin olive oil- 1 tbsp. + 1 tsp.
- Chopped tomatoes- 2 cups
- Basil sprig- 1

Directions:
1. Press 'Sauté' on the Instant Pot and add 1 tbsp of olive oil to it then add the garlic to cook for 1 minute.
2. Mix in the tomatoes to cook for 1 minute then put the green beans on a steamer rack then season with salt and place it above the pot contents.
3. Seal the lid and set to cook for 5 minutes at high pressure.
4. Quick release the pressure and pour the beans into the pot mix and stir well.
5. Serve sprinkled with basil and drizzled with olive oil.

Braised Fava Beans With Bacon And Parsley

Servings: 4, **Prep +Cook time:** 18 minutes

Ingredients:
- Shelled fava beans- 3 Ib.
- White wine- ½ cup
- Salt and black pepper
- Extra virgin olive oil- 1 tsp.
- Water- ¾ cup
- Chopped bacon- 4 oz.

- Chopped parsley- 3 sprigs

Directions:
1. Press 'Sauté' on the Instant Pot and add the oil then brown the bacon and pour in the wine to cook for 2 minutes.
2. Pour in the water and add the fava beans then seal the lid to cook for 7 minutes at high pressure.
3. Quick release the pressure and serve beans sprinkled with parsley and salt and pepper.

Lemony Artichokes

Servings: 4, **Prep +Cook time:** 35 minutes

Ingredients:
- Trimmed medium artichokes- 2
- Salt to taste
- Lemon wedge- 1
- Water- 1 cup

Directions:
1. Rub the artichokes with the lemon wedge then place it on the steaming rack.
2. Pour the water into the Instant Pot and place the basket above the water then seal the lid and set to cook for 20 minutes at high pressure.
3. Natural release the pressure for 10 minutes then move the valve to venting position.
4. Serve artichokes sprinkled with salt as side with steak and dipping sauce.

Cheesy Asparagus

Servings: 4, **Prep +Cook time:** 12 minutes

Ingredients:
- Trimmed asparagus- 1 bunch
- Water- 1 cup
- Minced garlic- 1 clove
- Grated parmesan cheese- 3 tbsp.
- Butter- 3 tbsp.

Directions:
1. Pour the water into the Instant Pot and put the asparagus, garlic, and butter on a tin foil then curve the edges.
2. Put the foil with asparagus in the pot and seal the lid to cook for 8 minutes at high pressure.
3. Quick release the pressure and serve the asparagus sprinkled with parmesan.

Honey Carrots With Dill

Servings: 4, **Prep +Cook time:** 15 minutes

Ingredient:
- Baby carrots- 1 Ib.
- Salt
- Butter- 2 tbsp.
- Honey- ½ cup
- Water- ½ cup
- Dried thyme- 1 tsp.
- Dried dill- 1 tsp.

Directions:
1. Put the carrots on a steaming basket. Pour the water in the Instant Pot then place the steaming rack above the water in the pot.
2. Seal the lid and set to high pressure for 3 minutes.
3. Quick release the pressure and remove the water then put the carrots in a bowl.
4. Press 'Sauté' on the Instant Pot then add the butter to melt then mix in the thyme, honey, dill, and salt then add the carrots and mix to coat.
5. Cook for 1 minute then serve as side.

Tomatoes and Peppers With Parsley

Servings: 4, **Prep +Cook time**: 16 minutes

Ingredients:
- Thinly sliced yellow bell peppers- 2
- Thinly sliced green bell pepper- 1
- Thinly sliced red bell peppers- 2
- Chopped tomatoes- 2
- Thinly sliced red onion- 1
- Minced garlic- 2 cloves
- A drizzle of extra virgin olive oil
- Finely chopped parsley- 1 bunch
- Salt and black pepper

Directions:

1. Press 'Sauté' on the Instant Pot then add the oil and the onions to cook for 3 minutes.
2. Mix in the bell peppers to cook for 5 minutes then add the tomatoes and season with salt and pepper then seal the lid to cook for 6 minutes on high pressure.
3. Quick release the pressure, then scoop the peppers and tomatoes to a bowl.
4. Sprinkle with salt and pepper, garlic, parsley, and drizzle the oil on it then mix to coat.
5. Serve as side

Creamy Fennel

Servings: 3, **Prep +Cook time**: 10 minutes

Ingredients:
- Sliced big fennel bulbs- 2
- Salt
- A pinch of ground nutmeg
- Milk- 2 cups
- Butter- 2 tbsp.
- White flour- 1 tbsp.

Directions:

1. Press 'Sauté' on the instant mode and add the butter to melt then add the fennel and brown for a bit.
2. Pour in the milk then mix in the flour, nutmeg, salt, and pepper then seal the lid to cook for 6 minutes on low pressure.
3. Quick release the pressure and serve the fennel.

Cheesy Rice With Spinach And Pecans

Servings: 6, **Prep +Cook time**: 20 minutes

Ingredients:
- Softened goat cheese; crumbled- 4 oz.
- Salt and black pepper
- Lemon juice- 2 tbsp.
- Arborio rice- 1 ½ cups
- Chopped yellow onion- ¾ cup
- Extra virgin olive oil- 2 tbsp.
- Toasted and chopped pecans- 1/3 cup
- White wine- ½ cup
- Minced garlic- 2 cloves
- Hot veggie stock- 3 ½ cups
- Chopped spinach- 12 oz.

Directions:

1. Press 'Sauté' on the Instant Pot and add the oil then mix in the onions and garlic to cook for 5 minutes.
2. Mix in the rice to cook for 1 minute then pour in the wine and mix to cook till it has been absorbed.
3. Pour in 3 cups of the stock and seal the lid and cook for 4 minutes at high pressure.
4. Quick release the pressure then mix in the spinach and let it simmer for 3 minutes.
5. Pour in the rest of the stock then mix in the lemon juice, goat cheese, and season with salt and pepper.
6. Serve topped with pecans.

Chapter 7 Simple and Healthy Vegetable Recipes

Spicy Steamed Cabbage

Servings: 4 , **Prep + Cook Time:** 18 minutes

Ingredients:
- Cabbage, cut into 8 wedges: 1
- Apple cider vinegar: 1/4 cup
- Apple: 1 ¼ cups
- Water: 2 Tsps.
- Raw sugar: 1 Tsps.
- Cornstarch: 2 Tsps.
- Cayenne pepper: 1/2 Tsps.
- Red pepper flakes: 1/2 Tsps.
- Sesame seed oil: 1 tbsp.
- Carrot, grated: 1

Directions:
1. 'Sauté' oil in an instant pot
2. Carefully add cabbage them stir an let it cook for 3 minutes
3. Add carrots, 1 ¼ cups water, sugar, vinegar, cayenne and pepper flakes, stir and secure. let it cook for 5 minutes on high
4. Add cornstarch and 2 tbsp of water, stir and let it simmer till it boils
5. Top it with water and serve

Beet with Salad

Servings: 4 , **Prep + Cook Time:** 20 minutes

Ingredients:
- Beets: 1 ½ lb.
- Orange peel: 3 strips
- Cider vinegar: 2 tbsp.
- Orange juice: 1/2 cup
- Orange zest, grated: 2 Tsps.
- Brown sugar: 2 tbsp.
- Scallions; chopped: 2
- Mustard: 2 Tsps.
- Arugula and mustard greens: 2 cups

Directions:
1. Scrub, and cut the beets in half. Place them in a bowl
2. Mix orange peel strips with vinegar and orange juice in an instant pot and stir
3. Add the beets, secure the lid and cook for 7 minutes on high
4. 'Natural release' the steam and remove the lid then place the beets in a bowl
5. Add scallions and grated orange zest then toss them
6. Top it with the soup from the pot and mixed salad greens then serve.

Steamed Potatoes

Servings: 4 , **Prep + Cook Time:** 17 minutes

Ingredients:
- Gold potatoes, cubed: 1 lb.
- Parsley leaves; chopped: 1/4 cup
- Ghee: 2 tbsp.
- Juice from 1/2 lemon
- Water: 1/2 cup
- Salt and black pepper to the taste

Directions:
1. Place water in the instant pot and potatoes in the steamer basket, secure the lid and cook for 5 minutes on high
2. 'Natural release' the pressure and remove lid
3. Add ghee, lemon juice, parsley, salt and pepper, stir and sauté it for 2 minutes
4. Serve

Broiled Spicy Peppers

Servings: 4 , **Prep + Cook Time:** 30 minutes

Ingredients:

- Turkey meat, ground: 1 lb.
- Canned green chilies; chopped: 5 oz.
- Water: 1 cup
- Jalapeno pepper; chopped: 1
- Chili powder: 2 Tsps.
- Garlic powder: 1 Tsps.
- Cumin, ground: 1 Tsps.
- Green onions; chopped: 2
- Avocado; chopped: 1
- Salt to the taste
- Whole wheat panko: 1/2 cup
- Bell peppers, tops, and seeds discarded: 4
- Pepper jack cheese slices: 4
- Crushed tortilla chips
- Pico de gallo

For the chipotle sauce:

- Zest from 1 lime
- Juice from 1 lime
- Sour cream: 1/2 cup
- Chipotle in adobo sauce: 2 tbsp.
- Garlic powder: 1/8 Tsps.

Directions:

1. Mix sour cream with chipotle in adobo sauce, lime zest and lime juice and garlic powder in a bowl, stir and keep it in the fridge to make chipotle sauce
2. Mix turkey, green onions, green chilies, bread crumbs, jalapeno, cumin, salt, chili powder and garlic powder in another bowl, stir then stuff peppers with it
3. In the instant pot, place 1 cup of water. place the peppers in the steamer basket, secure the lid and cook for 5 minutes on high
4. 'Natural release' the steam for 10 minutes then release the remaining pressure by venting
5. Place the peppers in a pan, top it with cheese and broil it in a preheated broiler till the cheese become brown
6. Top it with chipotle sauce and serve

Tasty Eggplant

Servings: 2 , **Prep + Cook Time:** 18 minutes

Ingredients:

- Eggplant, cubed: 4 cups
- Extra-virgin olive oil: 1 tbsp.
- Garlic cloves; minced: 3
- Marinara sauce: 1 cup
- Water: 1/2 cup
- Garlic powder: 1 tbsp.
- Salt and black pepper to the taste

Directions:

1. 'Sauté' oil in an instant pot
2. Add garlic then stir and cook for 2 minutes
3. Gently stir while adding eggplant, salt, pepper, garlic powder, marinara sauce and water, secure the lid then cook for 8 minutes on high
4. 'Quick release' the steam. Remove the lid
5. Serve it with spaghetti

Simple Broccoli

Servings: 4 , **Prep + Cook Time:** 22 minutes

Ingredients:

- Broccoli head, cut into 4 pieces: 1
- Chinese rice wine: 1 tbsp.
- Water: 1/2 cup
- Peanut oil: 1 tbsp.
- Garlic cloves; minced: 6
- Salt to the taste

Directions:

1. Place the ½ cup of water in the instant pot and broccoli in the steamer, secure the lid and cook for12 minutes at low pressure
2. 'Quick release' the steam. Remove the lid
3. Place the broccoli in a bowl, add cold water to fill then drain
4. Heat an oiled pan over medium-high heat
5. In the pan add garlic then stir and cook for 3 minutes
6. Add salt and cook for 30 seconds then serve

Hot Potatoes

Servings: 4 , **Prep + Cook Time:** 15 minutes

Ingredients:

- Brussels sprouts washed and trimmed: 1 ½ lb.
- Bread crumbs: 1 ½ tbsp.
- Beef stock: 1/2 cup
- New potatoes; chopped: 1 cup
- Butter: 1 ½ tbsp.
- Salt and black pepper to the taste

Direction:

1. In your instant pot, place sprouts, potatoes, stock, salt and pepper, secure the lid and cook for 5 minutes on high
2. 'Quick release' the steam. Remove the lid
3. Add butter and breadcrumbs, toss and 'sauté' briefly then serve

Buttered Carrots

Servings: 4 , **Prep + Cook Time:** 12 minutes

Ingredients:

- Baby carrots: 16 oz.
- Dill; chopped: 2 tbsp.
- Molasses: 4 oz.
- Water: 2 oz.
- Butter: 2 tbsp.
- Salt and black pepper to the taste

Directions:

1. In an instant pot, place carrot, water, salt, pepper and molasses then stir, secure the lid. cook for 3 minutes on high
2. 'Quick release' the steam. Remove the lid
3. Add butter and dill then stir and serve

Sour Eggplant

Servings: 4 , **Prep + Cook Time:** 17 minutes

Ingredients:

- Eggplant, roughly chopped: 1
- Zucchinis, roughly chopped: 3
- Extra virgin olive oil: 3 tbsp.
- Tomatoes, sliced: 3
- Lemon juice: 2 tbsp.
- Thyme; dried: 1 Tsps.
- Oregano; dried: 1 Tsps.
- Salt and black pepper to the taste

Directions:

1. In an instant pot, place eggplant, zucchini and tomatoes
2. Mix lemon juice with salt, pepper, thyme, oregano and oil in a bowl then stir
3. Pour the mixture over the veggies, toss it, secure the lid and cook for 7 minutes on high
4. 'Quick release' the steam. Remove the lid then serve.

Sweet Brussels Sprouts

Servings: 4 , **Prep + Cook Time:** 16 minutes

Ingredients:

- Brussels sprouts; washed: 1 lb.
- Water: 1 cup
- Parmesan, grated: 3 tbsp.
- Juice from 1 lemon
- Butter: 2 tbsp.
- Salt and black pepper to the taste

Direction:

1. In an instant pot, place sprouts, salt, pepper and water, stir, secure the lid and cook for 3 minutes on high
2. 'Quick release' the steam and place the sprouts in a bowl; discard the water an clean the pot
3. 'Sauté' butter in the pot
4. Carefully add lemon and sprouts then stir
5. Top it with parmesan cheese, salt and pepper then serve.

Tasty Garlicky Potatoes

Servings: 4 , **Prep + Cook Time:** 30 minutes

Ingredients:
- Baby potatoes: 2 lb.
- Vegetable oil: 5 tbsp.
- Stock: 1/2 cup
- Rosemary spring: 1
- Garlic cloves: 5
- Salt and black pepper to the taste

Directions:
1. 'Sauté' oil in an instant pot
2. Carefully add potatoes, rosemary and garlic and stir. Let them cook for 10 minutes till they become brown
3. Prick each potato using a knife
4. Add stock, salt and pepper; secure the lid and cook for 7 minutes on high
5. 'Quick release' the steam. Remove the lid then serve

Fragrant Turnips

Servings: 4 , **Prep + Cook Time:** 30 minutes

Ingredients:
- Turnips; peeled and chopped: 20 oz.
- Garlic; minced: 1 Tsps.
- Ginger grated: 1 Tsps.
- Sugar: 1 Tsps.
- Cumin powder: 1 Tsps.
- Coriander powder: 1 Tsps.
- Green chilies; chopped: 2
- Turmeric powder: 1/2 Tsps.
- Water: 1 cup
- Butter: 2 tbsp.
- Yellow onions; chopped: 2
- Tomatoes; chopped: 2
- Salt to the taste
- A handful coriander leaves; chopped.

Directions:
1. 'Sauté' butter to melt
2. Carefully add green chilies, garlic and ginger, stir then cook for 1 minute
3. Add onions then stir and cook for 3 minutes
4. While stirring, add salt, tomatoes, turmeric, and cumin and coriander powder then stir and cook for 15 minute
5. 'Quick release' the steam. Remove the lid
6. Add sugar and coriander then stir and serve.

Delicious Beet Salad

Servings: 4 , **Prep + Cook Time:** 40 minutes

Ingredients:
- Beets: 4
- Garlic clove; chopped: 1
- Balsamic vinegar: 2 tbsp.
- Capers: 2 tbsp.
- Water: 1 cup
- Extra-virgin olive oil: 1 tbsp.
- A bunch of parsley; chopped.
- Salt and black pepper to the taste

Directions:
1. In a pot, place 1 cup of water and bets in the steamer basket, secure the lid and cook for 20 minutes on high
2. Mix parsley, garlic, salt, pepper, olive oil and capers in a bowl and stir
3. 'Quick release' the steam. Remove the lid
4. Place the beet in the cutting board, le then cool, peel and slice them
5. Top it with vinegar and dress it with parsley then serve.

Lemon-Sour Artichokes

Servings: 4 , **Prep + Cook Time:** 30 minutes

Ingredients:
- Artichokes: 4
- Tarragon; chopped: 1 tbsp.
- Chicken stock: 2 cups
- Lemons: 2
- Celery stalk; chopped: 1
- Extra virgin olive oil: 1/2 cup
- Salt to the taste

Directions:
1. Remove the celery stalks and petal tips
2. Cut zest lemon into 4 slices and place them in the instant pot
3. Add artichokes on each lemon slice
4. Add stock, secure the lid and cook for 20 minutes on high
5. Mix tarragon, lemon zest, and pulp from the second lemon, celery, salt and olive oil then pulse them well
6. Drizzle the mixture over artichokes and serve,

Endives Delicacy

Servings: 4 , **Prep + Cook Time:** 30 minutes

Ingredients:
- Endives, trimmed: 4
- Butter: 2 tbsp.
- White flour: 1 tbsp
- Slices ham: 4
- Nutmeg: 1/2 Tsps.
- Milk: 14 oz.
- Salt and black pepper to taste

Directions:
1. Place water in the instant pot and the endives in the steamer then cook them for 10 minutes on high
2. Heat an oiled pan over medium heat to melt it
3. Add flour, stir and cook for 3 minutes
4. While stirring, add milk, salt, pepper and nutmeg the cook for 10 minutes on low heat
5. Release the pressure from the heat, remove the lid and place them on a chopping board
6. Roll each of them in a ham slice,
7. Arrange endives in a pan then add milk and broil them in a preheated broiler for 10 minutes
8. Slice them and serve

Nutty Brussels Sprouts

Servings: 4 , **Prep + Cook Time:** 15 minutes

Ingredients:
- Brussels sprouts: 1 lb.
- Pine nuts, toasted: 1/4 cup
- Pomegranate, seeds separated: 1
- Salt and black pepper to the taste
- Extra virgin olive oil: 1 drizzle
- Water: 1 cup

Directions:
1. Place Brussels sprouts in the instant pot pressure cooker, add 1 cup of water, secure the lid. cook for 4 minutes on high
2. 'Quick release' the steam. Remove the lid then move the sprouts to a bowl
3. While stirring, add salt, pepper, pine nuts, pomegranate seeds and pine nuts
4. Top it with olive oil, toss it and serve

Sour Endives

Servings: 4 , **Prep + Cook Time:** 17 minutes

Ingredients:

- Lemon juice: 1 tbsp
- Endives, trimmed and cut into halves: 4
- Butter: 1 tbsp.
- Salt and black pepper to the taste

Directions:

1. 'Sauté' butter to melt
2. Arrange endives in the pot
3. Add salt and pepper and the lemon juice, secure the lid and cook for 7 minutes on high
4. 'Natural release' the steam an place the endives on a platter
5. Top with cooking soup and serve

Cheesy Fennel Risotto

Servings: 2 , **Prep + Cook Time:** 20 minutes

Ingredients:

- Arborio rice: 1 ½ cups
- Yellow onion; chopped: 1
- Butter: 2 tbsp.
- Extra-virgin olive oil: 1 tbsp.
- White wine: 1/4 cup
- Chicken stock: 3 cups
- Fennel bulb trimmed and chopped: 1.
- Thyme; dried: 1/2 Tsps.
- Tomato paste: 3 tbsp.
- Parmesan cheese, grated: 1/3 cup
- Salt and black pepper to the taste

Directions:

1. 'Sauté' butter to melt
2. Add fennel and onion, stir and 'sauté' for 4 minutes then transfer them to a bowl
3. Add oil to the pot and heat then add rice and cook for 3 minutes
4. Add tomato paste, stock, fennel, onions, wine, salt, pepper and thyme then stir and secure the lid. Cook for 8 minutes on high
5. 'Quick release' the steam. Remove the lid
6. Add cheese and stir then serve

Saucy Bell Peppers

Servings: 4 , **Prep + Cook Time:** 25 minutes

Ingredients:

- Beef meat, ground: 16 oz.
- White rice, already cooked: 1 cup
- Egg: 1
- Canned tomato soup: 10 oz.
- Bell peppers, tops and seeds removed: 4
- Milk: 1/2 cup
- Onions; chopped: 2
- Water: 8 oz.
- Salt and black pepper to the taste

Directions:

1. Take a pot and boil water over medium heat
2. Add bell peppers and blanch them for 3 minutes. Drain and transfer them to a working surface
3. Mix beef, rice, salt, pepper, egg, milk and onions in a bowl then stir
4. Stuff bell peppers with this mixture then place them in an instant pot
5. Add tomato soup and water, secure the lid and cook for 12 minutes on high
6. 'Quick release' the steam. Remove the lid
7. Top with tomato sauce and serve

Blended Eggplant

Servings: 6 , **Prep + Cook Time:** 15 minutes

Ingredients:
- Eggplant peeled and cut into medium chunks: 2 lb.
- Extra virgin olive oil: 1/4 cup
- Water: 1/2 cup
- Tahini: 1 tbsp.
- Olive oil: 1 drizzle
- Olives; pitted and sliced: 3
- Garlic cloves: 4
- Lemon juice: 1/4 cup
- Thyme; chopped: 1 bunch
- Salt and black pepper to the taste

Directions:
1. In an instant pot, put eggplant pieces and a ¼ cup of oil then 'sauté' it
2. Add garlic, water, salt and pepper, stir, secure the lid and cook for 3 minutes on high
3. 'Quick release' the steam. Remove the lid
4. Blend the eggplant, garlic, lemon juice, thyme and tahini, pulsing it well
5. Place it in a bowl then top it with olive slices and a drizzle of oil then serve

Peppered Kale

Servings: 2 , **Prep + Cook Time:** 20 minutes

Ingredients:
- Kale; chopped: 10 oz.
- Carrots, sliced: 3
- Chicken stock: ½ cup
- Garlic cloves; chopped: 5
- Yellow onion, thinly sliced: 1
- Balsamic vinegar: a splash
- Red pepper flakes: ¼ tbsp
- Kale: 1 tbsp.
- Salt and black pepper to the taste

Directions:
1. 'Sauté' ghee to melt in an instant pot
2. Add carrots and onions then stir and 'sauté' for 2 minutes
3. Add garlic and stir then let it cook for 1 minute
4. Add kale, stock, salt and pepper, stir, secure the lid and cook for 7 minutes on high
5. 'Quick release' the steam and remove the lid
6. Add vinegar and pepper flakes, toss it then serve

Spicy Okra

Servings: 4 , **Prep + Cook Time:** 35 minutes

Ingredients:
- Okra, sliced: 2 cups
- Water: 2 ¼ cups
- Paprika: 2 Tsps.
- Brown rice: 1 cup
- Bacon slices; chopped: 4
- Tomatoes; chopped: 1 cup
- Salt and black pepper to the taste

Directions:
1. 'Sauté' bacon and brown it for 2 minutes
2. While stirring, ad okra and cook for 5 minutes
3. Add paprika and rice then stir and cook for 2 minutes
4. As you stir, add salt, pepper, water and tomatoes, secure the lid and cook for 16 minutes on high
5. 'Quick release' the steam and remove the lid then serve

Sautéed Endives

Servings: 4 , **Prep + Cook Time:** 25 minutes

Ingredients:
- Endives, trimmed: 8
- Butter: 4 tbsp.
- Juice from 1/2 lemon
- Water: 1/2 cup
- Sugar: 1 Tsps.
- Parsley; chopped: 2 tbsp.
- Salt and black pepper to the taste

Directions:
1. In the instant pot, place the endives, 1 tablespoon butter, lemon juice, 1/2 cup water, sugar, salt and pepper then stir, secure the lid and cook for 10 minutes on high
2. 'Quick release' the steam and remove the lid. Transfer the endives to the plate
3. Heat a pan with 3 tbsp butter
4. Add endives salt, pepper and parsley then stir and cook for 5 minutes.
5. Serve

Sour-Garlicky Kale

Servings: 4 , **Prep + Cook Time:** 15 minutes

Ingredients:
- Garlic cloves; chopped: 3
- Juice from 1/2 lemon
- Kale, trimmed: 1 lb.
- Extra-virgin olive oil: 1 tbsp.
- Water: 1/2 cup
- Salt and black pepper to the taste

Directions:
1. 'Sauté' oil in an instant pot
2. Add garlic and cook for 2 minutes
3. Add kale and water, secure the lid and cook for 5 minutes on high
4. 'Quick release' and remove the lid
5. Add with salt and pepper and stir then serve

Tasty Collard Greens

Servings: 4 , **Prep + Cook Time:** 30 minutes

Ingredients:
- Collard greens, trimmed: 1 bunch
- Extra virgin olive oil: 2 tbsp.
- Tomato puree: 2 tbsp.
- Yellow onion; chopped: 1
- Garlic cloves; minced: 3
- Balsamic vinegar: 1 tbsp.
- Sugar: 1 Tsps.
- Chicken stock: 1/2 cup
- Salt and black pepper to the taste

Directions:
1. Mix stock, oil, garlic, vinegar, onion and tomato puree in your instant pot then stir
2. Roll them in cigar-shaped bundles then add collard greens
3. Add salt, pepper and sugar, secure the lid and cook for 20 minutes on high
4. 'Quick release' the steam. Remove the lid then serve

Sautéed Bacon and Collard Greens

Servings: 6 , **Prep + Cook Time:** 35 minutes

Ingredients:
- Bacon; chopped: 1/4 lb.
- Collard greens, trimmed: 1 lb.
- Water: 1/2 cup
- Salt and black pepper to the taste

Direction:
1. 'Sauté' bacon in the instant pot for 5 minutes
2. Add collard greens, salt, pepper and water, stir, secure the lid and cook for 20 minutes on high
3. 'Quick release' the steam and remove the lid then serve

Bacon and Brussels Sprouts Delicacy

Servings: 4 , **Prep + Cook Time:** 10 minutes

Ingredients:

- Brussels sprouts; trimmed then cut into halves: 1 lb.
- Dill; finely chopped: 2 tbsp.
- Bacon; chopped: 1/2 cup
- Mustard: 1 tbsp.
- Chicken stock: 1 cup
- Butter: 1 tbsp.
- Salt and black pepper to the taste

Directions:

1. 'Sauté' bacon in your instant pot until it turns crispy
2. Add sprouts then stir and cook for 2 minutes
3. Add stock, mustard, salt and pepper, stir, secure the lid and cook for 4 minutes on high
4. 'Quick release' the steam. Remove the lid
5. Add butter and dill then 'sauté' and serve

Cheesy, Tasty Tomatoes

Servings: 4 , **Prep + Cook Time:** 20 minutes

Ingredients:

- Tomatoes; tops cut off and pulp scooped: 4
- Yellow onion; chopped: 1
- Celery; chopped: 2 tbsp.
- Mushrooms; chopped: 1/2 cup
- Bread, crumbled: 1 slice
- Water: 1/2 cup
- Cottage cheese: 1 cup
- Butter: 1 tbsp.
- Caraway seeds: 1/4 Tsps.
- Parsley; chopped: 1 tbsp.
- Salt and black pepper to the taste

Directions:

1. Placed chopped tomatoes in a bowl
2. Heat a pan with butter over medium heat
3. Add onions and celery then stir and cook for 3 minutes
4. Add tomato pulp and mushrooms then stir and cook for 1 minute
5. While stirring, add salt, pepper, crumbled bread, cheese, caraway seeds and parsley then cook for 4 minutes
6. Place the mixture in the tomato and arrange them I the instant pot steamer basket
7. Add water, secure the lid and cook for 2 minutes on high
8. 'Quick release' the pressure and remove eh lid then serve

Corny Okra

Servings: 6 , **Prep + Cook Time:** 30 minutes

Ingredients:

- Okra, trimmed: 1 lb.
- Canned tomatoes; chopped: 28 oz.
- Scallions; chopped: 6
- Green bell peppers; chopped: 3
- Vegetable oil: 2 tbsp.
- Sugar: 1 Tsps.
- Salt and black pepper to the taste
- Corn kernels: 1 cup

Directions:

1. 'Sauté' oil in an instant pot
2. Add scallions and bell peppers then stir and cook for 5 minutes
3. Add okra, salt, pepper, sugar and tomatoes then stir, secure the lid and cook for 10 minutes on high
4. 'Quick release' the steam and remove the lid
5. Add corn, secure the lid and cook for 2 minutes on high
6. Release the pressure and serve

Grilled Artichoke

Servings: 4 , Prep + Cook Time: 50 minutes

Ingredients:

- Big artichokes, washed, stems and petal tips cut off: 4
- Lemon juice: 2 tbsp.
- Balsamic vinegar: 2 Tsps.
- Oregano: 1 Tsps.
- Extra virgin olive oil: 1/4 cup
- Water: 2 cups
- Garlic cloves; minced: 2
- Salt and black pepper to the taste

Directions:

1. Place the artichokes in the steamer basket of instant pot
2. Add 2 cups of water secure the lid and steam for 8 minutes
3. Mix lemon, vinegar, oil, salt, pepper, garlic and oregano in a bowl and stir well to make a vinaigrette
4. 'Quick release' the steam, place the artichokes in a plate and cut them in halves. Place the hearts on a platter
5. Top vinaigrette over the artichokes and leave them aside for 30 minutes
6. Grill them over medium heat for 3 minutes each side
7. Serve it warm

Tasty Fennel

Servings: 4 , Prep + Cook Time: 22 minutes

Ingredients:

- Fennel bulbs, trimmed and cut into quarters: 2
- Extra virgin olive oil: 3 tbsp.
- White wine: 1/4 cup
- Parmesan, grated: 1/4 cup
- Veggie stock: 3/4 cup
- Juice from 1/2 lemon
- Garlic clove; chopped: 1
- Dried red pepper: 1
- Salt and black pepper to the taste

Direction:

1. 'Sauté' oil in an instant pot
2. Add garlic and pepper and stir then cook it for 2 minutes. Discard the garlic afterward
3. Add fennel and stir then brown it for 4 minutes
4. Add salt, pepper, stock and wine, secure the lid and cook for 4 minutes on high
5. 'Quick release' the steam. Remove the lid
6. Add lemon juice, salt, cheese and pepper. Toss it and serve.

Bacon and Kale Delicacy

Servings: 4 , Prep + Cook Time: 20 minutes

Ingredients:

- Bacon slices; chopped: 6
- Kale leaves; chopped: 10 oz.
- Vegetable oil: 1 tbsp.
- Red chili, crushed: 1 Tsps.
- Liquid smoke: 1 Tsps.
- Onion, thinly sliced: 1
- Garlic cloves; chopped: 6
- Chicken stock: 1 ½ cups
- Brown sugar: 1 tbsp.
- Apple cider vinegar: 2 tbsp.
- Salt and black pepper to the taste

Directions:

1. 'Sauté' oil in an instant pot
2. Add bacon and stir then cook for 2 minutes
3. Add onions and stir then cook for 3 minutes
4. Add garlic and stir then cook for 1 minute
5. While stirring, add vinegar, stock, sugar, liquid smoke, red chilies, salt, pepper and kale and secure the lid. Cook for 5 minutes on high
6. 'Quick release' the steam and remove the lid then serve

Collard Greens with Smoked Turkey

Servings: 8 , **Prep + Cook Time:** 35 minutes

Ingredients:
- Sweet onion; chopped: 1
- Extra virgin olive oil: 2 tbsp.
- Brown sugar: 1 tbsp.
- Chicken stock: 2 cups
- Apple cider vinegar: 2 tbsp.
- Crushed red pepper: 1/2 Tsps.
- Smoked turkey wings: 2
- Garlic cloves, crushed: 3
- Collard greens; chopped: 2 ½ lb.
- Salt and black pepper to the taste

Directions:
1. 'Sauté' oil in an instant pot
2. Add onion and stir then cook for 2 minutes
3. Add garlic and stir then cook for 1 minute
4. While stirring, add stock, greens, vinegar, salt, pepper, crushed red pepper and sugar
5. Add smoked turkey, secure the lid and cook for 20 minutes on high
6. 'Quick release' the pressure and remove the lid then serve

Sweet Cabbage

Servings: 8 , **Prep + Cook Time:** 18 minutes

Ingredients:
- Chicken stock: 2 cups
- Green cabbage head; chopped: 1
- Butter: 1/4 cup
- Bacon slices; chopped: 3
- Salt and black pepper to the taste

Directions:
1. 'Sauté' bacon and cook for 4 minutes in an instant pot
2. Add butter to melt
3. While stirring, add cabbage, stock, salt and pepper then co for 3 minutes on high
4. 'Quick release' the steam. Remove the lid then serve

Spicy Carrots and Turnips

Servings: 4 , **Prep + Cook Time:** 15 minutes

Ingredients:
- Turnips, peeled and sliced: 2
- Small onion; chopped: 1
- Lemon juice: 1 Tsps.
- Cumin, ground: 1 Tsps.
- Carrots, sliced: 3
- Extra-virgin olive oil: 1 tbsp.
- Water: 1 cup
- Salt and black pepper to the taste

Directions:
1. 'Sauté' oil in an instant pot
2. Add onions and stir then cook for 2 minutes
3. While stirring, add turnips, carrots, cumin and lemon juice then cook for 1 minute
4. Add salt, pepper, and water, secure the lid and cook for 6 minutes on high
5. 'Quick release' the steam and remove the lid then serve

Prosciutto Asparagus Canes

Servings: 4 , **Prep + Cook Time:** 10 minutes

Ingredients:
- Prosciutto slices: 8 oz.
- Asparagus, trimmed: 1 lb.
- Water: 2 cups
- Salt: 1 pinch

Directions:
1. Wrap asparagus spears in prosciutto slices and place them in the steamer basket in the instant pot
2. Add 2 cups of water and salt, secure the lid and cook for 4 minutes on high
3. 'Natural release' the steam and remove the lid then serve

Tasty Carrots

Servings: 4 , **Prep + Cook Time:** 35 minutes

Ingredients:
- Baby carrots: 2 cups
- Butter: 1/2 tbsp.
- Brown sugar: 1 tbsp.
- Water: /2 cup
- Salt: 1 pinch

Directions:

1. Mix butter, water, salt and sugar in your instant pot and 'sauté' for 30 seconds
2. Add carrots, stir, secure the lid and cook for 15 minutes on high
3. 'Quick release' the steam. Remove the lid
4. 'Sauté' for 1 minute then serve hot

Cheesy Pecan

Servings: 8 , **Prep + Cook Time:** 60 minutes

Ingredients:
- Mixed cherry tomatoes, cut into halves: 1-pint
- Water: 1 ½ cups
- Apple cider vinegar: 1 cup
- Water: 1 cup
- Pickling juice: 2 Tsps.
- Small beets, trimmed: 8
- Red onion, sliced: 1
- Pecans: 2 oz.
- Extra virgin olive oil: 2 tbsp.
- Sugar: 2 tbsp.
- Goat cheese: 4 oz.
- Salt and black pepper to the taste

Directions:
1. Place beets and 1 ½ cups water in the steamer basket, secure the lid and cook for 20 minutes on high
2. 'Quick release' the steam and remove the lid
3. Let them cool, peel and chop them then place them in a bowl A
4. Put 1 cup of water, vinegar, sugar, pickling juice and salt in an instant pot, stir, secure the lid and cook for 2 minutes on high
5. 'Quick release' the steam, strain the liquid to a bowl B, add onions and leave it aside for 10 minute
6. Add tomatoes to bowl A and stir
7. Mix 4 tbsp of onion juice, 2 tbsps olive oil, salts and pepper in a bowl C and stir
8. Add contents of bowl C to bowl A
9. Top it with goat cheese and pecans then serve

Seasoned Shrimp Asparagus

Servings: 4 , **Prep + Cook Time:** 8 minutes

Ingredients:
- Shrimp, peeled and deveined: 1 lb
- Water: 1 cup
- Cajun seasoning: 1/2 tbsp.
- Extra virgin olive oil: 1 Tsps.
- Asparagus, trimmed: 1 bunch

Directions:

1. In the instant pot, pour water and put asparagus and shrimp in the steamer
2. Add olive oil and Cajun seasoning then stir, secure the lid and cook for 2 minutes on low
3. 'Natural release' the steam and remove the lid then serve

Chapter 8 Snacks and Appetizers

Lovely Endives

Servings: 4 , **Prep + Cook Time:** 17 minutes

Ingredients:
- Endives, trimmed and halved: 4
- Ghee: 1 tbsp.
- Lemon juice: 1 tbsp.
- Salt and black pepper to the taste

Directions:
1. 'Sauté' ghee in an instant pot
2. Add endives which have been seasoned with salt and pepper
3. Add lemon juice, secure the lid and cook for 7 minutes on high
4. Top it with cooking juice and serve

Sweet Squid

Servings: 4 , **Prep + Cook Time:** 25 minutes

Ingredients:
- Squid, tentacles from 1 squid separated and chopped: 4
- Mirin: 1 tbsp.
- Stevia: 2 tbsp.
- Coconut aminos: 4 tbsp.
- Cauliflower rice: 1 cup
- Fish stock: 14 oz.

Directions:
1. Mix chopped tentacles and cauliflower rice in a bowl and stir then use it to stuff eh squid
2. Place the squid in the instant pot then add the stock, aminos, mirin and stevia and stir, secure the lid and cook for 15 minutes on high
3. Serve

Cauliflower Dip for Veggies

Servings: 6 , **Prep + Cook Time:** 20 minutes

Ingredients:
- Cauliflower florets: 6 cups
- Coconut milk: 1/2 cup
- Veggie stock: 7 cups
- Ghee: 2 tbsp.
- Garlic cloves; minced: 8
- Salt and black pepper to the taste

Directions:
1. 'Sauté' ghee, garlic, salt and pepper in an instant pot for 2 minutes
2. Add stock and cauliflower then stir, secure the lid and cook for 7 minutes on high
3. Blend it with 1 cup of stock and milk
4. Serve with veggies

Chili Bacon

Servings: 3 , **Prep + Cook Time:** 15 minutes

Ingredients:
- Bacon slices: 3
- Water: 1 cup
- Cream cheese: 3 oz.
- Onion powder: 1/4 Tsps.
- Jalapeno peppers; chopped: 2
- Parsley; dried: 1/2 Tsps.
- Garlic powder: 1/4 Tsps.
- Salt and black pepper to the taste

Directions:
1. 'Sauté' bacon for a few minutes' drains the grease using paper towels and crumples it
2. Mix cream cheese with jalapenos, bacon, onion, garlic powder, parsley, salt and pepper in a bowl then stir and shape it into balls
3. Place water in the clean pot and the spicy balls in the steamer, secure the lid and cook for 2 minutes on high

Cheesy Mushroom Dip

Servings: 6 , **Prep + Cook Time:** 45 minutes

Ingredients:

- Shiitake mushrooms; chopped: 10 oz.
- Portobello mushrooms; chopped: 10 oz.
- Cremini mushrooms; chopped: 10 oz.
- Thyme; chopped: 1 tbsp.
- Coconut cream: 1/2 cup
- Yellow onion; chopped: 1
- 1/4 cup olive oil: 1
- Coconut flour: 1 tbsp.
- Parmesan cheese, grated: 1 oz.
- Parsley; chopped: 1 tbsp.
- Garlic cloves; minced: 3
- Chicken stock: 1 ¼ cup
- Salt and black pepper to the taste

Directions:

1. 'Sauté' oil, onion, salt, pepper, flour, garlic and thyme in an instant pot then stir and cook for 5 minutes
2. Add stock, shiitake, cremini and Portobello mushrooms then stir, secure the lid and cook for 25 minutes on high
3. Add cream, cheese and parsley then stir and simmer for 5 minutes
4. Serve

Fragrant Pumpkin

Servings: 18 , **Prep + Cook Time:** 30 minutes

Ingredients:

- Pumpkin puree: 3/4 cup
- Coconut flour: 1/4 cup
- Erythritol: 1/2 cup
- Nutmeg, ground: 1/2 Tsps.
- Ghee: 4 tbsp.
- Flaxseed meal: 2 tbsp.
- Baking powder: 1/2 Tsps.
- Baking soda: 1/2 Tsps.
- Water: 1 ½ cups
- Egg: 1
- Cinnamon powder: 1 Tsps.

Directions:

1. Mix ghee, pumpkin puree, egg, flaxseed meal, coconut flour, erythritol, baking soda, baking powder, nutmeg and cinnamon in a bowl then stir and divide it into a greased muffin pan
2. Place water in an instant pot and the muffin in the steamer basket, secure the lid and cook for 20 minutes on high
3. Serve

Chilled Zucchini

Servings: 4 , **Prep + Cook Time:** 16 minutes

Ingredients:

- Zucchini, roughly sliced: 1
- Tomato sauce: 1/4 cup
- Mozzarella, shredded: 1 cup
- Cumin, ground: 1 pinch
- Olive oil: a drizzle
- Salt and black pepper to the taste

Directions:

1. Mix zucchini, oil, tomato sauce, salt, pepper and cumin in an instant pot, toss it, secure the lid and cook for 6 minutes on high
2. Serve

Shrimp Sausage

Servings: 4 , **Prep + Cook Time:** 15 minutes

Ingredients:
- Shrimp, heads removed: 1 ½ lb.
- Sausage; cooked and chopped: 12 oz.
- Red pepper flakes, crushed: 1 Tsps.
- Old Bay seasoning: 1 tbsp.
- Chicken stock: 16 oz.
- Sweet onions cut into wedges: 2
- Garlic cloves; minced: 8
- Salt and black pepper to the taste

Directions:
1. Mix stock, old bay seasoning, pepper flakes, salt, black pepper, onions, garlic, sausage and shrimp in an instant pot and cook for 5 minutes on high
2. Serve

Sweet Zucchini

Servings: 4 , **Prep + Cook Time:** 20 minutes

Ingredients:
- Zucchini; chopped: 2 lb.
- Yellow onion; chopped: 1
- Olive oil: 1 tbsp.
- Garlic cloves; minced: 2
- Water: 1/2 cup
- Basil; chopped: 1 bunch
- Salt and white pepper to the taste

Directions:
1. 'Sauté' oil and doily in an instant pot for 3 minutes
2. Add zucchini, salt, pepper and water, stir, secure the lid and cook for 3 minutes on high
3. Add garlic and basil, blend and simmer for a few minutes till thick
4. Serve

Grilled Artichokes

Servings: 4 , **Prep + Cook Time:** 25 minutes

Ingredients:
- Big artichokes, trimmed: 4
- Water: 2 cups
- Balsamic vinegar: 2 Tsps.
- Salt and black pepper to the taste
- Lemon juice: 2 tbsp.
- Olive oil: 1/4 cup
- Garlic cloves; minced: 2
- Oregano; dried; 1 Tsps.

Directions:
1. Place water in an instant pot and artichokes in the steamer basket, secure the lid and cook for 8 minutes on high
2. Mix lemon juice, vinegar, oil, salt, pepper, garlic and oregano in a bowl and stir well
3. Cut the artichokes in half, add lemon and vinegar then toss and grill them over medium heat for 3 minutes
4. Serve

Broiled Shrimp

Servings: 2 , **Prep + Cook Time:** 18 minutes

Ingredients:
- Big shrimp peeled and deveined: 1/2 lb.
- Worcestershire sauce: 2 Tsps.
- Creole seasoning: 1 Tsps.
- Olive oil: 2 Tsps.
- Juice from 1 lemon
- Salt and black pepper to the taste

Directions:
1. Mix shrimp, Worcestershire sauce, oil, lemon juice, salt, pepper and seasoning in an instant pot then stir, secure the lid and cook for 4 minutes on high
2. Place it in a lined baking sheet and broil in a preheated broiler for 4 minutes
3. Serve

Cheesy Artichoke

Servings: 6 , **Prep + Cook Time:** 15 minutes

Ingredients:

- Canned artichoke hearts: 14 oz.
- Parmesan cheese, grated: 16 oz.
- Spinach, torn: 10 oz.
- Onion powder: 1 Tsps.
- Cream cheese: 8 oz.
- Mozzarella cheese, shredded: 8 oz.
- Chicken stock: 1/2 cup
- Coconut cream: 1/2 cup
- Mayonnaise; 1/2 cup
- Garlic cloves; minced: 3

Directions:

1. Mix artichokes, stock, garlic, spinach, cream cheese, coconut cream, onion powder and mayo in an instant pot then stir, secure the lid and cook for 5 minutes on high
2. Add mozzarella and parmesan then stir and serve

Chilly Sausage

Servings: 4 , **Prep + Cook Time:** 15 minutes

Ingredients:

- Mexican cheese, cut into chunks: 2 cups
- Italian sausage; cooked and chopped: 1 cup
- Canned tomatoes and green chilies; chopped: 5 oz.
- Water: 4 tbsp.

Directions:

1. Mix sausage, cheese, tomatoes, chilies and water in an instant pot, secure the lid and cook for 5 minutes on high
2. Blend it and serve

Tomato Delicacy

Servings: 20 , **Prep + Cook Time:** 25 minutes

Ingredients:

- Tomatoes; peeled and chopped: 2 lb.
- Apple; cored and chopped: 1
- Yellow onion; chopped: 1
- Dates chopped: 3 oz.
- Whole spice: 3 Tsps.
- Balsamic vinegar: ½ pints
- Stevia: 4 tbsp.
- Salt to the taste

Directions:

1. Place tomatoes, apple, onion, dates, salt, whole spice and half of the vinegar in your instant pot then stir, secure the lid and cook for 10 minutes on high
2. Simmer and add the rest of the vinegar and stevia then stir. Cook till it thickens then serve

Steamed Prosciutto

Servings: 4 , **Prep + Cook Time:** 10 minutes

Ingredients:

- Asparagus spears: 8
- Prosciutto slices: 8 oz.
- Water: 2 cups
- Salt: 1 pinch

Directions:

1. Wrap asparagus spears in prosciutto slices
2. Place water with salt in an instant pot and asparagus in the steamer basket, secure the lid and cook for 4 minutes on high
3. Serve

Lovely Salmon Patties

Servings: 4 , Prep + Cook Time: 17 minutes

Ingredients:
- Salmon meat; minced: 1 lb.
- Olive oil: 1 Tsps.
- Egg; whisked: 1
- Coconut flour: 4 tbsp.
- Lemon zest, grated: 2 tbsp.
- Salt and black pepper to the taste
- Arugula leaves for serving

Directions:
1. Blend salmon and place it in a bowl
2. Add salt, pepper, lemon zest, coconut and egg then stir and shape it into small patties
3. 'Sauté' oil in an instant pot and add the mixture. Cook for 3 minutes each side
4. Top it with salmon patties and serve

Steamed Mushrooms shrimps

Servings: 5 , Prep + Cook Time: 25 minutes

Ingredients:
- White mushroom caps: 24 oz.
- Curry powder: 1 Tsps.
- Cream cheese, soft: 4 oz.
- Shrimp, cooked, peeled, deveined and chopped: 1 cup
- Mayo: 1/4 cup
- Garlic powder: 1 Tsps.
- Small yellow onion; chopped: 1
- Coconut cream: 1/4 cup
- Mexican cheese, shredded: 1/2 cup
- Water: 1 ½ cups
- Salt and black pepper to the taste

Directions:
1. Mix mayo, garlic powder, onion, curry powder, and cream cheese, cream, Mexican cheese, shrimp, salt and pepper in a bowl then stir and use it to stuff mushrooms
2. Place water in the instant pot and mushrooms in the steamer basket, secure the lid and cook for 14 minutes on high
3. Serve

Quick Spicy Salsa

Servings: 4 , Prep + Cook Time: 13 minutes

Ingredients:
- Avocados, pitted; peeled and chopped: 2
- Red onion; chopped: 1
- Lime juice: 2 tbsp.
- Cumin powder: 2 tbsp.
- Tomato; chopped: ½
- Jalapeno pepper; chopped: 3
- Salt and black pepper to the taste

Directions:
1. Mix onions, avocados, peppers, salt, black pepper, cumin, lime juice and tomato in an instant pot, stir, secure the lid and cook for 3 minutes on high
2. Serve

Sour Cranberry

Servings: 4 , Prep + Cook Time: 15 minutes

Ingredients:
- Lemon zest, grated: 2 ½ Tsps.
- Lemon juice: 3 tbsp.
- Cranberries: 12 oz.
- Stevia: 4 tbsp.

Directions:
1. Mix lemon juice, stevia, lemon zest and cranberries in an instant pot, secure the lid and cook for 2 minutes on high
2. Simmer it, and stir for a few minutes then serve with biscuits

Cheesy Crab

Servings: 8 , **Prep + Cook Time:** 30 minutes

Ingredients:
- Bacon strips, sliced: 8
- Cream cheese: 8 oz.
- Crab meat: 12 oz.
- Garlic cloves; minced: 4
- Green onions; minced: 4
- Parmesan cheese, grated: 1 cup
- Poblano pepper; chopped: 2
- Lemon juice: 2 tbsp.
- Mayonnaise: 1/2 cup
- Coconut cream: 1/2 cup
- Salt and black pepper to the taste

Directions:
1. 'Sauté' bacon in an instant pot till it gets crispy, drain the excess grease using paper towels
2. Mix coconut cream, cream cheese, mayo, half of the parmesan, poblano peppers, garlic, lemon juice, green onions, salt, pepper, crab meat and bacon in a bowl and stir
3. In an instant pot place crab mix and top it with parmesan, secure the lid and cook for 14 minutes on high
4. Serve

Broiled Chicken Wings

Servings: 6 , **Prep + Cook Time:** 27 minutes

Ingredients:
- Chicken wings, cut into halves: 6 lb.
- Egg: 1
- Parmesan cheese, grated: 1/2 cup
- Italian seasoning: 1/2 Tsps
- Garlic powder: 1 Tsps.
- Ghee: 2 tbsp.
- Water: 2 cups
- Salt and black pepper to the taste
- Red pepper flakes, crushed: 1 pinch

Directions:
1. Place water in the instant pot and the chicken wings on the trivet, secure the lid and cook for 7 minutes on high
2. Blend ghee, cheese, egg, salt, pepper, pepper flakes, garlic powder and Italian seasoning well
3. Arrange chicken wings on a lined basket, top it with cheese sauce and broil each side in a preheated broiler for 5 minutes
4. Serve

Seasoned Cajun Shrimp

Servings: 4 , **Prep + Cook Time:** 7 minutes

Ingredients:
- Shrimp, peeled and deveined: 1 lb.
- Cajun seasoning: 1/2 tbsp.
- Water: 1 cup
- Extra virgin olive oil: 1 Tsps.
- Asparagus, trimmed: 1 bunch.

Directions:
1. Place shrimp and asparagus in an instant pot
2. Add Cajun seasoning and oil then toss it, secure the lid and cook for 3 minutes on high
3. Serve

Coconut Cream Mushrooms

Servings: 4 , **Prep + Cook Time:** 20 minutes

Ingredients:
- Mushrooms; chopped: 6 oz.
- Olive oil: 3 tbsp.
- Thyme sprigs: 1
- Garlic clove; minced: 1
- Beef stock: 4 oz.
- Mustard: 1 tbsp.

- Coconut cream: 2 tbsp.
- Parsley; finely chopped: 2 tbsp.
- Balsamic vinegar: 1 tbsp.

Directions:
1. 'Sauté' oil, thyme, mushrooms and garlic in an instant pot then stir, cooking for 4 minutes
2. Add vinegar and stock, stir, secure the lid and cook for 3 minutes
3. Discard the thyme, add coconut, coconut cream and parsley then stir and simmer for 3 minutes. Serve.

Surprising Oysters

Servings: 3 , **Prep + Cook Time:** 16 minutes

Ingredients:
- Big oysters, shucked: 6
- Melted ghee: 2 tbsp.
- Water: 1 ½ cups
- Lemon cut into wedges: 1
- Parsley: 1 tbsp.
- Garlic cloves; minced: 3
- Sweet paprika: 1 pinch

Directions:
1. Place ghee, parsley, paprika and garlic in every oyster
2. Place water in an instant opt and oysters in the steamer basket, secure the lid and cook for 6 minutes on high
3. Serve with lemon on the side

Tasty Turkey Meatballs

Servings: 16 p , **Prep + Cook Time:** 16 minutes

Ingredients:
- Turkey meat, ground: 1 lb.
- Egg: 1
- Garlic powder: 1/2 Tsps.
- Mozzarella cheese, shredded: 1/2 cup
- Olive oil: 2 tbsp.
- Tomato paste: 1/4 cup
- Basil; chopped: 2 tbsp.
- Coconut flour: 1/4 cup
- Sun-dried tomatoes; chopped: 2 tbsp.
- Salt and black pepper to the taste

Directions:
1. Mix turkey, salt, pepper, egg, flour, garlic powder, sun-dried tomatoes, mozzarella and basil n a bowl and stir, shape them into meatballs
2. 'Sauté' oil and the meatballs in an instant pot for 2 minutes each side
3. Top it with tomato paste, toss it, secure the lid and cook for 8 minutes on high
4. Serve

Spicy Clams

Servings: 4 , **Prep + Cook Time:** 14 minutes

Ingredients:
- Clams; shucked: 24
- Parsley; chopped: 1/4 cup
- Parmesan cheese, grated: 1/4 cup
- Water: 2 cups
- Garlic cloves; minced: 3
- Oregano; dried: 1 Tsps.
- Almonds, crushed: 1 cup
- Ghee: 4 tbsp.
- Lemon wedges

Directions:
1. Mix almonds, parmesan, oregano, parsley, butter and garlic in a bowl then stir and divide them into exposed clams
2. Place water in an instant pot and clams in the steamer basket, secure the lid and cook for 4 minutes on high
3. Serve with lemon wedges on the side

Broiled Spinach

Ingredients:

- Bacon slices; cooked and crumbled: 6
- Garlic; minced: 1 tbsp.
- Spinach: 5 oz.
- Water: 1 ½ cups
- Coconut cream: 1/2 cup
- Cream cheese, soft: 8 oz.
- Parsley; chopped: 1 ½ tbsp.
- Parmesan, grated: 2.5 oz.
- Lemon juice: 1 tbsp.
- Olive oil: a drizzle
- Salt and black pepper to the taste

Directions:

1. 'Sauté' oil and spinach in an instant pot for 1 minute then transfer to a bowl
2. Add cream cheese, garlic, salt, pepper, coconut cream, parsley, bacon, lemon juice and parmesan then stir and divide it into 6 ramekins
3. Place water in an instant pot and the ramekins in a steamer basket, secure the lid and cook for 15 minutes on high
4. Broil it for 4 minutes in n a preheated broiler

Delicious tomatoes

Ingredients:

- Canned tomatoes; chopped: 28 oz.
- Jalapeno peppers; chopped: 2
- White onion; chopped: 1/2 cup
- Basil; chopped: 1/2 cup
- Balsamic vinegar: 1/4 cup
- Veggie stock: 1/4 cup
- Olive oil: 1/4 cup
- Mussels; scrubbed: 2 lb.
- Red pepper flakes, crushed: 2 tbsp.
- Garlic cloves; minced: 2
- Salt to the taste

Directions:

1. 'Sauté' oil, tomatoes, onion, jalapenos, stock, vinegar, garlic and pepper flakes then stir and cook for 5 minutes
2. Add mussels, stir, secure the lid and cook for 4 minutes on low
3. Add salt and basil then stir and serve

Steamed Cod Puddings

Ingredients:

- Cod fillets, skinless, boneless cut into medium pieces: 1 lb.
- Parsley; chopped: 2 tbsp.
- Coconut flour: 4 oz.
- Lemon juice: 2 Tsps.
- Eggs; whisked: 2
- Ghee, melted: 2 oz.
- Coconut milk, hot: 1/2-pint
- Shrimp sauce: 1/2-pint
- Water: 1/2-pint
- Salt and black pepper to the taste

Directions:

1. Mix fish, flour, lemon juice, shrimp sauce, parsley, eggs, salt and pepper in a bowl then stir
2. Add milk and ghee, stir and let it aside. Divide it into ramekins
3. Place water in an instant pot and ramekins in the steamer basket, secure the lid and cook for 15 minutes on high. Serve

Spiced Mussels

Servings: 4 , Prep + Cook Time: 12 minutes

Ingredients:

- Mussels, scrubbed: 2 lb.
- Veggie stock: 12 oz.
- Olive oil: 1 tbsp.
- Spicy sausage; chopped: 8 oz.
- Sweet paprika: 1 tbsp.
- Yellow onion; chopped: 1

Directions:

1. 'Sauté' oil, onions and sausages in an instant pot and cook for 5 minutes
2. Add stock, paprika and mussels then stir, secure the lid and cook for 2 minutes. Serve.

Coconut Avocado

Servings: 4 , Prep + Cook Time: 12 minutes

Ingredients:

- Erythritol powder: 1/4 cup
- Avocados, pitted, peeled and halved: 2
- Juice from 2 limes
- Stevia: 1/4 Tsps.
- Coconut milk: 1 cup
- Water: 1 cup
- Cilantro; chopped: 1/2 cup
- Zest from 2 limes, grated

Directions:

1. Place water in an instant pot and avocado in the steamer basket, secure the lid and cook for 2 minutes on high
2. Blend it with lime juice and cilantro, pulse it well
3. Add coconut milk, lime zest, stevia and erythritol powder, pulse it and serve.

Olive Eggplant

Servings: 6 , Prep + Cook Time: 20 minutes

Ingredients:

- Eggplant peeled and cut into medium chunks: 2 lb.
- Olives; pitted and sliced: 3
- Olive oil: 1/4 cup
- Garlic cloves; minced: 4
- Water: 1/2 cup
- Lemon juice: 1/4 cup
- Thyme; chopped: 1 bunch
- Sesame seed paste: 1 tbsp.
- Salt and black pepper to the taste

Directions:

1. 'Sauté' oil an eggplant an instant pot for 5 minutes
2. Add garlic, water, salt and pepper then stir, secure the lid and cook for 3 minutes on high
3. Blend it with sesame seed paste, lemon juice and thyme; pulse it well
4. Top it with olive slices and serve warm

Steamed Mussels

Servings: 4 , Prep + Cook Time: 17 minutes

Ingredients:

- Mussels cleaned and scrubbed: 2 lb.
- Water: 1/2 cup
- White onion; chopped: 1
- Veggie stock: 1/2 cup
- Garlic cloves; minced: 2
- Extra virgin olive oil: 1 drizzle

Directions:

1. 'Sauté' oil, garlic and onion in an instant pot for 4 minutes
2. Add stock then stir and cook for 1 minute
3. Place water in the steamer basket and the mussels on the steam basket, secure the lid n cook for 2 minutes on high
4. Top it with cooking juice and serve

Zucchini Delicacy

Servings: 4 , **Prep + Cook Time:** 16 minutes

Ingredients:
- Zucchini; chopped: 4 cups.
- Veggie stock: 3 tbsp.
- Olive oil: 1/4 cup
- Lemon juice: 1/2 cup
- Cumin, ground: 1 tbsp.
- Sesame seeds paste: 3/4 cup
- Garlic cloves; minced: 4.
- Salt and black pepper to the taste

Directions:
1. 'Sauté' oil, zucchini and garlic in an instant pot for 2 minute
2. Add stock, salt and pepper, secure het lid and cook for 4 minutes
3. Blend it with oil, sesame seeds, lemon juice and cumin, pulse it well and serve.

Sour Mussels and Clams

Servings: 4 , **Prep + Cook Time:** 23 minutes

Ingredients:
- Mussels; scrubbed: 30
- Chorizo links, sliced: 2
- Yellow onion; chopped: 1
- Small clams: 15
- Veggie stock: 10 oz.
- Parsley; chopped: 2 tbsp.
- Olive oil: 1 Tsps.
- Lemon wedges for serving

Directions:
1. 'Sauté' oil, onions and chorizo in an instant pot for 3 minutes
2. Add clams, mussels and stock then stir well, secure the lid and cook for 10 minutes on high
3. Add parsley then stir and serve with lemon wedges

Baked Tuna Patties

Servings: 12 , **Prep + Cook Time:** 18 minutes

Ingredients:
- Canned tuna drained and flaked: 15 oz.
- Red onion; chopped: 1/2 cup
- Parsley; dried: 1 Tsps.
- Garlic powder: 1 Tsps.
- Water: 1 ½ cups
- Eggs: 3
- Dill; chopped: 1/2 Tsps.
- Salt and black pepper to the taste
- Olive oil: 1 drizzle

Directions:
1. Mix tuna, salt, pepper, dill, parsley, onion, garlic powder and eggs, stir in a bowl and make medium patties out of it
2. 'Sauté' oil and tuna patties for 2 minutes each side to make tuna cakes; transfer it to a plate
3. Place water in the pot and the tuna cakes on the steamer basket, secure the lid and cook for 4 minutes on high. Serve

Sautéed Leeks

Servings: 4 , **Prep + Cook Time:** 20 minutes

Ingredients:
- Leeks; washed, roots and ends cut off: 4
- Ghee: 1 tbsp.
- Water: 1/3 cup
- Salt and black pepper to the taste

Directions:
1. Place leeks, water, ghee, salt and pepper in the instant pot, secure the lid and cook for 5 minutes on high
2. 'Sauté' for a few minutes and serve

Chapter 9 Beans and Grains Recipe

Creamy Buckwheat Porridge

Servings: 4, **Prep + Cook Time:** 16 minutes

Ingredients:
- Rice milk - 3 cups
- Vanilla - 1/2 tsp.
- Cinnamon - 1 tsp.
- Raisins - 1/4 cup
- Buckwheat groats - 1 cup
- Banana 1 piece, sliced
- Cinnamon - 1 tsp. ground
- Chopped nuts

Directions:
1. Place the buckwheat in the instant pot. Pour down the milk then add the banana, raising, vanilla, and cinnamon. Mix well, secure the lid of the pot and then cook for 6 minutes at high pressure.
2. Do a natural release for 15 minutes. Gently open the lid of the pot, mix the porridge. Serve in separate bowls.

Natural Barley Salad

Servings: 4, **Prep + Cook Time:** 30 minutes

Ingredients:
- Hulled barley - 1 cup, rinsed
- Jarred spinach pesto - 3/4 cup
- Green apple - 1 piece, chopped
- Water -2 ½ cups
- Celery - 1/4 cup, chopped
- Seasoning - salt and white pepper

Directions:

1. Mix the water, barley, salt, and pepper in the instant pot. Secure the lid of the pot and cook for 20 minutes at high pressure.
2. Do a quick release and then gently open up the lid of the pot. Using a strainer, strain the barley and then set aside in a bowl.
3. Put the apple, celery, spinach and then add more salt and pepper if preferred. Serve fresh and enjoy.

Spicy Seafood White Beans

Servings: 8, **Prep + Cook Time:** 45 minutes

Ingredients:
- White beans - 1 lb. soaked for 8 hours and drained
- Garlic - 1 clove, minced
- Green bell pepper – 1 piece, chopped
- Celery rib – 1 piece, chopped
- Parsley springs – 4 pieces, chopped
- Yellow onions – 2 pieces, chopped
- Seafood stock - 2 cups
- Shrimp - 1 lb. peeled and deveined
- Bay leaves – 2 pieces
- Canola oil - 3 tbsp.
- Creole seasoning
- Cooked rice
- Hot sauce

Directions:

1. Select Sauté in the instant pot then pour down the oil to heat.
2. Once the oil is hot, put the onions and Creole. Mix well and cook for 5 minutes.
3. Put the garlic, bell pepper, and celery in the pot and cook for another 5 minutes. Then add the beans, water, and stock.
4. Put the parsley and bay leaves. Mix well and then secure the pot's lead. Cook it for 15 minutes at high pressure.
5. Do a quick release, then gently open up the lid of the pot. Put the shrimp, then again secure the lid. Set aside for 10 minutes.
6. After 10 minutes you can now serve it on separate bowls or plates with rice. Top it up with hot sauce.

Special Fava Beans

Servings: 6, **Prep + Cook Time:** 35 minutes

Ingredients:
- Fava bean - 1 lb. rinsed
- Yellow onion - 1 cup, chopped
- Bay leaf – 1 piece
- Extra virgin olive oil - 1/4 cup
- Garlic – 1 clove, minced
- Lemon juice - 2 tbsp.
- Water - 4 ½ cups
- Seasoning - salt

Directions:
1. Place the fava beans inside the instant pot and then pour down 4 cups of water. Put salt and the bay leaf. Secure the lid of the pot then cook it for 18 minutes at high pressure.
2. Do a natural release and then gently open up the lid of the pot. Remove the water and bay leaf. Bring back the beans in the pot then pour down the remaining ½ cup of water, add garlic, onion, and salt.
3. Close the lid of the pot again then cook it for 5 minutes. After cooking, release the pressure and then gently open up the lid. Place the beans in a food processor, pour down olive oil and lemon juice. Blend until beans are fully liquefied.
4. Refrigerate and serve cold.

Black Curry

Servings: 4, **Prep + Cook Time:** 55 minutes

Ingredients:
- Cumin seeds - 1/2 tsp.
- Garlic - 6 cloves, minced
- Ginger - 1-inch piece, minced
- Turmeric - 1 tsp.
- Tomatoes – 2 pieces, chopped
- Avocado oil - 2 tbsp.
- Bay leaf – 1 piece
- Garam masala - 1 tsp.
- Water - 3 cups
- Yellow onion -1 piece, chopped
- Cayenne pepper - a pinch only
- Seasoning - salt and black pepper
- Cilantro leaves, chopped

Directions:
1. Select Sauté in your instant pot and then add the oil to heat. Put the cumin seeds and then fry for 2 minutes.
2. Put the bay leaf and onion and then cook for another 8 minutes.
3. Put the garlic, turmeric, cayenne, salt, pepper, garam masala, and ginger. Mix well and then cook for 2 minutes.
4. Put the tomatoes and peas and then pour down the water. Mix well and then secure the lid of the pot. Cook it for 30 minutes at high pressure.
5. Do a quick release and then gently open up the lid of the pot. Put the cilantro and then season with salt and pepper if preferred. Mix well and then serve in separate bowls.

Morning Jaggery

Servings: 2, **Prep + Cook Time:** 22 minutes

Ingredients:
- Cracked wheat - 2 cups
- Jaggery - 2 cups
- Cloves – 3 pieces
- Milk - 1 cup
- Fennel seeds - 1 tsp.
- Clarified butter - 2 ½ cups
- Water - 3 cups
- Salt - a pinch only
- Almonds, chopped

Directions:
1. Select Sauté in your instant pot and then put the butter to heat.
2. Put the cracked wheat, mix well and then cook for 5 minutes. Add the cloves and

fennel seeds. Mix well and then cook for another 2 minutes.
3. Put the jaggery, milk, water, and a pinch of salt. Mix well and then secure the lid of the pot. Cook it for 10 minutes at high pressure.

4. Do a quick release and then gently open up the lid of the pot. Serve in bowls and top it up with some almonds.

Spicy Split Pea Dish

Servings: 4, **Prep + Cook Time:** 45 minutes

Ingredients:
- Split peas - 7 oz.
- Olive oil - 1 tbsp.
- Canned coconut milk - 15 oz.
- Curry paste - 4 tbsp.
- Canned tomatoes - 15 oz. chopped
- Black onion seeds - 2 tsp.
- Coriander leaves - a bunch of, chopped
- Zest and juice of lime – 1 piece lime only
- Yellow onions – 2 pieces, chopped
- Bell peppers – 2 pieces, chopped
- Seasoning - salt and black pepper
- Coconut yogurt - 5 oz.
- Naan bread

Directions:

1. Select Sauté in your instant pot and then pour down the oil to heat.
2. Put the onions and bell peppers. Mix well and cook for 10 minutes.
3. Put the curry paste and black onion seeds. Mix well and then cook for another minute. Add the coconut milk, coriander, tomatoes, and split peas. Season with salt and pepper. Mix well.
4. Secure the lid of the pot and then cook it for 25 minutes at high pressure.
5. Do a quick release and then open up the pot. Season with salt and pepper again if preferred. Pour down the lime zest and juice and the coconut yogurt. Mix well.
6. Serve in separate bowls with naan bread.

Couscous Chicken Mix

Servings: 4, **Prep + Cook Time:** 25 minutes

Ingredients:
- Chicken thighs - 8 pieces, skinless
- Canned stewed tomatoes -15 oz., chopped
- Couscous - 3/4 cup
- Zucchini - 1 piece, chopped
- Mushrooms - 1 ½ cups, cut into halves
- Carrots - 1 ½ cups, chopped
- Chicken stock - 1/2 cup
- Green bell pepper - 1 piece, chopped
- Yellow onion -1 piece, chopped
- Garlic - 2 cloves, minced
- Seasoning - salt and black pepper
- Parsley - a handful only, chopped

Directions:
1. Mix up the chicken thighs, mushrooms, bell pepper, carrots, onion, tomatoes, garlic, and stock inside your instant pot. Secure the lid and then cook for 8 minutes at high pressure.
2. Do a quick release and then gently open up the lid of the pot. Put the zucchini, couscous, pepper, and salt. Mix well, then secure the lid again. Cook for 6 minutes at low pressure.
3. Release the pressure after cooking and then open up the pot. Top up with parsley and then serve in separate bowls.

Cranberry Beans Surprise

Servings: 6, **Prep + Cook Time:** 25 minutes

Ingredients:

- Cranberry beans - 1 ½ cups, soaked for 8 hours and drained
- Kale - 8 cups, chopped
- Shiitake mushrooms - 4 oz. chopped
- Kombu - 4-inch piece, sliced
- Bacon - 4 slices, chopped
- Garlic powder - 1/2 tsp.
- Extra virgin olive oil - 1 tsp.
- Seasoning - salt and black pepper

Directions:

1. Place the beans inside the instant pot and then add water, salt, pepper, and kombu. Secure the pot's lid and then cook for 8 minutes at high pressure.
2. Let the pressure come out of the pot after cooking and then gently open up the pot. Set aside the beans and the liquid from the pot in a separate bowl. Select Sauté in your instant pot and then pour down the oil to heat.
3. Put garlic powder, mushrooms, pepper, salt and a ¾ cup of the liquid (the one set aside). Mix well and then cook for a minute.
4. Secure the lid of the pot again and then cook for 3 minutes at high pressure. After cooking, do a quick release.
5. Put the beans and kale. Serve in separate bowls.

Salt and Pepper Millet Dish

Servings: 4, **Prep + Cook Time:** 30 minutes

Ingredients:

- Millet - 1 cup, chopped
- Split Mung beans - 1 cup
- Bay leaf – 1 piece
- Carrot - 1 cup, chopped
- Ginger -1/2 tsp. grated
- Lime juice - 1 tbsp.
- Cilantro - 1/4 cup, chopped
- Ghee - 1 tbsp.
- Cumin seeds -1/2 tsp. ground
- Turmeric powder -1/2 tsp.
- Coriander seeds - 1 tsp. ground
- Fennel seeds - 1 tsp. ground
- Celery - 1 cup, chopped
- Cardamom pods - 4 pieces
- Water - 6 cups
- Fresh peas - 1 ½ cups
- Seasoning - salt and black pepper

Directions:

1. Select Sauté in your instant pot and then put the Mung beans. Mix well and cook until the beans turn golden.
2. Put the miller, bay leaf, celery, cardamom, water, salt, pepper, and carrot. Mix well and then secure the lid of the pot. Cook for 10 minutes at high pressure. Do a quick release after cooking and then open up the pot and set it to simmer.
3. In a saucepan, heat up the ghee on medium heat. Place the coriander, cumin, fennel, ginger, and turmeric on the saucepan. Mix well and then cook for 2 minutes.
4. Mix the ghee with the ingredients inside the instant pot. Season with more salt and pepper if preferred. Add the peas and lime juice and let it simmer for 5 minutes.
5. Serve in separate bowls with cilantro as toppings.

Sour and Spicy Black Beans

Servings: 4, **Prep + Cook Time:** 50 minutes

Ingredients:

- Black beans - 2 cups, soaked for 8 hours and drained
- Garlic - 4 cloves, minced
- Water - 3 cups
- Smoked paprika - 1 tsp.
- Red palm oil - 2 Tsp.
- Chili powder - 1 tbsp.
- Yellow onion – 1 piece, chopped
- Seasoning - salt
- Juice from lime – 1 piece lime only

Directions:

1. Select Sauté in your instant pot and then pour down the oil to heat.
2. Place the garlic and onion and then sauté for 2 minutes.
3. Put the chili powder, beans, paprika, salt, and water. Mix well and then secure the lid of the pot. Cook for 40 minutes at high pressure.
4. Do a natural release after cooking and then open up the lid of the pot. Pour down the lime juice and season with salt. Mix well and then serve in separate bowls.

Middle East Style Fava Beans

Servings: 2, **Prep + Cook Time:** 35 minutes

Ingredients:

- Cooked fava beans - 2 cups
- Tomato – 1 piece, finely chopped
- Yellow onion – 1 piece, cut into thin rings
- Cumin - 1 tsp.
- Water - 1/2 cup
- Roasted garlic - 4 cloves, chopped
- Small red onion – 1 piece, chopped
- Hard-boiled egg – 1 piece, peeled and sliced
- Olive oil - 1 tbsp.
- Seasoning - salt and black pepper
- Lemon juice from lemons – 2 pieces lemon
- Red chili flakes - a pinch only
- Paprika - a pinch only

Directions:

1. Select Sauté in your instant pot and then pour down the oil to heat. Put the red onions, mix well and then sauté for 3 minutes.
2. Put the cumin and garlic. Mix well and cook for a minute. Put the beans, salt, pepper, and water. Mix well and then secure the lid of the pot. Cook for 15 minutes at high pressure.
3. Do a quick release right after cooking, open up the lid of the pot. Press simmer and then cook for another 10 minutes.
4. Put the contents of the pot to a bowl. Season with salt and pepper and then pour down the lemon juice. Mash the ingredients using a potato masher.
5. Top up with egg slices, yellow onion rings, red chili flakes, paprika, and tomato slices. Serve and enjoy!

Countryside Cranberry Beans

Servings: 6, **Prep + Cook Time:** 30 minutes

Ingredients:

- Cranberry beans - 1 lb. soaked for 8 hours and drained
- Yellow onion – 1 piece, chopped
- Cumin - 1 ½ tsp.
- Cilantro - 1/3 cup, chopped
- Water - 3 ¼ cups
- Garlic - 4 cloves, minced
- Chili powder - 1 tbsp.
- Oregano - 1 tsp. dried
- Seasoning - salt and black pepper
- Cooked rice

Directions:

1. Place the beans inside the instant pot, pour down water and then add the garlic and onion. Secure the lid of the pot and cook it for 20 minutes at high pressure.
2. Do a quick release and then gently open up the lid of the pot. Put cumin, cilantro, oregano, chili powder, salt, and pepper. Mix it using a potato masher. Serve in separate plates.

Curry Lentils with Tomato Sauce

Servings: 4, **Prep + Cook Time:** 30 minutes

Ingredients:

- Lentils - 1 ½ cups
- Yellow onion – 1 piece, chopped
- Celery – 1 piece, chopped
- Tomatoes - 1 ½ cups, chopped
- Olive oil - 1 tbsp.
- Green bell pepper – 1 piece, chopped
- Curry powder - 1 tsp.
- Water - 2 cups
- Seasoning - salt and black pepper

Directions:

1. Select Sauté in your instant pot and then pour down the oil to heat.
2. Put the celery, bell pepper, tomatoes, and onion. Mix well and sauté for 4 minutes.
3. Put the salt, pepper, curry, and water. Mix them well and then secure the lid of the pot. Cook it for 15 minutes at high pressure.
4. Do a quick release and then open up the lid of the pot. Serve the lentils in a separate bowl dressed with tomato sauce.

Chickpeas with Tomatoes and Garlic

Servings: 4, **Prep + Cook Time:** 45 minutes

Ingredients:

- Chickpeas - 2 cups, rinsed
- Tomatoes – 2 pieces, chopped
- Small cucumbers – 2 pieces, chopped
- Bay leaves – 2 pieces
- Garlic - 4 cloves
- Water
- Olive oil - 1 tsp.
- Seasoning - salt and black pepper

Directions:

1. Place the chickpeas inside the instant pot. Pour down water and then add the garlic and bay leaves. Mix well and then secure the lid of the pot, cook for 35 minutes at high pressure.
2. Do a natural release for 10 minutes. Turn the valve to "Venting" in order to release the remaining pressure. Gently open up the lid of the pot, remove the water and then place the chickpeas and garlic in a separate bowl.
3. Put cucumber, salt, pepper, oil, and tomatoes. Mix well and then serve.

Salty White Beans

Servings: 8, **Prep + Cook Time:** 45 minutes

Ingredients:

- White beans - 1 lb.
- Yellow onion -1 piece, chopped
- Green bell pepper – 1 piece, chopped
- Water - 5 cups
- Celery ribs – 2 pieces, chopped
- Bay leaves – 2 pieces
- Oregano - 1 tsp.
- Thyme - 1 tsp.
- Soy sauce - 1 tbsp.
- Tabasco sauce - 1 tbsp.
- Garlic - 4 cloves, minced
- Seasoning - salt and white pepper

Directions:

1. Pour water inside the instant pot and then add the beans, onion, celery, garlic, bell pepper, oregano, thyme, salt, white pepper and soy sauce. Secure the lid and cook for 15 minutes at high pressure.
2. Do a natural release for 15 minutes and then gently open up the lid of the pot. Press simmer and then season with salt and pepper.
3. Put Tabasco sauce, mix well and then cook for 20 minutes. Serve in separate bowls.

Boozed Beans with Bacon

Servings: 8, **Prep + Cook Time:** 1 hour and 10 minutes

Ingredients:

- Butter beans - 1 lb. soaked for 8 hours and drained
- Cumin - 1/2 tsp. ground
- Garlic - 1 clove, minced
- Beer - 12 oz.
- Bacon - 1 lb. chopped
- Jalapeno pepper – 1 piece, chopped
- Water - 4 cups
- Seasoning - salt and black pepper

Directions:

1. Select Sauté in your instant pot and then put the bacon. Cook it for 10 minutes. Set aside the bacon in a plate with paper towels to drain the grease.
2. Pour down water and beer in the instant pot and then add cumin. Mix well, put the beans and then secure the lid of the pot. Cook it for 30 minutes at high pressure.
3. Do a quick release, open up the lid of the pot and then put the bacon, garlic, jalapeno, salt, and pepper. Mix well and then secure the lid again. Cook for another 3 minutes at high pressure.
4. Release the pressure and then gently open up the lid. Serve in separate bowls.

Sweet Navy Beans

Servings: 8, **Prep + Cook Time:** 50 minutes

Ingredients:

- Navy beans - 1 ½ cups, soaked for 8 hours and drained
- Bacon slices – 6 pieces, chopped
- Cabbage head – 1 piece, chopped
- White wine vinegar - 3 tbsp.
- Cloves - 1/4 tsp.
- Yellow onion – 1 piece, chopped
- Honey - 3 tbsp.
- Bay leaf – 1 piece
- Chicken stock - 3 cups
- Seasoning - salt and black pepper

Directions:

1. Select Sauté in your instant pot and then put the bacon slices. Cook it for 6 minutes.
2. Put the onions and then cook it for 4 minutes. Pour down the chicken stock and then add the cloves, beans, and bay leaf. Mix well and then secure the pot's lid. Cook for 35 minutes at high pressure.
3. Do a quick release and then gently open up the lid of the pot. Pour down the vinegar and honey and then add the cabbage. Mix well and then again secure the lid. Cook for another 12 minutes at high pressure.
4. Release the pressure and then again gently open up the lid. Season with salt and pepper, mix well. Serve in separate bowls and enjoy.

Morning Berry Salad

Servings: 6, **Prep + Cook Time:** 45 minutes

Ingredients:

- Wheat berries - 1 ½ cups
- Extra-virgin olive oil - 1 tbsp.
- Water - 4 cups
- Seasoning - salt and black pepper
- Balsamic vinegar - 1 tbsp.
- Olive oil - 1 tbsp.
- Green onions, chopped
- Feta cheese - 2 oz. crumbled
- Kalamata olives -1/2 cup, pitted and chopped
- Basil leaves - 1 handful, chopped
- Parsley leaves - 1 handful, chopped
- Cherry tomatoes - 1 cup, cut into halves

Directions:

1. Select Sauté in your instant pot and then pour down the oil to heat. Put the wheat berries, mix well and then cook for 5 minutes.

2. Pour down water and then season with salt and pepper. Secure the lid of the pot and then cook it for 30 minutes at high pressure.
3. Do a natural release for 10 minutes and then turn the valve to "Venting" to release the remaining pressure. Gently open up the lid of the pot and then drain the wheat berries.

4. Put the wheat berries in a large bowl. Add the 1 tablespoon oil, balsamic vinegar, tomatoes, green onions, olives, cheese, basil, parsley, salt, and pepper. Mix well and then serve immediately.

Potato Chickpeas Curry

Servings: 8, **Prep + Cook Time:** 30 minutes

Ingredients:
- Canned tomatoes - 28 oz. chopped
- Potatoes – 3 pieces, cubed
- Cooked chickpeas - 3 cups, drained and rinsed
- Yellow onion – 1 piece, finely chopped
- Garam masala - 2 tsp.
- Coriander - 2 tsp. ground
- Turmeric - 2 tsp. ground
- Cumin seeds - 4 tsp.
- Water - 1/2 cup
- Olive oil - 8 tsp.
- Garlic - 4 tsp. minced
- Seasoning - salt and black pepper
- Cooked basmati rice
- Cilantro, chopped

Directions:
1. Select Sauté in your instant pot and then add the oil to heat. Put the cumin seeds. Mix well and then cook for 30 seconds. Add the onion, mix well and then cook for 5 minutes.
2. Put the garlic, garam masala, coriander, turmeric, tomatoes, potatoes, chickpeas, water, salt, and pepper. Mix well and then secure the lid of the pot. Cook it for 15 minutes at high pressure.
3. Do a quick release and then gently open up the lid of the pot. Serve the chickpeas on separate plates with rice then top it up with cilantro.

Buttered-Barley with Cheesy Mushrooms

Servings: 4, **Prep + Cook Time:** 35 minutes

Ingredients:
- Pearl barley - 1 ½ cups, rinsed
- Extra-virgin olive oil - 1 tbsp.
- Butter - 1 tbsp.
- Mushrooms - 1/3 cup, chopped
- Veggie stock - 4 cups
- Water - 2 ¼ cups
- White onion – 1 piece, chopped
- Parsley - 3 tbsp. chopped
- Parmesan cheese - 1 cup, grated
- Garlic - 1 clove, minced
- Celery stalk – 1 piece, chopped
- Seasoning - salt and black pepper

Directions:

1. Select Sauté in your instant pot and then put the butter to heat and melt. Put the onions and garlic, mix well and then cook for 18 minutes. Add the barley and celery, mix well until fully coated.
2. Put the mushrooms, salt, and pepper and then pour down the water and stock. Mix well and then secure the lid. Cook it for 18 minutes at high pressure.
3. Do a quick release and then gently open up the lid of the pot. Put the cheese and parsley. Season with more salt and pepper if desired. Serve in separate bowls.

Hot and Spicy Red Kidney Beans

Servings: 8, **Prep + Cook Time:** 35 minutes

Ingredients:

- Red kidney beans - 1 lb. soaked for 8 hours and drained
- Smoked Cajun Tasso - 8 oz. chopped
- Celery rib – 1 piece, chopped
- Garlic - 2 tbsp. minced
- Green bell pepper – 1 piece, chopped
- Thyme - 2 tsp. dried
- Green onions – 4 pieces, chopped
- Yellow onions – 2 pieces, chopped
- Extra virgin olive oil - 3 tbsp.
- Bay leaves – 2 pieces
- Cajun seasoning
- Hot sauce

Directions:

1. Select Sauté in your instant pot and then put the oil to heat. Put the Tasso and mix well. Cook for 5 minutes and then put it in a bowl.
2. Put onions and Cajun seasoning in the pot. Mix well and then cook for 10 minutes. Add garlic and mix well. Cook for another 5 minutes.
3. Put the bell pepper and celery. Mix well and cook for 5 minutes.
4. Put the beans, thyme, and bay leaves. Pour down the water in the pot. Secure the lid of the pot and then cook for 15 minutes at high pressure.
5. Do a quick release and then gently open up the lid if the pot. Put the Tasso and then set aside for 5 minutes.
6. Serve in separate plates.

Tangy Bulgur Salad

Servings: 4, **Prep + Cook Time:** 25 minutes

Ingredients:

- Bulgur - 1 cup, rinsed
- Soy sauce - 1 tbsp.
- Scallions - 2/3 cup, chopped
- Brown sugar - 2 tsp.
- Zest from 1 orange
- Juice from 2 oranges
- Water - 1/2 cups
- Almonds - 1/3 cup, chopped
- Garlic - 2 cloves, minced
- Canola oil - 2 Tsp.
- Ginger - 2 tbsp. grated
- Seasoning - salt

Directions:

1. Select Sauté in your instant pot and then add the oil to heat. Put the garlic and ginger. Mix well and cook for a minute.
2. Put the sugar, water, orange juice, and bulgur. Mix well and then secure the lid of the pot. Cook for 5 minutes at high pressure.
3. Do a natural release and then gently open up the lid of the pot. Set aside the bulgur.
4. Cook almonds in a pan over medium heat for 3 minutes. Add the salt, soy sauce, scallions, and orange zest. Mix well and cook for another minute.
5. Put all the contents of the pan on the bulgur. Mix well and then serve.

Healthy Dumplings and Chickpeas

Servings: 4, **Prep + Cook Time:** 27 minutes

Ingredients:

- Chickpeas - 2 cans
- Carrots – 4 pieces, chopped
- Yellow onion – 1 piece, chopped
- Green onions 2 pieces, chopped
- Celery stalks - 2 pieces, chopped
- Baking powder - 1 ¾ tsp.
- White flour - 3/4 cup
- Dill - 1/2 Tsp. dried
- Milk - 1/2 cup
- Red baby potatoes – 4 pieces, chopped
- Garlic - 2 cloves, minced
- Veggie stock - 28 oz.
- Veggie bouillon cube – 1 piece
- Cayenne pepper - a pinch only

- Seasoning - salt and black pepper

Directions:

1. Select Sauté in your instant pot and then add the onion, garlic and a few amounts of stock. Mix well and cook for 3 minutes.
2. Put the potatoes, chickpeas, carrots, stock, bouillon cube, pepper, cayenne pepper, and salt. Mix well and then secure the lid of the pot. Cook for 7 minutes at high pressure.
3. Do a quick release and then open up the lid of the pot. Put the green onions and celery. Mix well and then set aside.
4. Get a separate bowl. In the bowl, mix up the baking powder and flour. Add a pinch of salt then put the milk and dill. Mix well.
5. Form 10 dumplings from the mixture. Back on the instant pot, press simmer and then place the dumplings inside the pot. Secure the lid and then steam it for 10 minutes.
6. Gently open up the lid and then season with salt and pepper. Mix well and then serve in separate bowls.

Sour Fava Bean

Servings: 6, **Prep + Cook Time:** 40 minutes

Ingredients:

- Fava beans - 2 cups, soaked
- Garlic - 2 cloves, crushed
- Vegetable oil - 2 tbsp.
- Cumin powder - 2 tsp.
- Harissa - 1 Tsp.
- Zest from 1 lemon
- Water - 3 cups
- Tahini - 2 Tsp.
- Olive oil - 1 tbsp.
- Paprika - 1 tsp.
- Juice of 1 lemon
- Seasoning - salt and black pepper

Directions:

1. Select Sauté in your instant pot and then add the vegetable oil to heat. Put the garlic, mix well and then cook for 3 minutes.
2. Put the fava beans and then pour down the 3 cups of water. Mix well and then secure the lid of the pot. Cook for 12 minutes at high pressure.
3. Do a natural release for 10 minutes. Gently open up the pot's lid and then drain the liquid. Press Sauté again.
4. Put the cumin, tahini, pepper, salt, lemon zest, and harissa. Mix well using an immersion blender. Put paprika, lemon juice, and olive oil. Mix well.
5. Serve in separate bowls.

Healthy Breakfast Oats

Servings: 4, **Prep + Cook Time:** 25 minutes

Ingredients:

- Steel cut oats - 1 cup
- Water - 1 ½ cups
- Carrot – 1 piece, chopped
- Canola oil - 1 ½ tbsp.
- Curry leaves – 2 pieces
- Mustard seeds - 1/4 tsp.
- Green bell pepper - ½ piece, chopped
- Ginger - 1-inch piece, grated
- Thai green chili – 1 piece, chopped
- Urad dal - 1/2 tsp.
- Turmeric powder - a pinch only
- Asafetida powder - a pinch only
- Seasoning - salt

Directions:

1. Place the oats inside the instant pot, pour down water and then secure the lid. Cook for 7 minutes at high pressure.
2. Heat up oil in a pan over medium heat and then put the mustard seeds, urad dal, asafetida powder, turmeric, chili pepper, curry leaf, ginger, bell pepper, and carrot. Mix well and then cook for 5 minutes.
3. Do a quick release in the instant pot and then gently open up the lid. Place the oats on the pan. Season with salt, mix well and then serve in separate bowls.

Classic Salt and Pepper Mung Beans

Servings: 4, **Prep + Cook Time:** 27 minutes

Ingredients:

- Mung beans - 3/4 cup, soaked for 15 minutes and drained
- Canned tomatoes - 28 oz. crushed
- Brown rice - 1/2 cup, soaked for 15 minutes and drained
- Small red onion – 1 piece, chopped
- Cumin seeds - 1/2 tsp.
- Coriander - 1 tsp. ground
- Turmeric - 1 tsp.
- Garam masala - 1/2 tsp.
- Coconut oil - 1/2 tsp.
- Lemon juice - 1 tsp.
- Water - 4 cups
- Garlic - 5 cloves, minced
- Ginger - 1-inch piece, chopped
- Cayenne - a pinch only
- Seasoning - salt and black pepper

Directions:

1. Mix the tomatoes, ginger, onions, garlic, coriander, cayenne, turmeric, pepper, garam masala, and salt in a food processor.
2. Select Sauté in your instant pot and then add the oil to heat. Put the cumin seeds and then Sauté for 2 minutes. Put the tomatoes, mix well and then cook for another 15 minutes.
3. Put the beans, rice, salt, pepper, lemon juice, and water. Mix well and then secure the lid of the pot. Cook for 15 minutes at high pressure.
4. Do a natural release for 10 minutes. Turn the valve to "Venting" in order to release the remaining pressure. Gently open up the lid of the pot. Serve in separate bowls.

Tasty Mushroom Risotto with Parmesan

Servings: 4, **Prep + Cook Time:** 40 minutes

Ingredients:

- Dried mushrooms - 1.5 oz.
- Yellow onions - 2 cups, chopped
- Dry sherry - 1/3 cup
- Pearl barley - 1 cup
- Fennel seeds - 1 tsp.
- Water - 1 ½ cups
- Olive oil - 1 tbsp.
- Black barley - 2 tbsp.
- Chicken stock - 3 cups
- Seasoning - salt and black pepper
- Parmesan - 1/4 cup, grated

Directions:

1. Select Sauté in your instant pot and then add the oil to heat. Put the onions and fennel. Mix well and then cook for 4 minutes.
2. Put the mushrooms, stock, water, pepper, salt, barley, and black barley. Mix well. Secure the lid of the pot and cook it for 18 minutes at high pressure.
3. Do a quick release and then open up the pot. Press simmer, put salt and pepper. Mix well and then cook for 5 minutes.
4. Serve in separate bowls.

Cranberry Beans Pasta

Servings: 8, **Prep + Cook Time:** 30 minutes

Ingredients:

- Canned tomatoes - 26 oz. chopped
- Basil - 3 tsp. dried
- Smoked paprika - 1/2 tsp.
- Oregano - 2 tsp. dried
- Dried cranberry beans - 2 cups, soaked for 8 hours and drained
- Garlic - 7 cloves, minced
- Water - 6 cups
- Celery ribs – 2 pieces, chopped
- Yellow onion – 1 piece, chopped
- Small pasta - 2 cups
- Nutritional yeast - 3 tbsp.

- Rosemary - 1 tsp. chopped
- Red pepper flakes - 1/4 tsp.
- Seasoning - salt and black pepper
- Kale leaves - 10 oz.

Directions:

1. Select Sauté in your instant pot and then put the celery, garlic, pepper flakes, rosemary, a pinch of salt, and onion. Cook it for 2 minutes. Then add the tomatoes, oregano, basil, and paprika. Mix well and then cook for 1 minute.
2. Put the beans and the water inside the pot. Secure the lid of the pot and then cook it for 10 minutes at high pressure.
3. Do a quick release and then open up the lid of the pot. Put the pasta, kale, salt, and pepper mix well and then press Sauté again.
4. Cook it for another 5 minutes and then serve in separate bowls.

Hawaiian Curry and Pea

Servings: 4, Prep + Cook Time: 45 minutes

Ingredients:

- Peas - 1 cup, soaked in water for a few hours and drained
- Water - 4 cups
- Cashew butter - 1/4 cup
- Cinnamon - 1/4 tsp.
- Cumin - 1/2 tsp.
- Extra virgin olive oil - 3 tbsp.
- Turmeric - 1/2 tsp.
- Canned pineapple - 2/3 cup, cut into chunks
- Yellow onion – 1 piece, chopped
- Brown lentils - 1 cup
- Curry powder - 1 tsp.

Directions:

1. Put some water in a bowl and then put the cashew butter, mix well and then set aside.

Place the lentils and beans inside the instant pot, pour down 3 ½ cups water. Mix well and then secure the lid of the pot. Cook it for 25 minutes at high pressure.
2. Do a quick release and then drain the peas and lentils. Set aside the two ingredients in a bowl. Select Sauté in your instant pot and then add the oil to heat.
3. Put the turmeric, curry powder, cumin, cinnamon, mix well and then cook for 3 minutes. Add the onions, mix well and then cook for 4 minutes.
4. Press Simmer on the instant pot. Put the peas and lentils, pineapple, cashew butter, and a ½ cup of water. Mix well and then simmer for 5 minutes. Serve in separate bowls.

Spicy Lentils Tacos

Servings: 4, Prep+ + Cook Time: 25 minutes

Ingredients:

- Brown lentils - 2 cups
- Water - 4 cups
- Salt - 1 tsp.
- Garlic powder - 1 tsp.
- Tomato sauce - 4 oz.
- Cumin - 1/2 tsp.
- Chili powder - 1 tsp.
- Onion powder - 1 tsp.
- Taco shells

Directions:

1. Pour water in your instant pot and then add the lentils, cumin, garlic powder, chili powder, onion powder, and tomato sauce, mix them well. Secure the lid of the pot and then cook for 15 minutes at high pressure.
2. Do a quick release and then gently open up the pot's lid. Put the lentils in the taco shells. Serve while hot.

Grand Pesto and Chickpeas

Servings: 4, **Prep + Cook Time:** 30 minutes

Ingredients:

- Parmesan cheese - 1/4 cup, grated
- Pine nuts - 1 tbsp. roasted
- Extra virgin olive oil - 1/4 cup
- Basil - 1 ½ cups
- Garlic - 1 clove, minced
- Chickpeas - 12 oz. soaked for 8 hours
- Canned tomatoes - 14 oz.
- Carrots – 2 pieces, chopped
- Extra virgin olive oil - 2 tbsp.
- Parmesan - 1/4 cup, grated
- Chicken stock - 4 cups
- Yellow onion – 1 piece, chopped

Directions:

1. Blend the basil, 1 garlic clove, pine nuts, and ¼ cup oil and salt in a blender (this will make the pesto). Set aside the blended ingredients.
2. Select Sauté in your instant pot and then put two tablespoons of oil to heat. Put the onion and salt, mix well and then cook for 3 minutes.
3. Put the chickpeas, carrots, tomatoes, stock, salt, and pepper. Mix well and then secure the pot's lid. Cook for 10 minutes at high pressure.
4. Do a quick release and then carefully open up the lid of the pot. Put the chickpeas in a bowl.
5. Put the pesto at the top of the chickpeas and then top it up with the parmesan. Serve and enjoy.

Easy Lentils Salad

Servings: 4, **Prep + Cook Time:** 18 minutes

Ingredients:

- Parsley - 2 tbsp. chopped
- Red onion - 1/4 cup, chopped
- Celery - 1/2 cup, chopped
- Red bell pepper - 1/4 cup, chopped
- Oregano - 1/2 tsp. dried
- Chicken stock - 2 cups
- Lentils - 1 cup
- Bay leaf – 1 piece
- Thyme - 1/2 tsp. dried
- Extra virgin olive oil - 2 tbsp.
- Garlic - 1 tbsp. minced
- Juice of 1 lemon
- Seasoning - salt and black pepper

Directions:

1. Place the lentils in the instant pot. Add the bay leaf, thyme, and stock, mix well and then secure the lid of the pot. Cook for 8 minutes at high pressure.
2. Do a quick release and then open up the lid of the pot. Drain the lentils and then set aside in a bowl.
3. Put the onion, bell pepper, celery, garlic, parsley, oregano, lemon juice, olive oil, salt, and pepper in the bowl. Mix them well until fully coated. Serve fresh.

Chapter 10 Rice Recipes

Cheesy Rice with Artichoke Hearts

Servings: 4, Prep + Cook Time: 30 minutes

Ingredients:

- Canned artichoke hearts - 15 oz. chopped
- Arborio rice - 5 oz.
- Cream cheese - 16 oz.
- Extra-virgin olive oil - 1 tbsp.
- Grated parmesan cheese - 1 tbsp.
- White wine - 1 tbsp.
- Graham cracker crumbs - 6 oz.
- Water - 1 ¼ cups
- Thyme - 1 ½ tbsp. chopped
- Garlic - 2 cloves, crushed
- Chicken broth - 1 ¼ cups
- Seasoning - salt and black pepper

Directions:

1. Select Sauté in your instant pot and then put the oil to heat. Cook the rice for 2 minutes. Add the garlic, mix well and then cook for a minute. Place the rice mix in a bowl.
2. Pour over the stock, salt, pepper, wine, and crumbs on the bowl and then cover it with a tin foil. Put the bowl in a steamer basket and then put the basket on the instant pot.
3. Put water on the pot and then secure the lid. Cook for 8 minutes at high pressure. After cooking, do a quick release and then remove the bowl from the pot.
4. Remove the tin foil and then put the cream cheese, artichoke hearts, thyme, and parmesan. Mix well and serve hot.

Salty Jasmin Rice

Servings: 8, Prep + Cook Time: 15 minutes

Ingredients:

- Jasmine rice - 2 cups.
- Sea salt - 1/2 tsp.
- Water - 3 ¼ cups
- Millet - 1/2 cup

Directions:

1. Mix all the ingredients in your instant pot. Secure the lid and then press the Rice function.
2. Cook for 10 minutes and then serve right after.

Rice with Salmon Fillets

Servings: 2, Prep + Cook Time: 10 minutes

Ingredients:

- Wild salmon fillets – 2 pieces, frozen
- Jasmine rice - 1/2 cup
- Vegetable soup mix - 1/4 cup, dried
- Chicken stock - 1 cup
- Butter - 1 tbsp.
- Saffron - a pinch only
- Seasoning - salt and black pepper

Directions:

1. Pour the stock in your instant pot and then add the rice, soup mix, butter, and saffron. Mix well.
2. Sprinkle salt and pepper on the salmon fillets and then put the steamer basket inside the pot. Secure the lid and then cook for 5 minutes at high pressure.
3. Do a quick release and then serve the rice on separate plates.

Savory Beef Soup Rice

Servings: 6, **Prep + Cook Time:** 25 minutes

Ingredients:

- Beef meat - 1 lb. ground
- Garlic - 3 cloves, minced
- Yellow onion – 1 piece, chopped
- Canned garbanzo beans - 15 oz. rinsed
- Potato – 1 piece, cubed
- Frozen peas - 1/2 cup
- Canned tomatoes - 14 oz. crushed
- White rice - 1/2 cup
- Spicy V8 juice - 12 oz.
- Carrots – 2 pieces, thinly sliced
- Vegetable oil - 1 tbsp.
- Celery rib – 1 piece, chopped
- Canned beef stock - 28 oz.
- Seasoning - salt and black pepper

Directions:

1. Select Sauté in your instant pot and then add the beef. Mix well and then cook until the beef turns brown.
2. Put the oil on the pot and heat it. Add the onion and celery, mix well and then cook for 5 minutes. Add the garlic and then cook for another minute.
3. Pour the V8 juice, rice, tomatoes, beans, potatoes, carrots, beef, salt, stock, and pepper. Mix them well and then secure the lid of the pot. Cook for 5 minutes at high pressure.
4. Do a quick release and then gently open up the lid of the pot. Press Simmer and then add more salt and pepper if desired.
5. Put the peas and mix well. Serve the rice hot.

Black Rice Pudding

Servings: 4, **Prep + Cook Time:** 45 minutes

Ingredients:

- Black rice - 2 cups, washed and rinsed
- Water - 6 ½ cups
- Sugar - 3/4 cup
- Cardamom pods – 5 pieces, crushed
- Cloves – 3 pieces
- Coconut - 1/2 cup, grated
- Chopped mango
- Cinnamon - 2 sticks
- Salt - a pinch only

Directions:

1. Place the rice in your instant pot and then add a pinch of salt and water, mix well.
2. Using a cheesecloth bag, fill it with cardamom and cinnamon, mix them well and then add the cloves. Tie the bag.
3. Put the bag in the pot together with the rice. Secure the lid of the pot and then cook for 35 minutes at low pressure.
4. Do a natural release and then open up the pot's lid. Put the coconut and then select Sauté. Cook for 10 minutes and then after cooking, remove the cheesecloth bag.
5. Serve the rice in separate bowls.

Buttered Brown Rice

Servings: 4, **Prep + Cook Time:** 30 minutes

Ingredients:

- Vegetable stock - 1 ¼ cups
- Brown rice - 2 cups
- Butter - 1 stick
- French Onion soup - 1 ¼ cups

Directions:

1. Mix up all the ingredients inside your instant pot.
2. Secure the lid of the pot and then select manual. Cook the rice for 22 minutes at high pressure.
3. After cooking the rice, do a natural release. Serve the rice on separate plates.

Hawaiian Style Rice

Servings: 4, **Prep + Cook Time:** 12 minutes

Ingredients:
- Crushed pineapple - 8 oz.
- Brown rice - 1 cup
- Pineapple juice - 1/4 cup
- Butter - 1 tbsp.

Directions:

1. Place all the ingredients inside the instant pot and then secure the lid.
2. Press manual and then cook the rice for 7 minutes.
3. After cooking the rice, wait for about 2 minutes and then do a quick release. Mix well and then serve hot.

Brown Rice with Black Beans

Servings: 4, **Prep + Cook Time:** 35 minutes

Ingredients:
- Onion - 1 cup, diced
- Brown rice - 2 cups
- Dry black beans - 2 cups
- Garlic - 4 cloves, crushed and then minced.
- Water - 9 cups
- Salt - 1 tsp.
- Lime – 1 or 2 pieces
- Avocado – 1 piece, sliced

Directions:

1. Place the garlic and onion in the Instant Pot. Add the brown rice and black beans and then pour the water and salt.
2. Select manual and then cook the rice for 28 minutes. After cooking the rice, do a natural release. Let it sit for about 20 minutes.
3. Serve the rice in separate bowls squeezed with lime wedges and then add the avocado slices.

Rice Combo

Servings: 4, **Prep + Cook Time:** 35 minutes

Ingredients:
- Sea salt - 1/2 tsp.
- .Short grain brown rice - 3/4 cup
- Red, wild or black rice - 2 to 4 tbsp.
- Water - 1 tbsp.
- Water - 1 ½ cups

Directions:

1. Put all the red, wild or brown rice or a mixture of the three in a 1-cup measuring cup. Put brown rice to fill the cup.
2. Rinse the rice and then put it in the instant pot. Add the 1 ½ cup and the 1 tbsp. water in the pot. Put some salt.
3. Mix and make sure that the rice is compressed in the pot. Secure the lid of the pot and then select Multigrain. Cook the rice for 23 minutes.
4. After cooking the rice, do a natural release for 5 minutes. You can also release the pressure naturally for 15 minutes but it is up to you.
5. Right after releasing the pressure, you can now serve the rice.

Breakfast Rice

Servings: 2, **Prep + Cooking Time:** 15 minutes

Ingredients:
- Eggs – 2 pieces
- Water - 1 ⅓ cup
- Scallions – 2 pieces, finely chopped
- Seasoning - salt and black pepper
- Sesame seeds - a pinch only
- Garlic powder - a pinch only
- Hot rice

Directions:
1. Mix up the eggs and 1/3 cup of water in a bowl. Strain the mixture in a microwavable bowl.
2. Put salt, pepper, garlic powder, sesame seeds, and scallions. Mix them well and then pour 1 cup of water in the instant pot.
3. Put the microwavable bowl in a steamer basket and then secure the lid of the pot. Cook for 5 minutes at high pressure.
4. Do a quick release and then gently open up the lid of the pot. Serve the rice in separate bowls and enjoy.

Rice Veggies Stew

Servings: 6, **Prep + Cook Time:** 35 minutes

Ingredients:
- Medium-sized onions – 3 pieces, peeled and sliced.
- Brown basmati rice - 6 oz. rinsed
- Cooked chickpeas - 30 oz.
- Orange juice - 8 oz.
- Olive oil - 1 tbsp.
- Vegetable broth - 4 cups
- Chopped cilantro - 4 oz.
- Sweet potato - 1 lb. peeled and diced.
- Salt - 1/4 tsp.
- Ground black pepper - 1/4 tsp.
- Ground cumin - 2 tsp.
- Ground coriander -2 tsp.

Directions:
1. Press Sauté in your instant pot and then put the oil and onion. Cook for 12 minutes. Add in the coriander and cumin while stirring it. Cook for 15 seconds more.
2. Put all the ingredients in the pot beside the black pepper and cilantro. Mix the ingredients well.
3. Select Cancel to stop sautéing. Secure the lid of the pot and then press manual. Cook for 5 minutes at high pressure.
4. After cooking, do a natural release for 10 minutes and then gently open up the lid of the pot.
5. Serve with cilantro and black pepper on top.

Easy Brown Rice

Servings: 6, **Prep + Cook Time:** 30 minutes

Ingredients:
- Brown rice - 2 cups
- Vegetable broth - 2 ½ cups
- Sea salt - 1/2 tsp.

Directions:
1. Place the rice in your instant pot and then pour down the broth. Secure the lid and then select manual.
2. Cook the rice for 22 minutes and then after cooking, do a natural release for 10 minutes.
3. Gently open up the lid and then serve the rice hot.

Rice and Vegetables Mix

Servings: 4, **Prep + Cook Time:** 20 minutes

Ingredients:
- Basmati rice - 2 cups
- Garlic – 3 cloves, minced
- Butter - 2 tbsp.
- Cinnamon – 1 stick
- Cumin seeds - 1 tbsp.
- Bay leaves – 2 pieces
- Whole cloves – 3 pieces
- Ginger, grated - 1/2 tsp.
- Mixed frozen carrots, peas, corn, green beans - 1 cup
- Water - 2 cups
- Green chili - 1/2 tsp. minced
- Black peppercorns – 5 pieces
- Whole cardamoms – 2 pieces
- Sugar - 1 tbsp.
- Seasoning - Salt

Directions:
1. Put the water inside the instant pot and then add the rice, mixed frozen veggies, green chili, grated ginger, garlic cloves, cinnamon stick, whole cloves, butter, cumin seeds, bay leaves, cardamoms, black peppercorns, salt, and sugar.
2. Mix the ingredients well and then secure the lid. Cook for 15 minutes at high pressure.
3. Do a quick release and then serve right after.

Spiced Natural Rice

Servings: 4, **Prep + Cook Time:** 20 minutes

Ingredients:
- Veggie stock - 3 ¾ cups
- Medium-sized halved acorn squash – 2 pieces
- Quinoa - 1/2 cup
- Vegan cheese - 1/2 cup
- Garlic – 2 cloves, minced
- Earth Balance spread - 1 tbsp.
- White rice - 1 cup.
- Chopped rosemary - 1 tsp.
- Chopped thyme - 1 tsp.
- Chopped sage - 1 tsp.
- Diced onion - 1 cup

Directions:
1. Select Sauté in your instant pot and then add the Earth Balance to melt. Put the onion and salt and then cook for 2 minutes.
2. Add the garlic and then cook for 1 minute. Put the rice, quinoa, herbs, and broth. Mix well.
3. Put the squash in the steamer basket with the cut-side up. Secure the lid and then press manual.
4. Cook for 6 minutes at high pressure. After cooking, do a quick release and then drain the liquids from the steamer basket.
5. Put the vegan cheese in the pot. Mix well and then serve with the rice.

Rice with Cauliflower

Servings: 6, **Prep + Cook Time:** 30 minutes

Ingredients:
- Rice - 2 cups
- Extra virgin olive oil - 2 tsp.
- Cauliflower – 1 piece, florets separated and chopped
- Pineapple - ½ piece, peeled and chopped
- Water - 4 cups
- Seasoning - salt and black pepper

Directions:
1. Mix up the pineapple, cauliflower, water, oil, salt, pepper, and rice inside your instant pot. Secure the lid and then cook for 20 minutes at low pressure.
2. Do a natural release for 10 minutes. Serve the rice topped with some salt and pepper.

Creamy Pumpkin Rice

Servings: 6, **Prep + Cook Time:** 1 hour,

Ingredients:
- Pumpkin spice mix - 1 Tsp.
- Brown rice - 1 cup
- Cinnamon – 1 stick
- Pumpkin puree - 1 cup
- Maple syrup - 1/2 cup
- Water - 1/2 cup
- Vanilla extract - 1 tsp.
- Cashew milk - 3 cups
- Dates - 1/2 cup, chopped
- Salt - a pinch only

Directions:
1. Place the rice inside the instant pot and then pour over boiling water (enough to cover the rice). Set aside for about 10 minutes before draining.
2. Pour water and milk in the instant pot and then add the cinnamon stick, dates, and salt. Secure the lid and cook for 20 minutes at high pressure.
3. Do a quick release and then gently open up the lid of the pot. Put the maple syrup, pumpkin spice, and pumpkin puree. Mix well and then press Simmer. Cook for another 5 minutes.
4. Remove the cinnamon stick and then add the vanilla. Mix well and serve in separate bowls.

Beef Basmati Rice

Servings: 6, **Prep + Cook Time:** 50 minutes

Ingredients:
- Basmati rice - 2 cups
- Dill - 1 cup
- Butter - 3 oz.
- Salt - 1 tbsp.
- Beef broth - 4 cups
- Spinach - 1 cup
- Olive oil - 1 tsp.
- Dried oregano - 1 tsp.
- Garlic - 1 tbsp. minced

Directions:
1. In your instant pot, mix the butter, rice, minced garlic, and olive oil.
2. Cook for 5 minutes while stirring. Pour down the beef broth.
3. Rinse the spinach and dill, chop them and then blend in a blender.
4. Add the mixture of spinach on the rice mixture. Put salt, butter, and dried oregano. Mix well.
5. Secure the lid of the pot and then press Rice. Cook for 20 minutes and then serve immediately.

Cheesy Arborio Rice

Servings: 6, **Prep + Cook Time:** 25 minutes

Ingredients:
- Chicken stock - 28 oz.
- Arborio rice - 12 oz.
- Olive oil - 1 ½ tbsp.
- Romano or Parmesan cheese - 3 tbsp.
- Medium onion – 1 piece, finely chopped
- Seasoning - salt and pepper

Directions:
1. Select Sauté in your instant pot and then add the oil to heat. Put the onion and cook until soft.
2. Put the rice and chicken stock in the pot. Secure the lid and then press Rice. Cook for 15 minutes.
3. Do a natural release and then open up the lid of the pot and then sprinkle black pepper.
4. Serve the rice with Parmesan or Romano cheese on top.

Fruity Rice

Servings: 6, Prep + Cook Time: 50 minutes

Ingredients:

- Maple syrup - 1 tbsp.
- Small apples – 2 pieces, peeled and chopped
- Pear – 1 piece, chopped
- Slivered almonds - 1/2 cup
- Apple juice - 2 tbsp.
- Veggie oil - 1 Tsp.
- Cinnamon - 1 tsp.
- Ground nutmeg - 1/2 tsp.
- Water - 3 ½ cups
- Wild rice - 1 ½ cups
- Mixed fruit - 1 cup, dried
- Seasoning - salt and pepper

Directions:

1. Pour water inside your instant pot and then add the rice. Secure the lid and then press manual. Cook the rice for 30 minutes at high pressure.
2. While the rice is cooking, soak the mixed fruits in the apple juice. Drain the fruits right after the rice stops cooking.
3. Press cancel and then do a natural release. Remove the liquids from the pot and then transfer the rice in a bowl.
4. Select Sauté in your instant pot and then put the veggie oil. Put the pears, apples, and almonds. Cook for 2 minutes.
5. Mix the cooked rice, mixed fruits, seasonings, and maple syrup. Serve right after.

Brown Rice with Lime Juice

Servings: 4, Prep + Cook Time: 35 minutes

Ingredients:

- Brown rice - 2 cups, rinsed
- Olive oil - 1 ½ tbsp.
- Salt - 1 tsp.
- Chopped cilantro - 1/2 cup
- Hot water - 2 ¾ cups
- Lime – 1 piece, juiced
- Small bay leaves – 4 pieces

Directions:

1. Put the race in your instant pot together with the bay leaves and water. Press Rice on the pot and then cover the lid. Cook the rice with the default time setting.
2. After cooking the rice, do a natural release for 10 minutes and then right after, do a quick release.
3. Gently open up the lid and then put the oil, lime juice, cilantro, and salt. Mix well and then serve.

Countryside Spicy Rice Casserole

Servings: 4, Prep + Cook Time: 35 minutes

Ingredients:

- Brown rice - 2 cups
- Water - 5 cups
- Soaked black beans - 1 cup
- Tomato paste - 6 oz.
- Chili powder - 2 tsp.
- Onion powder - 2 tsp.
- Garlic - 1 tsp.
- Salt - 1 tsp.

Directions:

1. Set aside the dry beans in a bowl with enough water for about 2 hours and then drain it after.
2. Put all the ingredients in the instant pot. Secure the lid of the pot and then press manual. Cook the rice for 28 minutes at high pressure.
3. Do a quick release after cooking and then season with garlic before serving.

Spicy Breakfast Basmati Rice

Servings: 6, **Prep + Cook Time:** 30 minutes

Ingredients:

- Basmati Rice - 2 cups,
- Tomato paste - 1/2 cup
- Salt - 2 tsp.
- White onion - 1/2, chopped
- Garlic - 3 cloves, minced
- Small jalapeño - 1 piece
- Water - 2 cups

Directions:

1. Select Sauté in your instant pot and then add the oil to heat. Put the garlic, onions, and rice once the oil is hot. Cook for 4 minutes.
2. Mix up the tomato paste and water. Pour down this mixture in the pot and then add the jalapeno.
3. Select Cancel to stop sautéing. Secure the lid of the pot and then cook the rice for 22 minutes at high pressure.
4. After cooking, do a natural release for 15 minutes and then gently open up the lid of the pot.
5. Serve the rice hot and enjoy!

Spicy Wild Rice with Chicken Soup

Servings: 6, **Prep + Cook Time:** 25 minutes

Ingredients:

- Chicken breasts – 2 pieces, skinless and boneless and chopped
- Yellow onion - 1 cup, chopped
- Chicken stock - 28 oz.
- Cream cheese - 4 oz. cubed
- Wild rice - 6 oz.
- Butter - 2 tbsp.
- Celery - 1 cup, chopped
- Milk - 1 cup
- Parsley - 1 tbsp. dried
- Cornstarch - 2 tbsp. (mixed with 2 tbsp. water)
- Carrots - 1 cup, chopped
- Red pepper flakes - a pinch only
- Seasoning - salt and black pepper

Directions:

1. Select Sauté in your instant pot and then put the butter to melt. Put the carrot, celery, and onion. Cook for 5 minutes.
2. Put the rice, chicken, stock, salt, parsley, and pepper. Mix well and then secure the lid of the pot. Cook for 5 minutes at high pressure.
3. Do a quick release and then gently open up the lid. Put the cornstarch with water. Mix well and then press Simmer.
4. Serve with milk, half and half, and cheese.

Chapter 11 Egg Recipes

Seasoned Egg Porridge for Breakfast.

Serving: 4 , Prep + Cook Time:50 minutes

Ingredients:
- rinsed and drained white rice - 1/2 cup.
- Black pepper to taste
- water - 2 cups.
- Eggs - 4
- salt - 1/2 tsp.
- Sugar - 1 tbsp.
- olive oil - 1 tbsp.
- soy sauce - 2 tsp.
- chopped scallions - 4
- chicken broth - 2 cups.

Directions:
1. Add water, broth, sugar, salt, and rice to the Instant Pot before closing the lid
2. Press "Porridge" and leave it on "High" pressure for 30 minutes.
3. As that continues to cook, heat the oil in a saucepan.
4. When cracking the eggs, ensure to do so one at a time, this is so they won't touch each other
5. Keep cooking till the whites become crispy on the edges, while the yolks remain runny. Add a pinch of salt and pepper to taste.
6. Immediately the Instant Pot timer goes off, you are to press the "Cancel" button and allow the pressure to go down by itself.
7. Now, if the porridge isn't thick enough, press the "Sauté" button and cook uncovered for about 5 to 10 minutes.
8. Finally, you can serve with scallions, soy sauce, and an egg for each bowl

Savory Feta Spinach Egg Cups.

Serving: 4 , Prep + Cook Time:22 minutes

Ingredients:
- feta cheese - 1/4 cup.
- chopped tomato – 1
- eggs - 6
- salt - 1/2 tsp.
- water - 1 cup.
- black pepper - 1 tsp.
- 1/2 cup. mozzarella cheese
- chopped baby spinach - 1 cup.

Directions:
1. Add water to the Instant Pot and lower in trivet
2. Place silicone ramekins with spinach.
3. Mix the remaining ingredients in a bowl and transfer to cups, allowing 1/4-inch head room
4. Introduce to the instant pot pressure cooker; note that you may have to cook in batches before adjusting time to 8 minutes on "High" pressure
5. Turn off the instant pot and quick-release immediately the time is up.

Tasty and Soft Boiled Egg.

Serving: 2 , **Prep + Cook Time:** 6 minutes

Ingredients:
- water - 1 cup.
- eggs - 4
- toasted English muffins – 2
- Salt and pepper to taste

Directions:
1. Add the 1 cup of water to the Instant Pot and insert the steamer basket. Transfer four canning lids to the basket, then place the eggs on top of them, in order to ensure they are separated
2. Ensure the lid is secured.
3. Hit the STEAM setting and select a time of 4 minutes
4. Quick-release the steam valve once you are ready.
5. Remove the eggs using tongs and move them to a bowl containing cold water.
6. Wait for about one or two minutes.
7. Then peel and serve with one egg for each half of a toasted English muffin
8. Add salt and pepper as seasoning.

Poached Tomatoes with Eggs.

Serving: 4 , **Prep + Cook Time:** 15 minutes

Ingredients:
- eggs – 4
- salt - 1 tsp.
- paprika - 1/2 tsp
- olive oil - 1 tbsp.
- white pepper - 1/2 tsp.
- red onion – 1
- medium tomatoes - 3
- fresh dill - 1 tbsp.

Directions:
1. Add the olive oil inside to the ramekins by spraying.
2. Then, make sure to beat the eggs into every ramekin.
3. Mix the paprika, white pepper, fresh dill, and salt together in the mixing bowl. Ensure to stir the mixture gently as you mix.
4. Follow this by cutting the red onion into the mix.
5. Cut the tomatoes into the small pieces and then mix the pieces with the onion. Once again, stir the mixture gently and well.
6. Then sprinkle tomato mixture on the eggs.
7. Add spice mixture and move the eggs to the Instant Pot.
8. Close the lid and set the Instant Pot to STEAM mode
9. Cook the dish for about 5 minutes before removing the dish from the Instant Pot and let it chill for a while.
10. Serve the dish immediately and enjoy your meal!

Tasty and Simple French Toast.

Serving: 4 , Prep + Cook Time:35 minutes

Ingredients:
- butter - 1 tsp.
- stale cinnamon-raisin bread - 3 cups; cut into cubes
- water - 1 ½ cups.
- whole milk - 1 cup.
- pure vanilla extract - 1 tsp
- maple syrup - 2 tbsp.
- sugar - 1 tsp.
- Big and beaten eggs – 3

Directions:
1. Add water to your Instant Pot and lower in the steam rack
2. Grease a 6 to 7-inch soufflé pan.
3. Mix milk, vanilla, maple syrup, and eggs in a clean bowl.
4. Add the bread cubes and let them soak for 5 minutes.
5. Pour the soaked bread cubes to the pan; ensure that the bread is totally submerged.
6. Make sure the instant pot pressure cooker is set.
7. Then select "Manual" and adjust the time settings to 15 minutes on "High" pressure
8. Quick-release the pressure immediately the time is out.
9. Top with sugar by sprinkling, then broil in the oven for about 3 minutes

Bacon and Egg with Cheese Muffins.

Serving: 8 , Prep + Cook Time:25 minutes

Ingredients:
- green onion - 1, diced.
- lemon pepper seasoning - 1/4 tsp.
- cheddar or pepper jack cheese - 4 tbsp., shredded.
- Bacon - 4 slices; cooked and crumbled.
- water - 1 ½ cup; for the pot
- eggs - 4

Directions:
1. Add water to the Instant Pot container and then place a steamer basket to the pot. Break the eggs in a large measuring bowl using a pour pout.
2. Add the lemon pepper and beat properly. Cut the bacon, cheese, and green onion between 4 silicone muffin cups.
3. Pour the egg mix into each muffin cups; using a fork, stir using a fork to mix well. Place the muffin cups into the steamer basket, and make sure to close the lid.
4. Set the pressure on "High" pressure and the timer to 8 minutes
5. Immediately the timer beeps, turn off the pot. Then wait for about 2 minutes before turning the steam valve in order to quick release the pressure.
6. Open the pot lid gently, and lift the steamer basket right from the container, and then do away with the muffin cups.
7. Serve warm and enjoy your meal!

Tips: These muffins can be stored in the refrigerator for more than 1 week. When ready to serve, just microwave for 30 seconds on "High" to reheat

Hard Boiled Large Eggs Recipe.

Serving: 6 , **Prep + Cook Time:** 10 minutes

Ingredients:
- water - 1 cup.
- large white eggs - 12

Directions:
1. Pour about 1 cup of water into the bowl in the Instant Pot.
2. Insert the stainless steamer basket inside the pot
3. Place the eggs in the steamer basket
4. Boil on manual "High" pressure for about 7 minutes.
5. Then quick release valve to ensure that the pressure is released
6. Open the lid and remove the eggs using tongs and move them into a bowl containing cold water.

Spinach, Sliced Bacon with Eggs.

Serving: 4 , **Prep + Cook Time:** 15 minutes

Ingredients:
- Bacon - 7 oz.
- cream - 3 tbsp.
- spinach - 1/2 cup.
- eggs - 4, boiled
- ground white pepper - 1/2 tsp.
- cilantro - 1 tsp.
- butter - 2 tsp.

Directions:
1. Slice the bacon neatly and sprinkle the ground white pepper on it as well as cilantro. Stir the mixture gently.
2. Remove the egg shells, then wrap them in the spinach leaves
3. Follow this by wrapping the eggs with the sliced bacon
4. Select the Instant Pot MEAT/STEW mode and move the wrapped eggs
5. Then add butter and cook the dish for about 10 minutes.
6. Remove the eggs from the Instant Pot and sprinkle the cream on them, immediately the time is up.
7. Ensure to serve the dish while it is still hot.

Breakfast Jar with Bacon.

Serving: 3 , **Prep + Cook Time:** 25 minutes

Ingredients:
- eggs – 6
- Tater tots
- sharp cheese or shredded cheese - 9 slices; divided
- mason jars - 3 pieces; that can hold about 2-cup worth ingredients
- bacon - 6 pieces; cooked of your preferred breakfast meat, such as sausage
- peach-mango salsa - 6 tbsp.; divided

Directions:
1. Add about 1 ¼ cups of water to the Instant Pot. Then add enough tater tots to ensure the bottom of the mason jars is covered.
2. Break 2 eggs into each Mason jar you have. Then poke the egg yolks with a fork; you can also use the tip of a long knife.
3. Place a couple of your preferred meat to the mason jars. Then add 2 slices of cheese to each Mason jar; this should cover the ingredients.
4. Pour 2 tablespoon of salsa into each jar, right on top of the cheese. Also, add a couple more tater tots right on top of the salsa.
5. Then top the mix with 1 slice of cheese. Ensure to cover each jar using foil, make sure the cover is tight enough to prevent moisture from escaping into the jars.
6. Place the jars into the water in the Instant Pot. Close the lid of the instant pot.
7. Select "High" pressure and set the timer to clock out at 5 minutes; ensure the valve of the Instant Pot is also in pressure cooker mode.
8. Turn the steam valve to release pressure immediately the timer beeps; make sure to quick release the pressure.
9. Open the Instant Pot and gently remove the jar.

Tasty Scrambled Eggs & Bacon.

Serving: 4 , **Prep + Cook Time:** 15 minutes

Ingredients:
- fresh parsley - 1/4 cup.
- cilantro - 1 tbsp.
- butter - 1 tbsp.
- Eggs – 7
- basil - 1 tsp.
- milk - 1/2 cup.
- salt - 1 tsp.
- paprika - 1 tsp.
- bacon - 4 oz.

Directions:
1. Beat the eggs in a clean mixing bowl and whisk them well.
2. Also, add milk, basil, salt, paprika, and cilantro and stir the mixture gently. Chop the bacon and parsley.
3. Choose the Instant Pot "Sauté" mode and move the chopped bacon. Cook it for about 3 minutes
4. Also, add whisked egg mixture and cook the dish for another 5 minutes.
5. Follow that by mixing up the eggs gently using a wooden spoon
6. Then sprinkle some chopped parsley on the dish and cook it for another 4 minutes.
7. Remove them from the Instant Pot when the eggs are done.
8. Serve the dish immediately while the dish is still hot. Enjoy!

Tomato Spinach Quiche with Parmesan Cheese.

Serving: 6 , **Prep + Cook Time:** 30 minutes

Ingredients:
- fresh ground black pepper - 1/4 tsp.
- large green onions - 3, sliced
- tomato slices – 4; for topping the quiche
- milk - 1/2 cup.
- large eggs - 12
- Tomato - 1 cup; seeded, diced
- salt - 1/2 tsp.
- Water - 1 ½ cup; for the pot
- Parmesan cheese - 1/4 cup; shredded.
- fresh baby spinach - 3 cups; roughly chopped

Directions:
1. Add water to the Instant Pot container. Whisk the eggs with the milk, pepper, and salt in a large-sized bowl.
2. Then add the tomato, spinach, and the green onions into a 1 ½ quart-sized baking dish; stir the mix well.
3. Add the egg mix on the vegetables; stir until properly mixed. Put the tomato slices gently on top
4. Sprinkle the shredded parmesan cheese on the mix. Place the baking dish into the rack using a handle.
5. Place the rack into the Instant Pot and ensure the lid is locked. Put the pressure on "High" and set the timer to 20 minutes.
6. Immediately the timer clocks out, wait for about 1o minutes then turn the steamer valve to "Venting" in order to release the rest of the pressure. Open the lid of the pot gently.
7. Hold the rack handles carefully and remove the dish out from the pot
8. Broil till the top of the quiche turns to light brown color, if you like.

TIP: You can cover the baking dish with foil to prevent moisture from gathering on the quiche top. You can cook uncovered; just soak the moisture using a paper towel

Seasoned Cheesy Hash Brown.

Serving: 8 , Prep + Cook Time:10 minutes

Ingredients:
- Eggs - 8
- chopped bacon - 6 slices
- frozen hash browns - 2 cups.
- salt - 1 tsp.
- black pepper - 1/2 tsp.
- shredded cheddar cheese - 1 cup.
- milk - 1/4 cup.

Directions:
1. Set your Instant Pot to "Sauté" and cook the bacon until it gets crispy.
2. Add hash browns and stir for about 2 minutes or until they start to thaw
3. Whisk the eggs, milk, cheese, and seasonings in a bowl.
4. Transfer the hash browns to the pot, then lock and seal lid
5. Hit "Manual" button and adjust time to 5 minutes.
6. Select "Cancel" and quick-release the pressure when the time is up
7. Ensue to serve in slices.

Seasoned Creamy Sausage Frittata.

Serving: 4 , Prep + Cook Time:40 minutes

Ingredients:
- 1/2 cup. cooked ground sausage
- water - 1 ½ cups.
- grated sharp cheddar - 1/4 cup.
- beaten eggs - 4
- sour cream - 2 tbsp.
- butter - 1 tbsp.
- Black pepper to taste
- Salt to taste

Directions:
1. Pour water into the Instant Pot and lower in the steamer rack.
2. Grease a 6 to 7-inch soufflé dish
3. Whisk the eggs and sour cream together in a bowl.
4. Add cheese, sausage, salt, and pepper. Stir
5. Pour the mix into the dish and wrap with foil all over; ensure to wrap tightly.
6. Lower right into the steam rack and close the lid of the pot.
7. Press "Manual" and then put it on "Low" pressure for 17 minutes.
8. Quick-release the pressure when the time is up. Serve the dish while still hot!

Seasoned Egg Side Dish Recipe.

Serving: 6 , Prep + Cook Time:20 minutes

Ingredients:
- eggs - 8
- ground white pepper - 1 tsp.
- mustard - 1 tbsp.
- minced garlic - 1 tsp.
- mayo sauce - 1 tsp.
- dill - 1/4 cup.
- cream - 1/4 cup.
- salt - 1 tsp.

Directions:
1. Introduce the eggs in the Instant Pot, then add water to the pot.
2. Cook the eggs at high pressure for about 5 minutes
3. Then take out the eggs from the Instant Pot and chill
4. Remove the egg shells and cut them into 2 parts
5. Remove and do away with the egg yolks and mash them together.
6. Then add the mustard, cream, salt, mayo sauce, ground white pepper, and minced garlic in the mashed egg yolks
7. Cut the dill and sprinkle the chopped dill on the egg yolk mixture.
8. Mix it up gently until you get a smooth and homogenous mass
9. Then move the egg yolk mixture into a pastry bag.
10. Fill up the egg whites with the yolk mixture
11. Serve the dish as soon as possible. Enjoy your meal!

Chapter 12 Yogurt Recipes

Slow Cooked and Fruity Yogurt.

Serving: 4 , Prep + Cook Time: 12 hours

Ingredients:
- Milk - 5 ⅔ cups.; organic, reduced fat or whole
- water - 1 ½ cup.; for the pot
- dry milk powder - 4 tbsp.; non-fat; divided
- fresh fruit - 2 cups.; chopped
- yogurt culture - 4 tbsp.; plain; divided
- sugar - 4 tbsp.; all natural; divided

Equipment:
- wide mouth pint jars - 4

Directions:
1. Add water to the Instant Pot and then place a rack/grate in the pot.
2. Pour 1 and 1/3 cup of milk into each jar, then cover the jar loosely with their lids. Then transfer the jars onto the rack/grate
3. Set your Instant Pot to Pressure Cycle, then set it at a time of 2 minutes; this will heat the milk and nullify any pathogens present in the milk
4. Turn the steam valve to quick release the pressure when the cycle is completed.
5. Use a jar lifter to open the lid, then remove the jars from the pot. Place those jars in cool water and remove the jar lids gently.
6. The moment the milk reach a temperature below 100F; add about 1 tbsp of yogurt culture, 1 tbsp of dry milk powder and 1 tbsp of sugar to each jar; stir gently and well.
7. Add about 1/2 cups of fresh fruits gently into each jar; ensure that they are not over filled. Make sure to leave at least 1/ 8-inch clear from the top each jar. Also, place the jar lids back
8. Check and ensure that there is still about 1 ½ cup of water left at the bottom of the Instant Pot
9. Finally, place the jars back onto the rack/ grate. Select the yogurt cycle and set the timer at a time between the ranges of 8 - 12 hours.
10. Place the jars in the refrigerator when the cycle is done; this is to stop the cooking and also cool them down

Tips: Making the yogurt in jars enables you to make plain or different flavored yogurt at the same time s

Tasty Strawberry Yogurt.

Serving: 4 , Prep + Cook Time: 20 minutes

Ingredients:
- raw honey - 1 tbsp.
- full cream milk - 2 cans
- strawberry puree - 1 cup
- high-quality probiotic - 4 capsules
- vanilla paste - 1 tsp.
- gelatin powder - 2 tbsp.

Directions:
1. Add milk to the instant pot.
2. Lock and seal the lid and press the yogurt button; also hit the adjust button until the point that the display states boil.
3. Turn off the pot when the Instant Pot beeps, then unlock and remove the lid. Proceed to take out the metal bowl
4. Use a candy thermometer to measure the temperature of the milk till it reaches 239 F.
5. The moment the milk gets cooled below239 F; pour the entirety of the probiotic capsules in the milk
6. Place the metal bowl back into the pot; close the lid and seal it and hit the yogurt button once again.
7. Make use of the + button to change the time to 14hours. Taste the yogurt to make sure it is tart when the Instant pot beeps.
8. Move the yogurt to the blender or a food processor, then sprinkle gelatin powder into

the blender/food processor; also add the rest of the ingredients.
9. Pulse the yogurt in a food blender until it is perfectly smooth

10. Pour the yogurt into different glasses or different bowls; then refrigerate them for about 2 to 3 hours

Tasty Blueberry Oats Yogurt.

Serving: 6 , **Prep + Cook Time:**20 minutes

Ingredients:
- full cream milk - 2 cans
- blueberry puree or pulp - 1 cup
- gelatin powder - 2 tbsp.
- vanilla paste - 1 tsp.
- high-quality probiotic - 4 capsules
- roasted oats - 1/2 cup
- raw honey - 1 tbsp.

Directions:
1. Add milk to the instant pot.
2. Cover the pot with the lid and lock it; then press the yogurt button and hit the adjust button till the display shows boil
3. Turn off the pot when the Instant Pot beeps, then open the lid and remove the metal bowl
4. Make use of a candy thermometer measure the temperature of the milk till it reaches a temperature of 239 F.

5. Pour the contents of probiotic capsules into the milk immediately the milk is cooled below 239 F.
6. Move the metal bowl back to the pot, then close and seal the lid tight; then hit the yogurt button again.
7. Press the + button to change the time to 14hours. Taste the yogurt to make sure it is tart as soon as the Instant pot beeps.
8. Move the yogurt to the blender or food processor, then add gelatin powder and add rest of the ingredients.
9. Pulse the yogurt in a food blender until it becomes smooth
10. Transfer the yogurt into different glasses or different bowls and refrigerate the same for 2 - 3 hours

Tasty Pumpkin Spice Yogurt.

Serving: 4 , **Prep + Cook Time:**20 minutes

Ingredients:
- high-quality probiotic - 4 capsules
- raw honey - 1 tbsp.
- pumpkin spice - 1 tbsp.
- full cream milk - 2 cans
- vanilla paste - 1 tsp.
- gelatin powder - 2 tbsp.

Directions:
1. Add milk to the instant pot.
2. Cover the pot with the lid and lock it; then press the yogurt button and hit the adjust button till the display shows boil
3. Turn off the pot when the Instant Pot beeps, then open the lid and remove the metal bowl
4. Make use of a candy thermometer measure the temperature of the milk till it reaches a temperature of 239 F.

5. Pour the contents of probiotic capsules into the milk immediately the milk is cooled below 239 F.
6. Move the metal bowl back to the pot, then close and seal the lid tight; then hit the yogurt button again.
7. Press the + button to change the time to 14hours. Taste the yogurt to make sure it is tart as soon as the Instant pot beeps.
8. Move the yogurt to the blender or food processor, then add gelatin powder and add rest of the ingredients.
9. Pulse the yogurt in a food blender until it becomes smooth
10. Transfer the yogurt into different glasses or different bowls and refrigerate the same for 2 - 3 hours

Yummy Chocolate Yogurt.

Serving: 4 , **Prep + Cook Time:** 20 minutes

Ingredients:
- high-quality probiotic - 4 capsules
- raw honey - 1 tbsp.
- full cream milk - 2 cans
- vanilla paste - 1 tsp.
- gelatin powder - 2 tbsp.
- melted dark chocolate - 1 cup
- cocoa powder - 2 tbsp.

Directions:
1. Add milk to the instant pot. Then add cocoa powder.
2. Cover the pot with the lid and lock it; then press the yogurt button and hit the adjust button till the display shows boil
3. Turn off the pot when the Instant Pot beeps, then open the lid and remove the metal bowl
4. Make use of a candy thermometer measure the temperature of the milk till it reaches a temperature of 239 F.
5. Pour the contents of probiotic capsules into the milk immediately the milk is cooled below 239 F.
6. Move the metal bowl back to the pot, then close and seal the lid tight; then hit the yogurt button again.
7. Press the + button to change the time to 14hours. Taste the yogurt to make sure it is tart as soon as the Instant pot beeps.
8. Move the yogurt to the blender or food processor, then add gelatin powder and add rest of the ingredients.
9. Pulse the yogurt in a food blender until it becomes smooth
10. Transfer the yogurt into different glasses or different bowls and refrigerate the same for 2 - 3 hours

Cinnamon Yogurt with Honey.

Serving: 6 , **Prep + Cook Time:** 20 minutes

Ingredients:
- vanilla paste - 1 tsp.
- high-quality probiotic - 4 capsules
- Ceylon cinnamon - 2 tsp.
- full cream milk - 2 cans
- raw honey - 1 tbsp.
- gelatin powder - 2 tbsp.

Directions:
1. Add milk to the instant pot.
2. Cover the pot with the lid and lock it; then press the yogurt button and hit the adjust button till the display shows boil
3. Turn off the pot when the Instant Pot beeps, then open the lid and remove the metal bowl
4. Make use of a candy thermometer measure the temperature of the milk till it reaches a temperature of 239 F.
5. Pour the contents of probiotic capsules into the milk immediately the milk is cooled below 239 F.
6. Move the metal bowl back to the pot, then close and seal the lid tight; then hit the yogurt button again.
7. Press the + button to change the time to 14hours. Taste the yogurt to make sure it is tart as soon as the Instant pot beeps.
8. Move the yogurt to the blender or food processor, then add gelatin powder and add rest of the ingredients.
9. Pulse the yogurt in a food blender until it becomes smooth
10. Transfer the yogurt into different glasses or different bowls and refrigerate the same for 2 - 3 hours

Yummy Kiwi Yogurt.

Serving: 4 , **Prep + Cook Time:** 20 minutes

Ingredients:
- vanilla paste - 1 tsp.
- kiwi puree - 3/4 cup
- full cream milk - 2 cans
- raw honey - 1 tbsp.
- high-quality probiotic - 4 capsules
- gelatin powder - 2 tbsp.

Directions:
1. Add milk to the instant pot.
2. Cover the pot with the lid and lock it; then press the yogurt button and hit the adjust button till the display shows boil
3. Turn off the pot when the Instant Pot beeps, then open the lid and remove the metal bowl
4. Make use of a candy thermometer measure the temperature of the milk till it reaches a temperature of 239 F.
5. Pour the contents of probiotic capsules into the milk immediately the milk is cooled below 239 F.
6. Move the metal bowl back to the pot, then close and seal the lid tight; then hit the yogurt button again.
7. Press the + button to change the time to 14hours. Taste the yogurt to make sure it is tart as soon as the Instant pot beeps.
8. Move the yogurt to the blender or food processor, then add gelatin powder and add rest of the ingredients.
9. Pulse the yogurt in a food blender until it becomes smooth
10. Transfer the yogurt into different glasses or different bowls and refrigerate the same for 2 - 3 hours

Sweet Mango Yogurt.

Serving: 4 , **Prep + Cook Time:** 30 minutes

Ingredients:
- gelatine - 2 tbsp.
- mango puree or pulp - 1 cup
- high-quality probiotic
- raw honey - 1 tbsp.
- full cream milk - 2 cans
- vanilla extract - 1 tsp.

Directions:
1. Add milk to the instant pot.
2. Cover the pot with the lid and lock it; then press the yogurt button and hit the adjust button till the display shows boil
3. Turn off the pot when the Instant Pot beeps, then open the lid and remove the metal bowl
4. Make use of a candy thermometer measure the temperature of the milk till it reaches a temperature of 239 F.
5. Pour the contents of probiotic capsules into the milk immediately the milk is cooled below 239 F.
6. Also, stir in the mange puree
7. Move the metal bowl back to the pot, then close and seal the lid tight; then hit the yogurt button again.
8. Press the + button to change the time to 14hours. Taste the yogurt to make sure it is tart as soon as the Instant pot beeps.
9. Move the yogurt to the blender or food processor, then add gelatin powder and add rest of the ingredients.
10. Pulse the yogurt in a food blender until it becomes smooth
11. Transfer the yogurt into different glasses or different bowls and refrigerate the same for 2 - 3 hours

Tasty Raspberry Yogurt.

Serving: 6 , **Prep + Cook Time:** 20 minutes

Ingredients:
- raspberry puree - 1 cup
- gelatin powder - 2 tbsp.
- vanilla paste - 1 tsp.
- full cream milk - 2 cans
- raw honey - 1 tbsp.
- high-quality probiotic - 4 capsules

Directions:
1. Add milk to the instant pot.

2. Cover the pot with the lid and lock it; then press the yogurt button and hit the adjust button till the display shows boil
3. Turn off the pot when the Instant Pot beeps, then open the lid and remove the metal bowl
4. Make use of a candy thermometer measure the temperature of the milk till it reaches a temperature of 239 F.
5. Pour the contents of probiotic capsules into the milk immediately the milk is cooled below 239 F.
6. Move the metal bowl back to the pot, then close and seal the lid tight; then hit the yogurt button again.

7. Press the + button to change the time to 14hours. Taste the yogurt to make sure it is tart as soon as the Instant pot beeps.
8. Move the yogurt to the blender or food processor, then add gelatin powder and add rest of the ingredients.
9. Pulse the yogurt in a food blender until it becomes smooth
10. Transfer the yogurt into different glasses or different bowls and refrigerate the same for 2 - 3 hours

Tasty Vanilla Yogurt.

Serving: 4 , Prep + Cook Time:20 minutes

Ingredients:
- gelatin powder - 2 tbsp.
- raw honey - 1 tbsp.
- full cream milk - 2 cans
- vanilla paste - 3 tsp.
- high-quality probiotic - 4 capsules

Directions:
1. Add milk to the instant pot.
2. Cover the pot with the lid and lock it; then press the yogurt button and hit the adjust button till the display shows boil
3. Turn off the pot when the Instant Pot beeps, then open the lid and remove the metal bowl
4. Make use of a candy thermometer measure the temperature of the milk till it reaches a temperature of 239 F.

5. Pour the contents of probiotic capsules into the milk immediately the milk is cooled below 239 F.
6. Move the metal bowl back to the pot, then close and seal the lid tight; then hit the yogurt button again.
7. Press the + button to change the time to 14hours. Taste the yogurt to make sure it is tart as soon as the Instant pot beeps.
8. Move the yogurt to the blender or food processor, then add gelatin powder and add rest of the ingredients.
9. Pulse the yogurt in a food blender until it becomes smooth
10. Transfer the yogurt into different glasses or different bowls and refrigerate the same for 2 - 3 hours

Tasty Passionfruit Yogurt.

Serving: 4 , Prep + Cook Time:20 minutes

Ingredients:
- full cream milk - 2 cans
- gelatin powder - 2 tbsp.
- vanilla paste - 1 tsp.
- high-quality probiotic - 4 capsules
- raw honey - 1 tbsp.
- passionfruit pulp - 1 ½ cups

Directions:
1. Add milk to the instant pot.
2. Cover the pot with the lid and lock it; then press the yogurt button and hit the adjust button till the display shows boil

3. Turn off the pot when the Instant Pot beeps, then open the lid and remove the metal bowl
4. Make use of a candy thermometer measure the temperature of the milk till it reaches a temperature of 239 F.
5. Pour the contents of probiotic capsules into the milk immediately the milk is cooled below 239 F.
6. Move the metal bowl back to the pot, then close and seal the lid tight; then hit the yogurt button again.

7. Press the + button to change the time to 14hours. Taste the yogurt to make sure it is tart as soon as the Instant pot beeps.
8. Move the yogurt to the blender or food processor, then add gelatin powder and add rest of the ingredients including the pulp.
9. Pulse the yogurt in a food blender until it becomes smooth
10. Transfer the yogurt into different glasses or different bowls and refrigerate the same for 2 - 3 hours

Tasty White Chocolate Yogurt.

Serving: 4 , **Prep + Cook Time:**20 minutes

Ingredients:
- gelatin powder - 2 tbsp.
- full cream milk - 2 cans
- vanilla paste - 1 tsp.
- raw honey - 1 tbsp.
- melted white chocolate - 1 cup
- high-quality probiotic - 4 capsules

Directions:
1. Add milk to the instant pot.
2. Cover the pot with the lid and lock it; then press the yogurt button and hit the adjust button till the display shows boil
3. Turn off the pot when the Instant Pot beeps, then open the lid and remove the metal bowl
4. Make use of a candy thermometer measure the temperature of the milk till it reaches a temperature of 239 F.
5. Pour the contents of probiotic capsules into the milk immediately the milk is cooled below 239 F.
6. Move the metal bowl back to the pot, then close and seal the lid tight; then hit the yogurt button again.
7. Press the + button to change the time to 14hours. Taste the yogurt to make sure it is tart as soon as the Instant pot beeps.
8. Move the yogurt to the blender or food processor, then add gelatin powder and add rest of the ingredients including white chocolate.
9. Pulse the yogurt in a food blender until it becomes smooth
10. Transfer the yogurt into different glasses or different bowls and refrigerate the same for 2 - 3 hours

Vegan Soy Yogurt Culture Recipe.

Serving: 4 , **Prep + Cook Time:**12 hours

Ingredients:
- soy milk - 1-quart; use only made soybeans and water; no vitamins or sugar added
- vegan yogurt culture - 1 packet
- Sweetener; if desired

Directions:
1. Add the soymilk into the wide mouth of a 1-quart Mason jar with lid or you can pour into multiple heatproof containers with each container having a lid.
2. Pour the vegan yogurt culture to the jar or container. Close and seal the lid and shake to ensure the ingredients mix. Open the lid from the jar because at this point you don't need it anymore.
3. Place the Mason jar directly into the Instant Pot container. Close and lock the Instant Pot lid. At this point, you are to leave the steam valve at "Sealing" or "Releasing" mode; this won't affect the cooking in any way. Hit the YOGURT button and set the timer to clock in at 12 hours.
4. Gently remove the Mason jar from the pot when the timer beeps immediately the cooking cycle is completed, then cover with the lid; then place in the refrigerator and keep it there for at least 6 hours
5. You can sweeten and/ or flavor, if you so desire. This will allow it stay in the refrigerator for up to 6 days.

Tips: This thick, creamy, unsweetened, tart soy yogurt can be used as a sour cream substitute or in recipes. You can enjoy it topped with pears and cinnamons; with bananas, shredded coconut and pecans, with jam or sweetened with coconut sugar. You can also strain it overnight to make yogurt cheese

Chapter 13 Sauce Recipes

Cold Apple sauce

Serving: 4 , Prep + Cook Time:18 minutes

Ingredients:
- Apples – 8; cored and chopped.
- cinnamon powder - 1 tsp.
- cinnamon oil - 2 drops
- water - 1 cup

Directions:

1. Place apples in your instant pot, then add water and close the pot by placing the lid on top. Cook at High for about 10 minutes.
2. Do a quick release of the pressure and gently open the lid of the instant pot. Also, add oil and cinnamon, then puree with an immersion blender. Serve the dish cold.

Seasoned Chili Jam

Serving: 12 , Prep + Cook Time:50 minutes

Ingredients:
- cranberries - 17 oz.
- sugar - 4 oz.
- red chili peppers – 4; seeded and chopped.
- garlic cloves - 4; minced.
- red onions - 2; finely chopped
- red wine vinegar - 2 tbsp.
- water -3 tbsp.
- A drizzle of olive oil
- Salt and black pepper to the taste

Directions:
1. Put your instant pot on Sauté mode; then add oil and turn on the heat.

2. Also, add onions, garlic and chilies, stir gently and cook for 8 minutes.
3. Proceed by adding cranberries, vinegar, water and sugar; then stir gently. Close the lid and cook at High mode for about 15 minutes.
4. Do a quick release the pressure and gently open the lid; mash sauce with the help of an immersion blender, then put the pot on Simmer mode and cook for about 15 minutes.
5. Season with salt and pepper, then transfer to jars and serve on demand.

Tasty Rhubarb Sauce Recipe

Serving: 6 , Prep + Cook Time:25 minutes

Ingredients:
- Rhubarb - 8 oz., trimmed and chopped.
- raisins - 1/4 cup
- water - 1/4 cup
- honey - 1/3 cup
- cider vinegar - 1 tbsp.
- small onion - 1; chopped.
- jalapeno peppers - 2; chopped.
- A pinch of cardamom, ground.
- garlic clove - 1; minced.

Directions:
1. Mix rhubarb with vinegar, onion, cardamom, garlic, jalapenos, honey, water, and raisins in your instant pot; then stir well. Seal the instant pot lid tight and cook at High for a little above 5 minutes.
2. Do a quick release of the pressure and gently open the lid; put it on Simmer mode and cook for another 3 minutes.
3. Serve on demand.

Tasty Orange Sauce

Serving: 6 , **Prep + Cook Time:**17 minutes

Ingredients:

- orange juice - 1 cup
- white wine vinegar - 1/4 cup
- agave nectar - 2 tbsp.
- veggie stock - 1/4 cup
- cornstarch - 2 tbsp.
- ginger paste - 1 tsp.
- tomato paste - 2 tbsp.
- Sugar - 3 tbsp.
- sesame oil - 1 tsp.
- chili sauce - 1 tsp.
- soy sauce - 2 tbsp.
- Garlic - 1 tsp.; finely chopped

Directions:

1. Put your instant pot on Sauté mode; then add oil and turn on the heat
2. Add garlic and ginger paste, stir gently and cook for 2 minutes.
3. Add tomato paste, sugar, orange juice, vinegar, agave nectar, soy and chili sauce; then stir well. Seal the instant pot lid tight and cook at High for another 3 minutes.
4. Do a quick release of the pressure and gently open the lid; also add stock and cornstarch; then stir gently. Close the instant pot lid tight again and cook at High mode for 4 minutes
5. Release pressure once more and serve your sauce right away.

Yummy Spaghetti Sauce

Serving: 6 , **Prep + Cook Time:**50 minutes

Ingredients:

- canned tomatoes - 28 oz., crushed.
- Beef - 1 ⅔ lb., ground.
- Carrots - 2; chopped.
- bay leaves - 2
- olive oil - 1 tbsp.
- garlic cloves - 4; minced.
- celery ribs - 2; chopped.
- yellow onion - 1; chopped.
- A pinch of oregano; dried
- A splash of red wine
- A pinch of basil; dried
- Salt and black pepper to the taste

For the chicken stock mix:

- 1 cup chicken stock
- 2 tbsp. soy sauce
- 3 tbsp. tomato paste
- 2 tbsp. fish sauce
- 1 tbsp. Worcestershire sauce

Directions:

1. Place the instant pot on Sauté mode; then pour some beef, salt, pepper and the oil into the pot, stir gently and let it brown for 7 minutes.
2. Move beef to a bowl when it's brown and keep it away for a while.
3. Mix stock with fish sauce, soy sauce, tomato paste and Worcestershire sauce in a clean bowl and stir gently.
4. Add heat to your instant pot once again, then add onions, garlic, bay leaves, basil and oregano to the pot. Stir gently and cook for 5 minutes.
5. Add celery, carrots, salt and pepper to the pot, stir gently and cook for 3 minutes.
6. Also, add red wine, chicken stock mix, beef and crushed tomatoes on top
7. Close the instant pot lid and seal it, then cook on High mode for 10 minutes
8. Do a quick release of the pressure, gently open the lid; if there is a need for it, you can add more salt and pepper. Place the pot on Simmer mode and cook the sauce for another 4 minutes.
9. When you want to serve, do so with your favorite pasta.

Seasoned Mango Sauce

Serving: 4 , Prep + Cook Time: 40 minutes

Ingredients:

- Mangos - 2; chopped
- Shallot - 1; chopped
- vegetable oil - 1 tbsp.
- salt - 2 tsp.
- raw sugar - 1 ¼ cup
- cider vinegar - 1 ¼ apple
- raisins - 1/4 cup
- cardamom powder - 1/4 tsp.
- Ginger - 2 tbsp.; minced.
- Cinnamon - 1/2 tsp.
- red hot chilies - 2; chopped.
- Apple – 1; cored and chopped.

Directions:

1. Put your instant pot on Sauté mode; add oil and turn on the heat
2. Add ginger and shallot, stir gently and cook for a time of 5 minutes
3. Add cinnamon, hot peppers and cardamom, stir gently and cook for 2 minutes.
4. Add mangos, apple, raisins, sugar and cider, stir and cook until the sugar disappears.
5. Place the lid on the pot and cook at High for 7 minutes.
6. Do a quick release of the pressure and gently open the lid. Move to a pan and simmer on medium heat for another 15 minutes. While cooking, stir occasionally.
7. Move to jars and serve on demand.

Tasty Fennel Sauce Recipe

Serving: 6 , Prep + Cook Time: 20 minutes

Ingredients:

- fennel bulb - 1, cut into pieces
- dry white wine - 1/4 cup
- thyme springs - 5
- olive oil - 3 tbsp.
- grape tomatoes - 2 pints', cut into halves
- A pinch of sugar
- Salt and black pepper to the taste

Directions:

1. Put your instant pot on Sauté mode; add oil and turn on the heat.
2. Add fennel, tomatoes, thyme, sugar, salt and pepper, stir gently and sauté for about 5 minutes.
3. Add white wine to the mix, close the lid and cook for another 4 minutes.
4. Do a quick release of the pressure and gently open the lid; remove the thyme, stir sauce properly and serve right away.

Yummy Bread Sauce recipe

Serving: 12 , Prep + Cook Time: 20 minutes

Ingredients:

- milk - 26 oz.
- bread - 6 slices, torn
- bay leaves - 2
- butter - 2 tbsp.
- garlic cloves - 2, crushed.
- yellow onion - 1; chopped.
- Cloves - 6
- Salt to the taste
- A splash of double cream

Directions:

1. Put your instant pot on Simmer mode, then add milk and turn up the heat.

2. Also, add garlic, cloves, onion, bay leaves and salt to the instant pot, stir well and cook for about 5 minutes.
3. Add bread; then stir once again. Seal the instant pot lid tight and cook at High mode for 4 minutes.
4. Do a quick release of the pressure, carefully open the lid; move sauce to a blender, then add butter and cream and do away with the bay leaf. Make sure to blend well.
5. Return sauce to the pot set it on Simmer mode and simmer sauce for another 3 minutes.

Sweet Asian Tomato Chutney

Serving: 6 , **Prep + Cook Time:** 20 minutes

Ingredients:

- Tomatoes - 3 lb.; peeled and chopped.
- Cinnamon - 3/4 tsp., ground.
- Cloves - 1/4 tsp.
- Coriander - 1/2 tsp., ground.
- chili powder - 1 tsp.
- red wine vinegar - 1 cup
- Sugar - 1 ¾ cups
- nutmeg - 1/4 tsp.
- Ginger - 1/4 tsp., ground.
- paprika - 1 pinch
- ginger piece - 1-inch, grated
- garlic cloves - 3; minced.
- Onions - 2; chopped.
- raisins - 1/4 cup

Directions:

1. Pour some tomatoes and grated ginger in your blender and mix, then pulse well and transfer the blend to your instant pot.
2. Follow this by adding vinegar, sugar, garlic, onions, raisins, cinnamon, cloves, coriander, nutmeg, ground ginger, paprika and chili powder; then stir gently. Close and seal the instant pot lid and cook at High mode for about 10 minutes
3. Do a quick release of the pressure and gently open the lid; move to different jars and serve on demand.

Yummy Grapes Sauce Recipe

Serving: 6 , **Prep + Cook Time:** 20 minutes

Ingredients:

- black grapes - 6 oz.
- water - 1/2 cup
- sugar - 2 ½ tbsp.
- corn flour - 1 cup
- A splash of lemon juice

Directions:

1. Introduce some grapes to your instant pot, then add water to cover it up. Cook at High mode for 7 minutes then release pressure, and let the mix cool down by leaving it aside for a while.
2. Blend the mix with the help of an immersion blender, strain sauce and put it aside for sometime.
3. Place a pan over medium-high heat, then add grapes mix, sugar, water and corn flour, stir gently and boil until it gets thicker.
4. Add lemon juice; then stir gently. Turn off the heat and serve on demand.

Sweet Barbeque Sauce Recipe

Serving: 8 , **Prep + Cook Time:** 20 minutes

Ingredients:

- white wine vinegar - 4 tbsp.
- plums - 5 oz.; dried and seedless
- sesame seed oil - 1 tbsp.
- tomato puree - 1/2 cup
- yellow onion - 1; chopped.
- honey - 4 tbsp.
- salt - 1 tsp.
- granulated garlic - 1/2 tsp.
- cumin powder - 1/8 tsp.
- liquid smoke - 1 tsp.
- Tabasco sauce - 1 tsp.
- clove powder - 1/8 tsp.
- water - 1/2 cup

Directions:

1. Put the instant pot on Sauté mode; then pour some oil into the pot and turn up the heat.
2. Then add some onions to the pot, stir gently and cook for about 5 minutes.
3. Also, pour some tomato puree, honey, water, vinegar, salt, garlic, Tabasco sauce, liquid smoke, cumin and clove powder to the pot and stir all of the ingredients well.

4. Add plums to the mix and stir again; ensure to stir well.
5. Close the instant pot lid tight and cook at High mode for 10 minutes

6. Do a quick release of the pressure and carefully remove the lid; pulse everything using an immersion blender, move the sauce to a bowl and serve right away.

Seasoned Giblet Gravy

Serving: 2 , Prep + Cook Time: 1 hour and 30 minutes

Ingredients:
- Turkey neck, gizzard, but and heart
- vegetable oil - 1 tbsp.
- butter - 4 tbsp.
- thyme springs - 2
- turkey stock - 1-quart
- bay leaf - 1
- white flour - 4 tbsp.
- dry vermouth - 1/2 cup
- yellow onion - 1; chopped.
- Salt and black pepper to the taste

Directions:
1. Put your instant pot on Sauté mode; add oil and turn on the heat.
2. Add turkey pieces and onion, stir gently and cook for 3 minutes.
3. Do the stirring again and cook for another 3 minutes.
4. Add vermouth, stock, as well as bay leaf and thyme; stir again.
5. Seal the instant pot lid tight and cook at High mode for a little above 30 minutes.
6. Let the pressure release naturally for 20 minutes then release the rest of the pressure by turning the valve to 'Venting', and gently opening the lid.
7. Strain the stock, reserve turkey gizzard, and heart, and allow them to cool; then remove gristle and cut it along with the heart.
8. Add heat to a pan containing the butter using medium heat, then add flour, stir gently and cook for 3 minutes
9. Add strained stock, stir gently and increase heat to medium high; then simmer for 20 minutes
10. Add salt and pepper as seasoning, then add heart and gizzard; stir well and serve on demand.

Tasty Strawberry Sauce

Serving: 8 , Prep + Cook Time: 12 minutes

Ingredients:
- Strawberries - 1 lb., cut into halves
- sugar - 1/8 cup
- vanilla extract - 1/2 tsp.
- orange juice - 1 oz.
- A pinch of ginger, ground.

Directions:
1. Mix strawberries with sugar in your instant pot, stir gently and keep them aside for 10 minutes
2. Add orange juice; then stir gently. Close the instant pot lid and cook at High mode for 2 minutes.
3. Let the pressure release naturally for 15 minutes then release the rest of the pressure by turning the valve to 'Venting', gently open the lid of the pot; then pour vanilla extract and ginger to the mix.
4. Puree with the help an immersion blender and keep it aside until it is cold enough.
5. Serve your strawberry sauce with as a side dish, preferably tasty pancakes

Seasoned Cilantro Sauce

Serving: 6 , **Prep + Cook Time:** 12 minutes

Ingredients:

- garlic cloves - 3; minced.
- olive oil - 1 tbsp.
- Scallions - 3; chopped.
- Tomatoes - 3; chopped.
- red chilies - 2; minced.
- Shallots - 3; minced.
- Cilantro - 2 tbsp.; chopped.
- water - 1/4 cup
- Salt and black pepper to the taste

Directions:

1. Put your instant pot on Sauté mode; add oil and turn on the heat
2. Add garlic, shallots and chilies, stir gently and cook for 3 minutes.
3. Add scallions, tomatoes, water, salt, pepper and cilantro; then stir well. Close the instant pot lid and cook on High mode for 3 minutes.
4. Do a quick release of the pressure and gently open the lid; pulse with the aid of an immersion blender and serve.

Tasty Carrot Sauce

Serving: 6 , **Prep + Cook Time:** 25 minutes

Ingredients:

- carrot juice - 2 cups
- butter - 4 tbsp.
- mixed chervil - 1 tbsp., chives and tarragon
- Salt and black pepper to the taste
- A pinch of cayenne pepper
- A pinch of cinnamon

Directions:

1. Place the carrot juice in your instant pot, place the pot on Simmer mode and bring to a boil.
2. Add butter, salt, pepper, cayenne and cinnamon to the mix; then stir gently. Seal the instant pot lid tight and cook at High mode for 5 minutes.
3. Do a quick release of the pressure and gently open the lid; add mixed herbs, stir gently and serve

Tasty Dates Sauce

Serving: 6 , **Prep + Cook Time:** 20 minutes

Ingredients:

- Dates - 2 cups; dried
- lemon juice - 1 tbsp.
- apple juice - 2 cups

Directions:

1. Mix apple juice with lemon juice and dates in your instant pot; then stir well. Close the

instant pot lid and cook at High mode for almost 10 minutes.

2. Do a quick release of the pressure and gently open the lid; pulse with the aid an immersion blender and move to a container

Tasty Chestnut Sauce

Serving: 6 , **Prep + Cook Time:** 30 minutes

Ingredients:

- Chestnuts - 1 ½ lb; cut into halves and peeled
- rum liquor - 1/8 cup
- sugar - 11 oz.
- water - 11 oz.

Directions:

1. Mix sugar with water, rum, and chestnuts in your instant pot.
2. Stir, then seal tight the instant pot lid and cook at High mode for 20 minutes.
3. Release pressure for about 10 minutes then remove the instant pot lid and blend all of it using an immersion blender.
4. Serve on demand.

Seasoned Broccoli Sauce Recipe

Serving: 4 , **Prep + Cook Time:** 16 minutes

Ingredients:
- broccoli florets - 3 cups
- water - 6 cups
- garlic cloves - 2; minced.
- nutritional yeast - 1 tbsp.
- coconut milk - 1/3 cup
- olive oil - 1 tbsp.
- white wine vinegar - 1 tbsp.
- Salt and black pepper to the taste

Directions:
1. Add water to your instant pot.
2. Add broccoli, salt, pepper and garlic to the pot; then stir gently. Seal the instant pot lid tight and cook at High mode for a little above 5 minutes.
3. Do a quick release of the pressure and gently open the lid; strain broccoli and garlic and move to a food processor.
4. Pour some coconut milk, vinegar, yeast, olive oil as well as salt and pepper to taste; ensure to blend very well.
5. Serve over pasta

Tasty Plum Sauce Recipe

Serving: 20 , **Prep + Cook Time:** 25 minutes

Ingredients:
- Plumps - 3 lb., pitted and chopped.
- Apples - 2, cored and chopped.
- Ginger - 4 tbsp., ground.
- Salt - 1 ½ tbsp.
- Onions - 2; chopped.
- Cinnamon - 4 tbsp.
- allspice - 4 tbsp.
- Vinegar - 1-pint
- Sugar - 3/4 lb.

Directions:
1. Place the plumps, apples, and chopped onions in your instant pot
2. Add ginger, cinnamon, allspice, salt and almost the entirety of the vinegar; then stir well. Close the instant pot lid tight and cook at High mode for 10 minutes.
3. Do a quick release of the pressure and gently open the lid; put it on Simmer mode, add the remaining vinegar and the sugar, stir gently `and cook until all of the sugar disappears.

Tasty Cherry Sauce Recipe

Serving: 4 , **Prep + Cook Time:** 15 minutes

Ingredients:
- lemon juice - 1 tbsp.
- sugar - 1 tbsp.
- water - 1/4 cup
- cherries - 2 cups
- kirsch - 1 tsp.
- cornstarch - 2 tbsp.
- A pinch of salt

Directions:
1. Mix water with lemon juice, salt, sugar, kirsch and cornstarch in your instant pot.
2. Add cherries; then stir gently. Seal the instant pot lid tight and cook at High mode for 5 minutes.
3. Do a quick release of the pressure and gently open the lid; move the sauce to a bowl and serve when it gets cold.

Seasoned Eggplant Sauce Recipe

Serving: 6 , **Prep + Cook Time:** 30 minutes

Ingredients:
- Eggplant - 1; chopped.
- canned tomato paste - 5 oz.
- ground meat - 1 lb.
- canned tomatoes - 28 oz.; chopped.
- garlic cloves - 5; minced.
- Parsley - 1/4 cup; chopped.
- sweet onion - 1; chopped.
- apple cider vinegar - 1 tbsp.
- turmeric - 1/2 tsp.
- bone stock - 1 cup
- dill - 1/2 tsp.; dried
- olive oil - 1/2 cup
- Salt and black pepper to the taste

Directions:
1. Put the instant pot on Sauté mode; add meat, brown for a few minutes before moving to a bowl.
2. Add heat to your instant pot containing oil, then add onion and some salt and cook for 2 minutes.
3. Add eggplant and garlic, stir gently and cook for 1 minute.
4. Add vinegar, stir again and gently; then cook for 2 minutes
5. Add tomato paste, tomatoes, meat, salt, pepper, parsley, dill, turmeric and stock; then stir well. Seal the instant pot lid tight and cook at High mode for 15 minutes.
6. Do a quick release of the pressure and gently open the lid; add more salt and pepper to taste as well as a splash of lemon juice. Finally, stir well and serve right away.

Seasoned Tomato Sauce

Serving: 20 , **Prep + Cook Time:** 25 minutes

Ingredients:
- Tomatoes - 2 lb.; peeled and chopped.
- Apple - 1, cored and chopped.
- whole spice - 3 tsp.
- brown sugar - 1/2 lb.
- vinegar - 1/2-pint
- yellow onion - 1; chopped.
- Sultanas - 6 oz.; chopped.
- dates chopped - 3 oz.
- Salt to the taste

Directions:
1. Add some tomatoes to your instant pot
2. Then add apple, onion, sultanas, dates, salt, whole spice and ½ of the vinegar and stir gently. Close the lid of the instant pot tight and cook at High mode for about10 minutes.
3. Do a quick release of the pressure, and gently open the lid; put it on Simmer mode, and pour the remaining the vinegar and sugar, stir gently and simmer until all the sugar becomes soluble.
4. Move to different jars and serve on demand.

Quince Sauce Served with Cake

Serving: 6 , **Prep + Cook Time:** 25 minutes

Ingredients:
- grated quince - 2 lb.
- sugar - 2 lb.
- water - 1/4 cup
- lemon juice - 1
- cloves - 10

Directions:
1. Mix quince with sugar in your instant pot and stir well
2. Add water to the pot and stir once again
3. Tie cloves in a cheesecloth and add to the pot as well
4. Cover the pot and cook at High mode for 10 minutes.
5. Release pressure for 10 minutes before you open the lid; then stir the sauce again and move to different jars.
6. Serve as toppings for cakes.

Sweetened Melon Sauce Recipe

Serving: 6 , **Prep + Cook Time:** 15 minutes

Ingredients:
- Sugar - 1 oz.
- butter - 1 tbsp.
- starch - 1 tsp.
- sweet wine - 1 cup
- Flesh of small melon – 1
- Lemon Juice – 1

Directions:
1. Introduce the melon and sweet wine to your instant pot, then seal the instant pot lid tight and cook at High mode for a little above 5 minutes
2. Do a quick release of the pressure, move sauce to a blender, then add lemon juice, sugar, butter and starch and pulse well.
3. Move the sauce back to your instant pot, then put it on Simmer mode and cook sauce for 3 minutes until it becomes thick.
4. Serve immediately.

Seasoned Parsley Sauce Recipe

Serving: 6 , **Prep + Cook Time:** 17 minutes

Ingredients:
- Parsley - 4 tbsp.; chopped.
- chicken stock - 2 cups
- flour - 2 tbsp.
- whole milk - 3/4 cup
- yellow onion - 1; finely chopped
- egg yolk – 1
- cup heavy cream - 1/4
- butter - 2 tbsp.
- Salt and white pepper to the taste

Directions:
1. Place stock and onion in your instant pot, then put the pot on Simmer mode and bring to a boil
2. Add medium-high heat to a pan containing butter, then add flour and stir well to mix properly.
3. Add the mix and whole milk on stock and stir very well.
4. Bring to a boil, then add parsley and stir well. Seal the instant pot lid tight and cook at High mode for 2 minutes.
5. Do a quick release of the pressure, then remove the lid of the instant pot and put it back on Simmer mode
6. Mix cream with egg yolk in a clean bowl together with some of the sauce from the pot.
7. Stir this gently, pour over the sauce and whisk well.
8. Add salt and pepper as seasoning, stir again and cook for a couple of minutes until it becomes thick. Serve with chicken and some rice.

Ginger and Orange Mix Sauce

Serving: 4 , **Prep + Cook Time:** 12 minutes

Ingredients:
- ginger piece - 1-inch; chopped
- olive oil - 1 tbsp.
- fish stock - 1 cup
- spring onions - 4; chopped.
- Salt and black pepper to the taste
- Zest and juice from 1 orange

Directions:
1. Mix fish stock with salt, pepper, olive oil, spring onions, ginger, orange juice and zest in your instant pot and stir gently.
2. Seal the instant pot lid tight and cook at High mode for a little over 5 minutes.
3. Do a quick release of the pressure and remove the instant pot lid and serve your sauce on demand.

Seasoned Leeks Sauce

Serving: 8 , **Prep + Cook Time:** 12 minutes

Ingredients:
- Leeks - 2, thinly sliced
- butter - 2 tbsp.
- whipping cream- 1 cup
- lemon juice - 3 tbsp.
- Salt and pepper to the taste

Directions:
1. Put your instant pot on Sauté mode; then add butter to it and melt it.
2. Add leeks to the pot, stir gently and cook for 2 minutes.
3. Add lemon juice to the mix; then stir gently. Seal the instant pot lid properly and cook at High mode for 3 minutes
4. Do a quick release of the pressure, and gently open the lid; move the sauce to your blender, then add whipping cream and pulse all of the mix.
5. Move the sauce back to the pot, then put the pot on Simmer mode. Also, add salt and pepper as seasoning, stir gently and cook for 2 minutes.
6. Serve with fish

Yummy Cheese Sauce Recipe

Serving: 4 , **Prep + Cook Time:** 15 minutes

Ingredients:
- processed cheese - 2 cups, cut into chunks
- Italian sausage; - 1 cup cooked and chopped.
- Water- 4 tbsp.
- canned tomatoes and green chilies - 5 oz.; finely chopped

Directions:
1. Mix sausage with cheese, tomatoes and chilies and water in your instant pot.
2. Stir gently, seal the instant pot lid tight and cook at High mode for 5 minutes.
3. Do a quick release of the pressure and gently open the lid; move the sauce back to a clean bowl and serve with your favorite macaroni.

Tasty Pineapple Sauce

Serving: 4 , **Prep + Cook Time:** 13 minutes

Ingredients:
- pineapple tidbits - 3 cups
- rum - 3 tbsp.
- Cinnamon - 1 tsp.
- ginger - 1 tsp.
- allspice - 1 tsp.
- nutmeg - 1 tsp.
- butter - 3 tbsp.
- brown sugar - 4 tbsp.

Directions:
1. Put your instant pot on sauté mode; then add butter and let it melt completely.
2. Then, add sugar, pineapple tidbits, rum, allspice, nutmeg, cinnamon and ginger to the pot of melted butter and stir well. Seal the instant pot lid tight and cook at High mode for 3 minutes.
3. Do a quick release of the pressure and gently open the lid; stir sauce once more and serve on demand.

Sweet Elderberry Sauce Recipe

Serving: 20 , **Prep + Cook Time:** 20 minutes

Ingredients:
- elderberries - 1 cup
- ginger piece - 1-inch, grated
- cloves - 5
- water - 4 cups
- cinnamon stick - 1
- honey - 1 cup
- vanilla bean - 1, split

Directions:
1. Mix elderberries with water, ginger, cinnamon, vanilla and cloves in your instant pot; then stir well. Close the instant pot lid and ensure it is sealed tight. Cook at High mode for 10 minutes.
2. Do a quick release of the pressure, then strain sauce and hold the sauce in jars.

Seasoned Corn Sauce Recipe

Serving: 4 , **Prep + Cook Time:** 16 minutes

Ingredients:
- corn kernels - 2 cups
- chicken stock - 1 ¾ cups
- white wine - 1/4 cup
- thyme spring - 1
- white flour - 1 tsp.
- butter - 2 tsp.
- Yellow onion – 1; chopped.
- olive oil - 1 tbsp.
- Thyme - 1 tsp.; finely chopped
- Salt and black pepper to the taste

Directions:
1. Put your instant pot on Sauté mode; then pour some oil into the pot and turn on the heat.
2. Add onion, stir gently and well; cook for 3 minutes.
3. Then add flour, stir well and cook for another minute.
4. Also, add wine, stir gently and cook for a minute.
5. Add thyme spring, stock and corn; then stir well. Cover the pot with the lid and seal tight; cook at High for 1 minute.
6. Do a quick release of the pressure and gently open the lid of the pot; do away with the thyme spring and move the corn sauce to a blender.
7. Sprinkle a pinch of salt and pepper to taste; then add butter as well as chopped thyme and pulse well.
8. Go back to the pot; then set it on Sauté mode again and cook for another 1 to 2 minutes.
9. Serve on demand

Guava Sauce with Fish

Serving: 6 , **Prep + Cook Time:** 30 minutes

Ingredients:
- guava shells and syrup - 1 can
- onions - 2; chopped.
- garlic cloves - 2; chopped.
- nutmeg - 1/2 tsp.
- bird chilies - 2; chopped.
- ginger piece - 1-inch; minced.
- vegetable oil - 1/4 cup
- Lemon juice – 2

Directions:
1. Place guava shells and syrup in your blender, pulse well and put it aside for a while.
2. Put the instant pot on Sauté mode; then pour some oil into the pot and turn on the heat.
3. Add onion and garlic, stir and cook for 4 minutes
4. Also, add guava mix, ginger, lemon juice, chilies and nutmeg to the pot; then stir gently. Close the instant pot lid and seal tight; cook on High mode for 15 minutes.
5. Do a quick release of the pressure, remove the instant pot lid and serve sauce with fish

Tasty Peach Sauce Recipe

Serving: 6 , **Prep + Cook Time:** 8 minutes

Ingredients:

- Peaches - 10 oz., stoned and chopped.
- cornstarch - 2 tbsp.
- sugar - 3 tbsp.
- water - 1/2 cup
- almond extract - 1/8 tsp.
- nutmeg - 1/8 tsp., ground.
- Cinnamon - 1/8 tsp.
- A pinch of salt

Directions:

1. Mix peaches with nutmeg, cornstarch, sugar, cinnamon and salt in your instant pot; stir well. Close the instant pot lid and ensure it is sealed tight; cook at High for 3 minutes.
2. Do a quick release the pressure, gently open the lid; add almond extract, stir well and serve the sauce.

Tasty Mustard Sauce Recipe

Serving: 4 , **Prep + Cook Time:** 18 minutes

Ingredients:

- Mushrooms - 6 oz.; chopped.
- beef stock - 3.5 oz.
- dry sherry - 3.5 oz.
- thyme spring - 1
- garlic clove - 1; minced.
- Parsley - 2 tbsp.; finely chopped
- olive oil - 3 tbsp.
- balsamic vinegar - 1 tbsp.
- mustard - 1 tbsp.
- crème fraiche - 2 tbsp.

Directions:

1. Put your instant pot on Sauté mode; pour some oil into the pot and turn on the heat.
2. Then add garlic, thyme and mushrooms to the pot, stir gently and cook for 5 minutes.
3. Also, add sherry wine, vinegar, stock to the mix and stir gently. Cover the pot with the lid and seal tight; then cook at High mode for 3 minutes.
4. Do a quick release of the pressure and gently open the lid; do away with the thyme, then add crème fraiche, mustard, and parsley. Ensure to stir the mix well.
5. Put the pot on Simmer mode and cook the sauce for about 3 minutes.
6. Serve immediately.

Chapter 14 Desserts

Eggnog Cheese Cake

Serves: 6, Prep + Cooking Time: 35 minutes

Ingredients:

- Cream cheese, soft-16 oz.
- 2 eggs
- Butter, melted-2 tbsp.
- Bum-1 tbsp.
- Ginger cookies, crumbled. - 1/2 cup
- Sugar-1/2 cup
- Water-2 cups
- Vanilla-1/2 tbsp.
- Nutmeg, ground. - 1/2 tbsp.

Directions:

1. Use butter to grease an already cleaned pan, put cookie crumbs and spread them in an even manner.
2. Beat cream cheese with a mixer using a bowl.
3. Add vanilla, rum, nutmeg, and eggs and stir thoroughly.
4. Transfer the mixture into the steamer basket of your instant pot, pour the water inside the pot, cover the instant pot with the lid and allow to cook at High for about 15 minutes.
5. Release the pressure quickly and carefully open the lid; bring the cheesecake out, and leave to stand till cool. Place in the fridge for about 4 hours prior to slicing and serving.

Recipe for Ricotta Cake

Serves: 6 , Prep + Cooking Time: 60 minutes

Ingredients:

- Dates, soaked for 15 minutes and drained-6 oz.
- Ricotta-1 lb.
- Honey softened-2 oz.
- 4 eggs
- Sugar-2 oz.
- Water-17 oz.
- Orange juice and zest from ½ orange
- Some vanilla extract

Directions:

1. Using a clean bowl, soften the ricotta by whisking continuously.
2. Using another clean bowl, whisk eggs thoroughly.
3. Combine the mixtures above and stir thoroughly.
4. Put dates, orange zest, honey, vanilla, and juice to the ricotta mixture and stir yet again
5. Transfer the batter into a heat resistant dish and cover with a clean tin foil
6. Position the dish in the steamer basket compartment of instant pot, pour water in the pot, cover the instant pot with the lid and allow to cook at High for about 20 minutes
7. Release the pressure quickly and carefully open the lid; allow the cake to cool, transfer to a neat platter, slice and serve.

Mix Berries Compote

Serves: 8, **Prep + Cooking Time:** 15 minutes

Ingredients:
- 1 cup blueberries
- Lemon juice-2 tbsp.
- Sugar-3/4 cup
- Cornstarch-1 tbsp.
- Water-1 tbsp.
- Strawberries, sliced-2 cups

Directions:
1. In a clean instant pot, mix blueberries with lemon juice and sugar; then stir thoroughly.
2. Cover the instant pot with the lid and allow it to cook at High for up to 3 minutes.
3. Allow the pressure to release naturally for up to 10 minutes and open the lid carefully
4. In a clean bowl, combine cornstarch and water, stir vigorously and pour into the instant pot.
5. Stir again, position the pot on Sauté mode and let compote cook for additional 2 minutes
6. Apportion into jars and keep in the fridge until you are ready to serve it.

Recipe for Pumpkin Chocolate Cake

Serves: 12 , **Prep + Cooking Time:** 55 minutes

Ingredients:
- Pumpkin pie spice-3/4 tbsp.
- Greek yogurt-1/2 cup
- 1 banana, mashed
- Canola oil-2 tbsp.
- A pinch of salt
- Whole wheat flour-3/4 cup
- Vanilla extract-1/2 tbsp.
- Chocolate chips-2/3 cup
- Baking soda-1 tbsp.
- One egg
- Sugar-3/4 cup
- Canned pumpkin puree-8 oz.
- Water-1-quart
- White flour-3/4 cup
- Baking powder-1/2 tbsp.
- Cooking spray

Directions:

1. Using a clean bowl, mix whole wheat flour with white flour, baking soda and powder, salt and pumpkin spice and stir.
2. Using another bowl, combine sugar, oil, yogurt, pumpkin puree, banana, vanilla, and egg then stir using a mixer.
3. Mix the 2 mixtures above, add chocolate chips then mix everything together.
4. Transfer the above into an already greased Bundt pan, seal pan with clean paper towels and foil then place in the steamer basket of the instant pot.
5. Pour 1-quart water into the pot, cover the instant pot with its lid and leave to cook at High for up to 35 minutes.
6. Let the pressure release naturally for about 10 minutes then release remaining part of the pressure by positioning the valve to 'Venting', open the lid carefully; leave the cake to stand to cool, cut then serve it.

Recipe for Poached Figs

Serves: 4 , **Prep + Cooking Time:** 17 minutes

Ingredients:
- Figs-1 lb.
- Red wine-1 cup
- Pine nuts, toasted-1/2 cup
- Sugar-1/2 cup

For the yogurt crème:
- Plain yogurt-2 lb.

Directions:
1. Pour the yogurt in a strainer, strain well and transfer to a clean bowl, keep inside the fridge overnight.
2. Pour the wine into the already washed instant pot, put figs inside the steamer basket, cover

the instant pot with the lid and allow to cook on Low for not less than 4 minutes.

3. Release the pressure quickly, open the lid carefully; evacuate the figs then arrange them on clean plates.

4. Put the instant pot on Simmer mode, add sugar then stir
5. Allow cooking until the sugar melts, then drizzle the sauce over figs
6. Also, put yogurt crème on the top or the side and serve immediately.

Recipe for Peach Compote

Serves: 6 , **Prep + Cooking Time:** 13 minutes

Ingredients:
- 1 vanilla bean, scraped
- Grape nuts cereal-2 tbsp.
- 8 peaches; chopped.
- Sugar-6 tbsp.
- Cinnamon, ground. - 1 tbsp.
- vanilla extract-1 tbsp.

Directions:

1. Transfer peaches into a clean instant pot then mix with vanilla bean, cinnamon, sugar and vanilla extract. Stir thoroughly, seal the lid and allow to cook at High for up to 3 minutes.
2. Let go the pressure for about 10 minutes put grape nuts, stir thoroughly and then transfer the compote into bowls and serve

Chocolate Cheese cake

Serves: 12 , **Prep + Cooking Time:** 2 hours,

Ingredients:
For the crust:
- Melted butter-4 tbsp.
- Chocolate cookie crumbs-1 ½ cups

For the filling:
- Cream cheese, soft-24 oz.
- Cornstarch-2 tbsp.
- Greek yogurt-1/2 cup
- Sugar-1 cup
- 3 eggs
- Vanilla extract-1 tbsp.
- Cooking sprays
- Bittersweet chocolate-4 oz.
- White chocolate-4 oz.
- Milk chocolate-4 oz.
- Water-1 cup

Directions:
1. Using a clean bowl, combine butter with cookie crumbs and stir thoroughly.
2. Use some cooking oil to spray springform pan, then line using a clean parchment paper, press butter and crumbs mix on the bottom and keep in the freezer for further use.
3. In another bowl, combine cream cornstarch, cheese and sugar and stir using a mixer.
4. Combine vanilla, eggs, and yogurt then stir once again to mix all the ingredients, then apportion into 3 bowls.

5. Add milk chocolate in a heat resistant bowl and heat it up in the microwave for close to 30 seconds
6. Combine what you get in step 5 with one of the bowls that have the batter you've made before and stir thoroughly
7. Pour white and dark chocolate in 2 heat resistant bowls and heat them up for 30 seconds using the microwave.
8. Combine the above with the other 2 bowls that have the cheesecake batter, stir and place them all in the fridge for about 30 minutes
9. Remove bowls out of the fridge and layer your cheesecake
10. Let the dark chocolate batter be at the center of the crust.
11. Use white chocolate batter as the topping and distribute evenly then add milk chocolate batter
12. Put the pan in the steamer basket of your pot, add 1 cup water in the pot, seal the instant pot lid and cook at High for 45 minutes
13. Release pressure for 10 minutes take the cake out of the pot, leave aside to cool down and serve.

Classic Rhubarb Compote

Serves: 8 , **Prep + Cooking Time:** 40 minutes

Ingredients:

- Strawberries; chopped. - 1 lb.
- Water-1/3 cup
- Honey-3 tbsp.
- Rhubarb; chopped. - 2 lb.
- Some fresh mint, torn

Directions:

1. Introduce water and rhubarb in your instant pot, seal the lid, then cook at High for about 10 minutes release pressure and open the lid carefully.
2. Introduce honey and strawberries; then stir thoroughly.
3. Put the pot on Simmer mode and allow compote to cook for 20 minutes.
4. Put mint; then stir again. Apportion into jars and serve.

Recipe for Pina Colada Pudding

Serves: 8 , **Prep + Cooking Time:** 15 minutes

Ingredients:

- Vanilla extract-1/2 tbsp.
- Milk-1/2 cup
- Sugar-1/2 cup
- Canned pineapple tidbits, drained and halved-8 oz.
- Canned coconut milk-14 oz.
- Coconut oil-1 tbsp.
- 2 eggs
- Water-1 ½ cups
- Arborio rice-1 cup
- A pinch of salt

Directions:

1. In a clean instant pot, combine oil, rice, water, and salt; then stir thoroughly. Cover the instant pot with its lid and leave to cook at High for close to 3 minutes.
2. Let the pressure release naturally for 10 minutes then release the remaining part of the pressure by turning the valve to 'Venting' position, open the lid carefully; add coconut milk and sugar then stir again.
3. Using a clean bowl, mix vanilla, eggs, and milk stir and pour the mixture over rice.
4. Stir again, put the pot on Sauté mode and leave to boil
5. Put pineapple tidbits; then stir again. Apportion into dessert bowls then serve

Recipe for Ruby Pears Delight

Serves: 4 , **Prep + Cooking Time:** 20 minutes

Ingredients:

- 4 Pears
- Grape juice-26 oz.
- Currant jelly-11 oz.
- 4 garlic cloves
- Juice and zest of 1 lemon
- 4 peppercorns
- 2 rosemary springs
- 1/2 vanilla bean

Directions:

1. Pour the jelly and grape juice in your instant pot and mix with lemon zest and juice
2. In the mix, dip each pear and wrap them in a clean tin foil and place them orderly in the steamer basket of your instant pot
3. Combine peppercorns, rosemary, garlic cloves and vanilla bean to the juice mixture,
4. Seal the lid and cook at High for 10 minutes.
5. Release the pressure quickly, and carefully open the lid; bring out the pears, remove wrappers and arrange them on plates. Serve when cold with toppings of cooking juice.

Instant Pot Banana Cake

Serves: 5 , **Prep + Cooking Time:** 60 minutes

Ingredients:
- 3 bananas, peeled and mashed
- Water-1 cup
- Sugar-1 ½ cups
- Cinnamon-1 tbsp.
- 1 stick butter, soft
- Nutmeg-1 tbsp.
- 2 cups flour
- Baking powder-2 tbsp.
- A pinch of salt
- 2 eggs

Directions:

1. Using a clean bowl, combine eggs with sugar and butter and stir thoroughly
2. Put salt, cinnamon, baking powder, and nutmeg stir well again.
3. Put the flour and bananas and stir once again.
4. Use butter to grease a springform pan, then transfer the batter into it and cover the pan with a clean paper towel and a tin foil.
5. Pour a cup of water into the instant pot, position the pan in the pot, cover the instant pot lid and cook at High for about 55 minutes
6. Release pressure quickly and remove the pot, let the cake stand to cool, slice and serve.

Recipe for Brownie Cake

Serves: 6, **Prep + Cooking Time:** 60 minutes

Ingredients:
- Borlotti beans, soaked for 8 hours and drained-1 cup
- Water-4 cups

For the cake:
- Almond extract-1/8 tbsp.
- Raw sugar-1/2 cup
- Almonds, sliced-1/4 cup
- Baking powder-2 tbsp.
- A pinch of salt
- Cocoa powder-1/2 cup
- Extra virgin olive oil-3 tbsp.
- 2 eggs

Directions:

1. In an already cleaned instant pot put beans and water then close the lid, allow to cook at High for about 12 minutes release pressure and open the lid carefully; transfer beans to a blender and puree them after straining.
2. Empty water from the pot and ensure to keep 1 cup
3. Using some olive oil, grease a heat-resistant bowl and put aside for later use.
4. Put the beans in the blender then add almond extract, honey cocoa powder, eggs, salt and oil and puree everything for 1 minute.
5. Place the mix in the already greased bowl, spread then put the bowl in the steamer basket of instant pot, add reserved water from cooking the beans,
6. Cover the instant pot with the lid and cook at High for about 20 minutes.
7. Quick-release pressure and take cake out of the pot put it aside for 15 minutes
8. Transfer cake to a plate then sprinkle the top with almonds, slice it then serve.

Dulce De Leche Recipe

Serves: 6 , **Prep + Cooking Time:** 35 minutes

Ingredients:
- Canned sweetened condensed milk. - 16 oz.
- Water to cover

Directions:

1. In the steamer basket compartment of your instant pot, put condensed milk can and add water in the pot, cover the instant pot with the lid and cook at High for about 20 minutes.
2. Let the pressure release naturally, and carefully open the lid; remove can from the pot and place aside to cool.

Carrot Cake Recipe

Serves: 6 , **Prep + Cooking Time:** 40 minutes

Ingredients:

- Baking soda-1/2 tbsp.
- 5 oz. flour
- A pinch of salt
- Yogurt-3 tbsp.
- Water-2 cups
- Cooking spray
- Carrots, grated-1/3 cup
- Sugar-1/2 cup
- Pineapple juice-1/4 cup
- Coconut oil, melted-4 tbsp.
- Cinnamon powder-1/2 tbsp.
- Baking powder-3/4 tbsp.
- Nutmeg, ground. - 1/4 tbsp.
- Allspice-1/2 tbsp.
- Pecans, toasted and chopped. - 1/3 cup
- Coconut flakes-1/3 cup
- One egg

Directions:

1. Using a clean bowl, combine flour with salt, cinnamon, baking soda and powder, salt, allspice, and nutmeg and stir.
2. In another clean bowl, combine the egg with pineapple juice, yogurt, sugar, oil, carrots, coconut flakes, and pecans and stir thoroughly.
3. Mix the two mixtures above and stir thoroughly again.
4. Grease a springform with some cooking spray then pour 2 cups water in your instant pot and put the form into the steamer basket of the pot.
5. Cover the pot with the lid and allow it to cook at High for about 32 minutes.
6. Endeavor to release pressure for about 10 minutes evacuate cake from the pot, and allow to stand for cooling, slice it and serve.

Recipe Peach Jam

Serves: 6 , **Prep + Cooking Time:** 15 minutes

Ingredients:

- Peaches, peeled and cubed-4 ½ cups
- 1 box fruit pectin
- Sugar-6 cups
- Crystallized ginger; chopped. - 1/4 cup

Directions:

1. Adjust instant pot to Simmer mode, put ginger, pectin, and peaches, stir and bring to a boil
2. Add sugar and stir thoroughly. cover the instant pot with the lid and cook at High for about 5 minutes.
3. Release the pressure quickly, and open the lid carefully, apportion jam into jars and serve.

Recipe of Chocolate Fondue

Serves: 4 , **Prep + Cooking Time:** 12 minutes

Ingredients:

- Dark chocolate, cut into chunks-3.5 oz.
- Water-2 cups
- Liquor-1 tbsp.
- Sugar-1 tbsp.
- Crème fraiche-3.5 oz.

Directions:

1. Using a heat resistant container, combine chocolate chunks with crème Fraiche, liquor and sugar.
2. In a clean instant pot, pour some water and place the container in the steamer basket, close the pot with the lid and cook at High for about 2 minutes.
3. Release pressure naturally and carefully open the lid; take the container out, stir fondue thoroughly and serve immediately with some fresh fruits.

Pots of Lemon Crème

Serves: 4 , **Prep + Cooking Time:** 35 minutes

Ingredients:

- Blackberry syrup for serving
- Fresh cream-1 cup
- Fresh blackberries-1/2 cup
- Zest from 1 lemon
- Whole milk-1 cup
- Sugar-2/3 cup
- 6 egg yolks
- Water-1 cup

Directions:

1. Place a clean pan over medium heat, add milk, cream, and lemon zest; and stir thoroughly. allow to boil, remove off heat and place aside for about 30 minutes.

2. Using a clean bowl, combine egg yolks with cold cream and sugar, mix and stir thoroughly

3. Turn the above mixture into ramekins and cover them with a tin foil, put them in the steamer basket of instant pot, put 1 cup water to the pot, cover the instant pot with its lid and allow to cook at High for about 5 minutes.

4. Reduce pressure naturally for about 10 minutes then release rest of the pressure by turning the valve to 'Venting', open the lid carefully; evacuate ramekins,

5. Allow them to cool and serve with toppings of blackberries and blackberry syrup

Candied Lemon Peel

Serves: 80 pieces , **Prep + Cooking Time:** 40 minutes

Ingredients:

- Water-5 cups
- 5 big lemons
- White sugar-2 ¼ cups

Directions:

1. Slice lemons into halves after washing, place juice aside for another use, then slice each half into quarters, remove the pulp and slice peel into thin strips

2. Pour strips in instant pot, then pour 4 cups water, cover the instant pot with the lid and allow to cook at High for about 3 minutes.

3. Quick-release pressure, open the lid carefully; strain peel, rinse it and pour it in a bowl.

4. Clean the instant pot and pour 1 cup water and 2 cups sugar.

5. Put the lemon strips; then stir thoroughly. set pot on Simmer mode and allow to cook for up to 5 minutes.

6. Cover the instant pot with lid, and cook at High for about 10 more minutes then release the pressure naturally for up to 20 minutes

7. Once again strain the peels and spread on a cutting board and leave to stand for about 10 minutes. Keep in jars until served

Pudding of Chocolate

Serves: 4 , **Prep + Cooking Time:** 30 minutes

Ingredients:

- Cardamom, ground. - 1/4 tbsp.
- Bittersweet chocolate; chopped. - 6 oz.
- Chocolate shavings for serving
- Brown sugar-1/3 cup
- Crème Fraiche for serving
- A pinch of salt
- Vanilla extract-2 tbsp.
- Water-1 ½ cups
- Milk-1/2 cup
- Heavy cream-1 ½ cups
- 5 egg yolks

Directions:

1. In a clean pot, put cream and milk and allow to a simmer over medium heat, off the heat, add chocolate and whisk thoroughly.

2. Using a clean bowl, combine egg yolks with cardamom, sugar, vanilla and a pinch of salt; then stir thoroughly. strain then mix with chocolate mix.
3. Transfer the above into a soufflé dish, seal with tin foil and place in the steamer basket of instant pot, pour water into the pot, seal the lid, then allow to cook on Low for about 18 minutes and release pressure naturally.
4. Remove pudding from the instant pot, leave to stand to coolness and keep in the fridge for up to 3 hours before serving it with toppings of crème Fraiche and chocolate shavings

Tasty Cobbler Recipe

Serves: 4 , **Prep + Cooking Time:** 22 minutes

Ingredients:
- Date syrup-1/4 cup
- 2 pears, cored and cut into chunks
- Steel-cut oats-1 cup
- 3 apples, cored and cut into chunks
- Cinnamon-1 tsp.
- Hot water-1 ½ cup
- Ice cream for serving

Directions:

1. Place pears and apples in instant pot and combine with cinnamon, oats, date syrup and hot water.
2. Stir and cover the instant pot with the lid and allow it to cook at High for about 12 minutes.
3. Reduce pressure naturally then transfer cobbler to bowls and serve with toppings of ice cream.

Stuffed Peaches

Serves: 6 , **Prep + Cooking Time:** 15 minutes

Ingredients:
- Maple syrup-1/4 cup
- Water-1 cup
- Coconut flour-1/4 cup
- 6 peaches, insides removed
- Coconut butter-2 tbsp.
- Almond extract-1 tbsp.
- Cinnamon powder-1/2 tbsp.
- A pinch of salt

Directions:

1. Using a clean bowl, mix flour with cinnamon, syrup, butter, salt and half of the extract gotten from almond, stir thoroughly.
2. Fill the peaches with the mix above and place them in steamer basket compartment of instant pot, pour the water and the remaining part of the almond extract to the instant pot, cover the instant pot with the lid and cook at High for about 4 minutes.
3. Let the pressure reduce naturally and apportion stuffed peaches on serving plates. Ensure to serve while warm.

Recipe for Samoa Cheese Cake

Serves: 6 , **Prep + Cooking Time:** 1 hour 15 minutes

Ingredients:
For the crust:
- Butter, melted-2 tbsp.
- Chocolate graham crackers, crumbled. - 1/2 cup

For the filling:
- Water-1 cup
- Cooking spray
- Vanilla extract-1 ½ tbsp.

- Sour cream-1/4 cup
- Heavy cream-1/4 cup
- Sugar-1/2 cup
- Cream cheese, soft-12 oz.
- Flour-1 tbsp.
- One egg yolk
- 2 eggs

For the topping:
- Chocolate; chopped. - 1/4 cup
- 12 caramels
- Heavy cream-3 tbsp.
- Coconut, sweet and shredded. - 1 ½ cups

Directions:
1. Use some cooking spray to grease an already cleaned springform pan and put it aside
2. Using a clean bowl, combine butter and crackers; then stir thoroughly. spread the mix in the pan and put it in the freezer for about 10 minutes.
3. Using another clean big bowl, mix heavy cream with vanilla, sugar, flour, cheese, sour cream and eggs and stir very well using a mixer.
4. Pour the mix in step 4 into the pan on top of the crust, then cover it with tin foil and put in the steamer basket of the instant pot.
5. Pour cup water in the pot, cover the instant pot with its lid and cook at High for about 35 minutes

6. Let the pressure release naturally for about 10 minutes then evacuate the remaining pressure by putting the valve to 'Venting', open the lid carefully; remove tin foil from the pan and leave the cake to cool down in the fridge for about 4 hours.
7. On a lined and cleaned baking sheet, carefully spread the coconut, place in the oven at 300 ^{0} F and bake for up to 20 minutes and ensure it is stirred often
8. Use a heat resistant bowl to collect the caramel, place in the microwave for about 2 minutes and stir every 20 seconds after which you will mix with the toasted coconut
9. Spread the resulting mix in step 8 on your cheesecake and put it aside for now.
10. In another heatproof bowl, put chocolate, then place in your microwave for some seconds until it melts and drizzles over your cake. Ensure to serve immediately.

Recipe for Zucchini Nut Bread

Serves: 6 , **Prep + Cooking Time:** 30 minutes

Ingredients:
- 2 cups zucchini, grated
- Baking cocoa-1/2 cup
- Baking soda-1 tbsp.
- Baking powder-1/4 tbsp.
- Applesauce-1 cup
- 3 eggs, whisked
- Vanilla extract-1 tbsp.
- Sugar-2 cups
- Walnuts; chopped. - 1/2 cup
- Chocolate chips-1/2 cup
- Salt-1 tbsp.
- White flour-2 ½ cups
- Cinnamon-1 tbsp.
- Water-1 ½ cups

Directions:

1. Using a clean bowl, combine zucchini with vanilla, eggs, applesauce, and sugar and stir well
2. Using another clean bowl, combine cinnamon with cocoa, salt, baking soda, walnuts, flour, chocolate chips, and baking powder then stir.
3. Mix the above 2 mixtures; then stir thoroughly. turn into a Bundt pan, position the pan in the steamer basket of your instant pot, pour water into the pot, cover the instant pot with the lid and allow to cook at High for up to 25 minutes.
4. Let the pressure release naturally, open the lid carefully; transfer the bread to a clean plate, slice it and serve.

Tasty Apple Cake

Serves: 8, **Prep + Cooking Time:** 30 minutes

Ingredients:
- One egg
- Vanilla extract-1 tbsp.
- Olive oil-3 tbsp.
- 1 apple, sliced
- White flour-1 cup
- 1 apple; chopped.
- Water-2 cup
- Ricotta cheese-1 cup
- Baking soda-1 tbsp.
- Baking powder-2 tbsp.
- Lemon juice-1 tbsp.
- Raw sugar-1/4 cup
- Cinnamon powder-1/8 tbsp.

Directions:
1. In a clean bowl, put chopped and the sliced apple, add lemon juice, then toss to coat and put aside for now.
2. Line a heat resistant dish with clean parchment paper, grease with some oil and sprinkle with some flour.
3. Sprinkle some sugar over the bottom and place sliced apple on the top.
4. In an already cleaned bowl, combine the sugar with vanilla extract, egg, cheese and oil and stir well.
5. Add baking powder, flour, soda and cinnamon, and stir.
6. Add chopped apple and toss to coat it and turn everything into the pan.
7. Put the pan in the steamer basket compartment of your instant pot, pour water inside the pot, cover the instant pot with the lid and allow to cook at High for about 20 minutes
8. Let the pressure release quickly, and carefully open the lid; arrange cake on a clean plate and serve warm.

Recipe for Berry Jam

Serves: 12 , **Prep + Cooking Time:** 50 minutes

Ingredients:
- Water-2 tbsp.
- Black currant-3.5 oz.
- A pinch of salt
- Zest from 1 lemon
- Cranberries-1 lb.
- Sugar-2 lb.
- Strawberries-1 lb.
- Blueberries-1/2 lb.

Directions:
1. Combine strawberries with blueberries, currants cranberries, lemon zest, and sugar in an already cleaned instant pot
2. Stir and leave to stand for 1 hour.
3. Add water and salt then set the pot on Simmer mode and allow to boil
4. Cover the instant pot with lid, then cook on Low for about 10 minutes and let go of the pressure for up to10 minutes
5. Open the lid carefully, then set it on Simmer mode once again, bring to a boil then simmer for not less 4 minutes. Apportion into jars, keep in the fridge until needed.

Recipe for Lemon Marmalade

Serves: 8 , **Prep + Cooking Time:** 25 minutes

Ingredients:
- Sugar-4 lb.
- Water-2 cups
- lemons, washed, sliced and cut into quarters-2 lb.

Directions:
1. Clean your instant pot and put lemon pieces, pour 2 cups water and cover the instant pot with a lid then cook at High for not less than 10 minutes.
2. Allow the pressure to release naturally, open the lid carefully; add sugar; then stir thoroughly. set the pot in Simmer mode and cook for about 6 minutes while stirring continuously
3. Apportion into jars and serve at your convenience.

Vacation Pudding

Serves: 4 , **Prep + Cooking Time:** 50 minutes

Ingredients:
- Butter-15 tbsp.
- Maple syrup-3 tbsp.
- Ginger powder-1 tbsp.
- Water-2 cups
- 4 oz. dried cranberries, soaked in hot water for 30 minutes drained and chopped.
- 4 eggs
- 1 carrot, grated
- Dried apricots; chopped. - 4 oz.
- A pinch of cinnamon powder
- A pinch of salt
- A drizzle of olive oil
- White flour-1 cup
- Baking powder-3 tbsp.
- Raw sugar-1 cup

Directions:
1. Use a drizzle of oil to grease a heat resistant pudding mold and put it aside for now
2. With the use of a blender, mix flour with cinnamon, baking powder, ginger, salt and sugar and pulse for some time.
3. Add pulse and butter once more.
4. Add eggs and maple syrup and pulse again.
5. Add carrot and dried fruits and fold into the batter
6. Spread this mix above into the already greased pudding mold, place it in the steamer basket compartment of your instant pot and pour 2 cups water in the pot.
7. Set the pot on Sauté mode and allow pudding to steam for 10 minutes.
8. Seal the pot and cook pudding at High for about 30 minutes.
9. Let the pressure release naturally for close to 10 minutes then release the remaining part of the pressure by turning the valve to 'Venting' position, carefully open the lid; evacuate pudding and put it aside to cool before it is served

Quick Pot Key Lime Pie

Serves: 6, **Prep + Cooking Time:** 25 minutes

Ingredients:

For the crust:
- Sugar-1 tbsp.
- crackers, crumbled. - 5 Graham
- butter, melted-3 tbsp.

For the filling:
- key lime zest, grated-2 tbsp.
- Cooking spray
- 4 egg yolks
- key lime juice-1/2 cup
- sour cream-1/3 cup
- canned condensed milk-14 oz.
- Water-1 cup

Directions:
1. Using a clean bowl, whisk egg yolks thoroughly
2. Add milk little by little and stir again.
3. Add sour cream, lime juice, and lime zest and stir once again
4. In another clean bowl, whisk butter with sugar and crackers, stir thoroughly and distribute evenly on the bottom of a spring form already greased with cooking spray.
5. Seal the pan with tin foil and put it inside the steamer basket of the instant pot.
6. Pour 1 cup water inside the pot, cover the instant pot with the lid and leave to cook at High for about 15 minutes.
7. Let the pressure release naturally for close to 10 minutes then release the remaining pressure by positioning the valve to 'Venting', then open the lid carefully; evacuate the pie, then put aside to cool and keep in the fridge for 4 hours, slice it and serve.

Recipe for Chocolate Cake

Serves: 6, **Prep + Cooking Time:** 50 minutes

Ingredients:
- 3 eggs, whites, and yolks separated
- Vanilla extract-1 tbsp.
- Baking powder-1/2 tbsp.
- Cocoa powder-3/4 cup
- White flour-3/4 cup
- Water-1 cup
- White sugar-1 ½ cups
- Butter-1/2 cup

Directions:
1. Beat egg whites with the aid of a mixer into a clean and dry bowl,
2. Using another clean bowl, beat egg yolks with the aid of a mixer
3. Using the third bowl, mix sugar with baking powder, flour, and cocoa powder.
4. Combine egg yolks, egg white, and vanilla extract then stir very well.
5. Get a springform pan and grease with butter, then line it with clean parchment paper, transfer the cake batter and arrange pan in the steamer basket of instant pot, pour a cup of water inside the pot, cover the instant pot with the lid and leave to cook on Low for about 40 minutes
6. Let the pressure release quickly, and carefully open the lid; evacuate the pan, then leave the cake to stand for cooling, transfer to a platter, slice and serve.

Recipe for Tomato Jam

Serves: 12, **Prep + Cooking Time:** 40 minutes

Ingredients:
- Tomatoes, cored and chopped. - 1 ½ lb.
- Lime juice-2 tbsp.
- White sugar-1 cup
- Ginger, grated-1 tbsp.
- A pinch of salt
- 1 jalapeno pepper; minced.
- Cinnamon-1 tbsp.
- Cumin-1 tbsp.
- Cloves, ground. - 1/8 tbsp.

Directions:
1. Combine tomatoes with sugar in an already cleaned instant pot, then add cinnamon, jalapeno pepper, cloves, salt, lime juice, ginger, and cumin; and stir thoroughly.
2. Cover the instant pot with the lid and allow it to cook at High for about 30 minutes.
3. Let the pressure release quickly, and carefully open the lid; apportion jam into jars and serve at your convenience

Recipe for Chocolate Lava Cake

Serves: 3 , **Prep + Cooking Time:** 15 minutes

Ingredients:
- Milk-4 tbsp.
- Flour-4 tbsp.
- Cocoa powder-1 tbsp.
- Sugar-4 tbsp.
- Olive oil-2 tbsp.
- A pinch of salt
- Water-1 cup
- Baking powder-1/2 tbsp.
- Orange zest-1/2 tbsp.
- One egg

Directions:

1. Combine the milk with flour, orange zest, sugar, oil, salt, cocoa powder, baking powder, and egg and stir thoroughly.
2. Pour the above into an already greased ramekins and arrange them in the steamer basket compartment of the instant pot that you have already washed.
3. Pour a cup of water into the pot, cover the instant pot with the lid and allow to cook at High for about 6 minutes.
4. Let the pressure release quickly, and carefully open the lid; evacuate the lava cakes and serve after it is a little bit cool.

Appendix 1: 30 Days Instant Pot Meal Plan

Meal Plan	Breakfast	Lunch	Dinner	Snacks
Day-1	Espresso Oatmeal	Chicken Pineapple Sandwiches	Lentils And Spinach Stew	Lovely Endives
Day-2	Pomegranate Oatmeal	Simple Lamb and Veggies mix	Chili endive and rice soup	Eggnog Cheese Cake
Day-3	Potato Ham Hash	Duck and Vegetable Stew	Spicy vinegar lamb stew	Sweet Squid
Day-4	Pumpkin Apple Medley	Cheesy Beef & Pasta Casserole	Leeks and corn soup	Cauliflower Dip for veggies
Day-5	Spinach Egg Bake	Chicken Eggplant Curry	Dark beet soup with lentils	Fragrant Pumpkin
Day-6	Italian Bacon Potatoes	Coconut Beef Curry	Creamy asparagus soup	Chilled Zucchini
Day-7	Sausage Eggs	Mushroom Cream Goose Curry	Beer lamb and potatoes soup	Shrimp Sausage
Day-8	Cinnamon Millet Meal	Instant pot Bacon and Collard	Cheesy cauliflower soup	Sweet Zucchini
Day-9	Breakfast Bell Pepper Hash	Colombian Potato Chicken	Beet with Salad	Grilled Artichokes
Day-10	Breakfast Ham Quiche	Garlic Pork Carnitas	Chicken with butternut squash soup	Chilly Sausage
Day-11	Creamy Egg & Ham Breakfast	Chicken Curry with Chickpeas	Simple Broccoli	Steamed Prosciutto
Day-12	Pear Walnut Oatmeal	Instant pot Beef Chili	Cheesy fennel and leek soup	Cheesy Crab
Day-13	Tofu &Brussel Sprouts Medley	Saucy Teriyaki Chicken	Spicy steamed Cabbage	Sour Cranberry

Day-14	Chickpeas Tahini Spread	Chipotle Pork Tamales	Hot Potatoes	Broiled Spinach
Day-15	Apple Lentil Breakfast	Chicken Shrimp Curry	Buttered Carrots	Spiced Mussels
Day-16	Cranberry Raisins Jam	Cinnamon Beef Brisket	Fragrant Turnips	Steamed Mussels
Day-17	Caper Mixed Chicken Liver	Chicken Lentil Stew	Sour Eggplant	Zucchini Delicacy
Day-18	Mixed Mushroom Cheese	Instant Pot Spiced Beef	Delicious Beet Salad	Baked Tuna Patties
Day-19	Berries Mixed Quinoa	Saucy Goose Satay	Endives Delicacy	Mix Berries Compote
Day-20	Pectin Blackberries Jam	Pork Meatball	Sour Endives	Recipe for Poached Figs
Day-21	Avocado Quinoa Salad	Sesame Chicken Satay	Cheesy Fennel Risotto	Chocolate Cheese cake
Day-22	Nutmeg Banana Cake	Mexican Stewed Lamb	Blended eggplant	Recipe for Brownie Cake
Day-23	Chia Almond Pudding	Chicken with Romano Cheese	Tasty Collard Greens	Recipe Peach Jam
Day-24	Tofu kale Medley	Sherry BBQ Pork	Cheesy, tasty Tomatoes	Pots of Lemon Crème
Day-25	Turkey Filled Tacos	Chicken Drumsticks with Corn	Soy burger veggie soup	Tasty Apple Cake
Day-26	Cheesy Butter Grits	Parmesan Meatloaf	Corny Okra	Vacation Pudding
Day-27	Millet Date Pudding	Balsamic Chicken Salad	Cheesy tomato soup	Recipe for Chocolate Cake
Day-28	Morning Tofu Scramble	Zesty Chicken Luncheon	Tasty Fennel	Recipe for Tomato Jam
Day 29	Mushroom Gouda Oatmeal	Sausage Wrapped Chicken	Okra and tomatoes beef stew	Recipe for Chocolate Lava Cake
Day 30	Curried Tofu Breakfast	Chicken with Apricot Sauce	Bacon and Kale Delicacy	Spicy Clams

Appendix 2: Recipes Index

CPSIA information can be obtained
at www.ICGtesting.com
Printed in the USA
BVHW012120011221
623057BV00012B/489